Why Education in the Later Years?

Louis Lowy
Boston University

AND

Darlene O'Connor

Lexington Books
D.C. Heath and Company/Lexington, Massachusetts/Toronto

Library of Congress Cataloging-in-Publication Data

Lowy, Louis.
  Why education in the later years?

  Bibliography: p.
  Includes index.
  1. Aged—Education—United States. 2. Gerontology—
United States. I. O'Connor, Darlene. II. Title.
LC5471.L69   1986   370'.880565   82–47966
ISBN 0–669–05721–5 (alk. paper)

Published simultaneously in Canada
Printed in the United States of America
Casebound International Standard Book Number: 0–669–05721–5
Library of Congress Catalog Card Number 82–47966

The paper used in this publication meets the minimum requirements of
American National Standard for Information Sciences—Permanence of
Paper for Printed Library Materials, ANSI Z39.48–1984. ∞™

86 87 88 89 90 8 7 6 5 4 3 2 1

To my wife, Ditta, who has been a source of infinite strength, love and support in all my life, particularly during my sickness-ordeal and who exemplifies the goals and ideas in this book through her recent decision to return to graduate school.

L.L.

To my parents, Frank and Eleanor O'Connor, who have inspired me with a love of learning and to my husband, Curt, who has nurtured this love and grown along with me.

D. O'C.

Contents

Figures and Tables

Coda: Old Age

The sun
in lengthening rays
refracted in intricate counterpoint
can play
light strings in fields of violets.

The thunder
when it rumbles
soft alterations in the west
can sound
unencumbered by crashing distraction.

The wind
in leaning reeds
now balancing in easy grace
can sing
love burdens light as wind-borne seed.

The water does not beat
a cateract of ragged song
but runs
an elegant cadenza to the sea.

—from *Pacing the Floor: Poems*
  Curt G. Curtin
  ©1979

Preface

There are times in the lives of people when fortuitous circumstances arise that bring fortuitous results. This was the case when Darlene O'Connor, a doctoral candidate at the Florence Heller School, Brandeis University, and a former student in my graduate course "Social Policy and Programs on Aging" at Boston University, accepted my offer to co-author this book on education in the later years.

Ideas for such a book had been in my head for quite a while. A tentative outline was drafted and a contract signed with D.C. Heath and Company in 1982. However, it was not to be, not yet! Two myocardial infarctions, which I barely survived, struck me down in 1983. After "making it," despite all odds to the contrary—largely owing to the devoted skills of physicians, nurses, social workers, and above all, the enormous socio-emotional support of my wife, my children, other family members, friends, colleagues and students—I was determined to get back to this book.

More than ever I felt that my traumatic experiences themselves were involuntary educational experiences in the later years. I had learned a great deal about illness, about hospital routines and management from the inside out, about great medical skills and caring dedication of physicians, residents, interns, nurses, physical therapists, and social workers. I had learned something about the myriad sets of problems which beset their efforts at coordination of service delivery and managing the recovery process. I had also learned how important the active participation of the patient is during all phases of the illness and recuperation, as is the psychological and physical support of family and friends.

Coping, contributive, expressive, and influencing needs reared their heads many times and required attention; so did my needs for contemplation and most of all some answer to my transcendental questions: Why all this? Is there any meaning in life which makes this struggle for survival worthwhile? It did not take me long to move from an ambivalent to an affirmative response.

After this traumatic episode, I did a good deal of reflecting and reminiscing. I shared my thoughts and feelings with family, friends, colleagues, students; I knew I was about to tackle the psycho-emotional tasks of later adulthood. I also knew that this delayed book would be somewhat different in conception than originally planned. It would focus essentially on "why" rather than on "what" and "how."

And here I had the good fortune to meet Ms. O'Connor, because her background in literature and philosophy complemented my background in philosophy, social work, and education. Our shared interests and ideas about social policy were thus given the chance to find fuller expression. We proceeded to transcend the earlier roles of teacher and student, probing and testing one another, questioning and challenging ideas in an atmosphere of mutual respect and desire for truth. Thus an intergenerational collaboration, indeed a "marriage of authors" was born.

The results of this "marriage" are evident in the pages that follow. It was an exciting adventure to collaborate on this book. Our drafts and dialogues proved enriching for both of us. We learned from one another continuously and practiced *"éducation permanente."* For my part, I conclude with Andre Gide's words, which sum up the barriers to realizing the potential of lifelong learning: "It is a rule of life that when one door closes, another always opens. But most of us spend so much time mourning the losses behind the closed doors that we seldom see—let alone grasp—the opportunities presented by the newly opened doors."

Louis Lowy

Acknowledgments

Acknowledgements are due to a number of graduate students at the Boston University School of Social Work, notably Vicki Vanderloop, Bonnie Schwartz-Glatt, and John Borzain for their invaluable assistance in obtaining reference materials. Thanks are also due to the staff of the Boston University Gerontology Center for their general assistance as well as their unflagging support and encouragement; thanks are particularly due to Knight Steel, the Center's Executive Director; Elizabeth Markson, Director of Social Research; and Gretchen Batra, Director of Education. And special thanks go to colleagues at the Boston University School of Social Work—notably Dean Hubie Jones, Julianne Wayne, Leonard Bloksberg, Louise Frey, and Marsha Seltzer—for ideas, support, and friendship. Thanks go also to Marie Gerace, secretary at the Boston University School of Social Work, who provided invaluable typing and other assistance throughout the project.

A book such as this is the product of much thought and discussion. We have done our best in the text to cite the specific ideas of various scholars; however, it is not always possible to trace the evolution of one's own consciousness. Many friends and colleagues have contributed to the shaping of the ideas in this book. Among those who deserve special mention are several lifelong learners at the Heller School, Brandeis University: Phyllis Bailey, William Crown, Walter Leutz, Robert Morris, James Schulz, and Kisang Sohn. These individuals, along with many others, have provided inspiration, challenge, and an honest willingness in their discussions to seek the truth. Their criticisms, encouragement, and friendship have, in a very real sense, made this book possible.

Special thanks are due to Curt G. Curtin, not only for the two elegant poems which are reprinted here but also for a critical reading of the text which helped us to refine and reshape the argument.

Last, but certainly not least, thanks are due to Margaret N. Zusky, editor at Lexington Books, D.C. Heath and Company, Karen E. Maloney, production editor and their coworkers for their forbearance, understanding, and steady cooperation during the odyssey of this volume.

We, of course, have full responsibility for the contents of this book which, we hope, will lead to further debate and clarification of the positions articulated here.

The authors gratefully acknowledge permission to reprint from: Curt G. Curtin for "Coda: Old Age," in *Pacing the Floor: Poems* (Westfield, MA: Little River Press, 1979) and "Eldersong," © 1985, Curt G. Curtin; Donna Roazen for excerpts from her interview with Curt G. Curtin in "College-Age Students: Fifty-Plus," unpublished manuscript, Westfield State College, Westfield, Massachusetts, February, 1985; H.R. Moody for various passages from his works (Moody, 1976, 1978, 1985); The Institute for Educational Leadership for excerpts from "Clarifying the Federal Role in Education" by Cora P. Beebe and John W. Evans, in *The Federal Role in Education: New Directions for the Eighties,* published by the Institute in 1981; *The Gerontologist* for an excerpt from "Agency-Family Collaboration," *The Gerontologist,* vol. 25 (August 1985); and Harcourt Brace Jovanovich, Inc. (U.S. rights) and Faber and Faber Ltd (world rights) for an excerpt from "East Coker" in *Four Quartets* by T.S. Eliot, © 1943 by T.S. Eliot, renewed 1971 by Esme Valerie Eliot.

Introduction

Although the expression "lifelong learning" has been in use for a long time, until recently the concept has not been assumed to apply to older people. Not until gerontology emerged as a field of practice and research in the middle of this century and the existing adult education movement became related to it was much thought given to older persons as potential students of lifelong education.

Education can be viewed as part of the broader field of social welfare, because *social welfare* in its most encompassing definition is viewed as "a system of laws, programs, benefits, and services which strengthen or assure provisions for meeting social needs recognized as basic for the well-being of the population and for the functioning of the social order" (Friedlander and Apte, 1974, p. 4).

Assuring and strengthening provisions to meet basic social needs can be achieved through a variety of mechanisms such as income support, employment, housing, health care, social services, recreation, and education. Within the context of social welfare, education with, for, and by people in their later years will be examined and analyzed. It is argued in this volume that through education the well-being of the older population is enhanced, and the well-being of society is also furthered.

It would be inaccurate to suggest that educational needs of older adults have not been addressed. Despite a late start, educational programs for older adults have become quite popular. Educational activities in Senior Centers began as early as the 1940s and have multiplied rapidly, especially in the past two decades. The history of Senior Centers for older people in the U.S. began in 1943, when the William Hodson Community Center was established in New York City by the Public Welfare Department under the direction of Harry Levine and Gertrude Landau. The idea for it arose among social workers who noticed how desperately older clients sought human contact and communication to escape the loneliness and isolation of their lives. Subsequently, other centers appeared in New York City, Bridgeport, and San Francisco. During the following forty years the concept of a multiservice center was adopted by an ever-increasing number of communities around the country. The multiservice senior center provided a single setting in which older people who came to the center or who were reached via outreach could take part in social activities as well as have access to essential services. The activities and services included nutrition, health, employment, transportation, social work, education, creative arts, recreation, leadership, and volunteer opportunities (Lowy, 1985a).

Morris Cohen, Grace Coyle, Rose Dobroff, Rebecca Eckstein, Margaret Hartford, Jerome Jordan, Alan Klein, Susan Kubie, Gertrude Landau, Louis Lowy, Geneva Mathiasen, Jean Maxwell, Ollie Randall, Marvin Schreiber, Peter Tarrell, Sebastian Tine, Florence Vickery and James Woods, among a host of others, had laid the groundwork for linking social group work with the Senior Center movement. Here was a major, tangible connection between social work and adult education.

The social welfare concept is clearly embodied in that of the Senior Center. Subsequently, the Senior Center became the "multiservice center," a host facility identified with older persons as their own institution. In the early seventies the Senior Center became identified and visible as an indigenous facility of the elderly:

> Children have their schools, young and middle-aged adults have their own institutions, whether in the world of work or in the world of leisure. . . . The Senior Center can indeed become a community institution for all the older adults, whether "needy" or not. It is identified with wellness and not with debility. This can be enhanced by linking it with younger people through joint projects which have meaning to old and young. Youth would work with the elderly on their own "home ground" and they in turn would reciprocate by working with young people on their "home ground." (Lowy, 1974)

Social group work, one of the classical practice methods of the profession of social work (the others are social case work and community organization), had a special place in the adult education movement, because many of its activities had been conducted in small, face-to-face groups. Essentially, social group work is a democratic approach or method in which individuals work together, sharing ideas, thoughts, programs and activities, settling conflicts, making decisions and compromises in the interest of the total group, and enhancing the growth and development of the individual member as part of the total group. Mutual support and mutual aid have been major goals in social group work (Shurman, 1984). The Senior Center adopted the social group-work method in its beginnings and has used it ever since in its many faceted operations when group activities have been called for (Lowy, 1985a).

Educational programs offered by local groups, community organizations, churches and synagogues, and local public school systems have also proliferated. Colleges and universities have been the slowest to respond to the educational needs of older learners, but nevertheless have done so through reduced tuition or service fees, discounts on cultural and educational offerings, specialized programs, and outreach. Much more needs to be done; efforts are uncoordinated and marked by wide regional and local variation, but it is no longer possible to assert that the educational needs of older adults are being ignored. The single example of the growth of the Elderhostel, the program in which older adults enroll for one or two weeks of studies at colleges and universities all over the world, gives profound testimony to the contrary (more on this later). Enrollment in programs sponsored by Elderhostel has grown from 200 to over 100,000 in just over a decade.

Organization of the Book

This volume contains a philosophical argument designed to answer the two-pronged question implied in the title: why should older adults and why should society invest in education for people in the later years? The book is divided into three parts, with chapter subdivisions. The following is a brief outline.

Part I outlines the philosophical principles which serve as the basis on which the analysis is grounded. After first providing a brief review of the rise of adult education and gerontology as fields of practice, *Chapter 1* outlines four stages of development in educational policy for older adults. Next, a variety of terms (e.g., social welfare system, education, educational gerontology) are defined in order that their use in the context of this book will be clear. A semantic analysis relates these concepts to similar terms in other languages in an effort to develop a broader understanding of these concepts. The chapter concludes with a discussion of conceptual analysis, a philosophical method which is employed in the following chapter to uncover the essential elements of a variety of philosophies of education.

Chapter 2 examines the philosophical underpinnings of educational theory, with particular emphasis on developments in the late nineteenth century in an attempt to explain how the emphasis on productivity and utilitarian purposes came to dominate contemporary educational philosophy in this country. A number of educational philosophies are reviewed in order to assess their relevance to education of older adults. This background provides a foundation for the discussion of one of the major questions which the book addresses in its later chapters: what are the appropriate philosophical bases and goals of education in the later years?

Part II provides an overview of the state-of-the-art in the field of educational gerontology. In order to design public policies and justify educational programs for older adults, policymakers need to know that older adults can learn, that they want to learn, that they have educational needs, and that certain programs are more successful than others in meeting those needs. Policymakers must also consider demographic trends which have important implications for future needs and desires of older learners. Moreover, it is essential that those who advocate educational reforms consider the nature of such reforms and how proposed changes are related to existing educational policies and precedents established in the past. Although the information assimilated in PART II is not sufficient to convince any policymaker to invest in education for older adults, this review attempts to establish that conditions necessary for meaningful lifelong education can be designed. Later chapters present arguments about why such investments should be made.

In keeping with the purpose of this section, *Chapter 3* reviews demographic changes and trends in the United States as they have occurred since the turn of the century, with particular emphasis upon present data. The increased attention to education of older adults comes at a time when the size and proportion of the elder population is growing dramatically. Of all the people in the history of the world who have lived past the age of 60, two thirds are living today. By the year 2000, persons over the age of 65 are expected to number 35 million in the United States and to account for 13.1 percent of the population. Moreover, the educational level of older adults is expected to rise from the median 9.7 years in 1980 to a median of about 12 years by the turn of the century. The coupling of these two factors alone would be enough to create a major challenge to our educational systems because those with higher levels of formal education tend to seek educational opportunities in the later years. It becomes evident that demography holds a key to certain human and societal destinies, particularly in the realm of relationship patterns among differing groupings of older people and their families and friends.

Chapter 4 looks at existing knowledge about education in the later years. Such questions as the following are addressed and answered: Can people in their later years learn? What are myths and what are facts about learning, retention, memory, recall? What do studies of cognitive abilities tell us? How do environment, background, attitudes, motivations, and feelings affect older learners? Do older people have specific educational needs?

Research on learning abilities of older adults has supported the emergence of educational activities for older adults in the latter half of the twentieth century. Whereas studies of cognitive abilities in the early part of the century had suggested that learning capacities declined after the early twenties, studies in the 1940s and 1950s began to reveal limitations in methods of testing which had emphasized speed of response and short-term memory, factors which had inappropriately disadvantaged older learners. By the 1960s, theories about memory storage and retrieval suggested strengths as well as limitations in learning abilities for older adults. Age increasingly has come to be seen as an irrelevant characteristic in determining learning abilities.

Whether or not they believed that older adults could learn, many educators and older adults themselves thought that elders did not need to learn, that there was no value in education in their later years. In recent times, however, research has identified various categories of learning needs which are at least as relevant for older adults as they are for younger people; coping, contributive, expressive, influencing, and transcendental needs, can all be met, in part, through educational activities. It has been shown that older adults have as wide a range of educational needs as younger and middle-aged persons, the children and grandchildren of the older population.

The discussion in *Chapter 5* seeks to uncover how the involvement of older adults in formal educational programs helps transform our assumptions about theories of learning and teaching. The review of the theoretical distinctions between pedagogy, andragogy, and geragogy attempts to assess the extent to which learning theory should be adapted to different age groups. It is suggested that what we have learned about education of adults and older adults may apply to all educational endeavors, notably in emphasizing the need to learn how to learn. Experiences of adult educators in the United States, Canada, France, Germany, Great Britain, and Switzerland are included to indicate how older learners can continue to transform educational systems.

Chapter 6 explores the potential forces which influence national policy in the United States. The fragmented nature of educational and social welfare policy is examined in the context of a historical review of the federal role in educational policy in this country. Existing federal programs serving older adults are described, and a summary of such programs is included in the Appendix. Two major sets of recommendations regarding the federal role in educational gerontology are reviewed and analyzed. Attention is given to developing strategies for establishing a national goal of lifelong learning and infusing this sense of purpose throughout the social welfare and educational systems.

Part III moves the discussion from this practical focus to developing the arguments about why investment in such education should be made. This is by no means a simple matter, however. Thousands of delegates to the 1971 White House Conference on Aging pointed out that education should be considered a basic right to which older adults are entitled. Such rhetoric, while useful in the context of a political event such as a White House Conference, does little to put muscle into the position of those who advocate educational programs in the later years. There is need to clarify the meaning of entitlement to education for all citizens, particularly in a society which does not unquestioningly affirm entitlement for these same citizens to such basics as food, clothing, shelter, health care and a socially defined "adequate" standard of living, but merely proclaims, especially in the present era, the existence of a vague "safety net" for the "truly needy." A declaration of educational rights is simply not sufficient to justify major public expenditures for education of older adults.

A commitment to lifelong learning in a post-industrialized society, such as the United States, must come from a reexamination of the purposes of education in general and education of older people in particular. Education of any person must be perceived as inherently valuable, not only to the individual but also to the society as a whole, in order to be worthy of significant public and private expenditure. The same position can be adopted with regard to older people. This was the view of the delegates to the 1981 White House Conference on Aging, who called for education to be seen as "a right and a necessity." The rhetoric, however, needs to be founded on philosophic arguments which justify such an emphasis. This book attempts to begin such an examination of the purposes, objectives, and approaches of education for and by older persons in the United States.

Chapter 7 analyzes the recommendations of the 1971 and 1981 White House Conferences on Aging in the context of a discussion of how entitlements, rights, and liberties are viewed in this country. The issue of education as a right is explored by attempting to go back to earlier U.S. positions on rights, liberties, and responsibilities. The nature of rights is examined, and a distinction is made between moral and legal rights. Questions about the positions of White House Conference delegates are raised in an effort to determine on what basis, if any, education should be considered a right of citizenship in general and for older people in particular. An attempt is made to go beyond vague talk of citizens' rights in order to prepare the argument for a more fundamental examination of the purposes and justification of education or lifelong learning for older adults.

Chapter 8 deals with the distinction between instrumental and expressive educational experiences, common in the literature of educational gerontology, and examines it for relevance to the development of a philosophic base for education in the later years. An argument is made for an educational philosophy to guide education as people grow older which includes both instrumental and expressive aspects of learning and which is based on principles that are fundamentally humanistic.

Chapter 9 attempts to answer the fundamental question of the book: Why education in the later years? The tension between individual and societal values is examined. It is noted that older persons can be a national resource in the economic, social, cultural, and spiritual sense and that education can be a bridge to develop this resource as part of the social welfare of the country. Along with the practical benefits of maximizing the use of human resources and improving the quality of collective political decisions, the chapter urges a serious societal commitment to a struggle for higher levels of human understanding. It is argued that the struggle for existence, evidenced in our domestic and foreign policies and exemplified in our social welfare policy's emphasis on minimum sufficiency, is without value unless there is some movement toward greater ethical development of human understanding and increasing growth of human consciousness. A case is made for the merger of the goals of social welfare and education (learning and teaching) in the struggle for social justice as well as the full development of human potential, in order to fulfill the substance of the broad definition of social welfare.

In the final chapter, the authors conclude that education of older adults can contribute significantly to our national thinking about the value and meaning of the social order and therefore its social welfare. A commitment to lifelong education is seen as essential to a society that seeks to continue to grow and to improve the quality of life for all its citizens at any age, and some questions are raised which have relevance for the development of policies to encourage lifelong learning.

Part I
Philosophical Foundations of Education in the Later Years

Home is where one starts from. As we grow older
The world becomes stranger, the pattern more complicated
Of dead and living. Not the intense moment
Isolated, with no before and after,
But a lifetime burning in every moment
And not the lifetime of one man only
But of old stones that cannot be deciphered.
There is a time for the evening under starlight,
A time for the evening under lamplight
(The evening with the photograph album).
Love is most nearly itself
When here and now cease to matter.
Old men ought to be explorers
Here and there does not matter
We must be still and still moving
Into another intensity
For a further union, a deeper communion
Through the dark cold and empty desolation,
The wave cry, the wind cry, the vast waters
Of the petrel and the porpoise. In my end is my beginning.

—T.S. Eliot, from *Four Quartets,* 1943

1
Foundations of Educational Gerontology

I see in the growth of the practice of adult education prodigious possibilities for the future of our nation, the only healthy way out from the frontiersman's emphasis on material values which still marks our young country. . . . The habit of study . . . is the only one which can provide that improvement *in the quality of individual minds* which is the only way in which the quality of any national thinking can be improved.

—Fisher, 1931, 42, original emphasis

In the latter part of this century there has been a renewed interest in adult education and a special emphasis on the education of older adults. Unlike Dorothy Canfield Fisher's forward-looking sense of national purpose for lifelong learning, actual practice in adult education has been fragmented, a slowly evolving product of a variety of forces without a clear purpose. Adult education has developed in many different settings: libraries, churches, community centers, local schools, workplaces, community colleges, universities, and numerous other locations. Sponsorship and financing have been equally diverse, ranging from local school systems, religious organizations, employers, unions and private foundations, along with some state and federal resources. Given such diversity, educational goals and specific programs often have been overlapping and uncoordinated, sometimes duplicating one another, sometimes leaving needs, interests, and requests unmet.

In spite of the variety and numbers of organizations and auspices involved, not much has been known about the extent to which the educational process continues throughout the lifespan of most people. It was not until 1926 that the American Association for Adult Education was organized. In those early days, the primary concern of most professional workers in adult education was with literacy education and classes for large groups of immigrants. Especially in the urban areas of the country, those who had recently come to the United States were expected by the dominant culture to equip themselves through such classes for the responsibilities of U.S. citizenship. Some form of adult education thus was deemed necessary to achieve assimilation into the society. Education was the seasoning added to the American melting-pot.

In the 1950s, the stated objectives of adult education could be summarized as follows:

to make adults aware of their civic responsibilities to one another, to the community, the nation, and the world;

to make adults economically more efficient;

to develop a sense of responsibility and a knowledge of how to proceed in making personal adjustments to home, life, and family relationships;

to promote health and physical fitness;

to provide the means for encouraging cultural development and an appreciation of the arts;

to supplement and broaden educational backgrounds;

to provide for the development of avocational interests through opportunities for self-expression.

(*Handbook on Adult Education,* 1949, 13–24)

In December 1951, the following statement appeared on the cover of *Adult Education:*

As seen by the Association, the fundamental goal of adult education is to enable adults to deal intelligently, demonstrably and peacefully with the problems posed for individuals and communities by the pervasive fact of change. (*Adult Education,* 1951)

The adult education movement in the United States set lofty goals and had idealistic visions of its future directions. The subsequent history of the adult education movement confirmed that its actuality was not consonant with its sense of purpose and its goals (Sheats, Jayne, and Spence, 1953.) Many pioneers attempted to anchor adult education in the American social and cultural fabric through philosophical statements as well as through demonstration projects which were based on the ideals of a citizen-participatory, democratic process. Mortimer Adler, Kenneth D. Benne, Leland Bradford, George S. Counts, Paul Essert, Lawrence Frank, Homer Kempfer, Kurt Lewin, Eduard C. Lindeman, Ronald Lippitt, Charles Loomis, Howard McClusky, Harry C. Overstreet, among many others, were key figures and pioneers in those days. However, the movement itself could not be sufficiently embedded, culturally and structurally, in the U.S. society (as it was, for example, in the Scandinavian countries' *folkshochschulen*) and achieve institutional sanction.

Lacking a coherent sense of purpose and widespread popular and institutional acceptance, adult education came to be justified increasingly in terms of its influence on developing the productive capacities of its students rather than on creative, artistic, or expressive processes and outcomes; its successes were more frequently measured instrumentally, such as in terms of jobs acquired or up-to-date skills achieved by graduates. Under such assumptions, education of people in their later years of life was generally seen as a frill, a dubious waste of scarce societal resources on people who had little, if any, ability to do *productive* work, or be "productive" somehow, in the future.

To counter the stereotype that education for older adults was frivolous, a number of programs focused on development of skills. Arts and craft courses were developed to enable older adults to create material things; community college courses offered vocational skills to older learners; university programs began to focus attention on "new careers" and other ways to enable middle-aged and people in their later years to remain productive in the work force, at least until mandatory retirement took them out of it.

At the other end of this continuum, away from the productive view of education, several gerontologists, educators, and social workers preferred to see education as a basic right for anyone—in the same vein as the right to life, liberty, and the pursuit of happiness. The proponents of this view argued that whatever education individuals wanted should be provided, that older adults had to be afforded equal entitlements to pursue their individual potentials through educational activities of whatever nature. This attitude seems somewhat ironic in a country that has not come to real terms with the concept of *entitlement*. Indeed, there is a need to clarify what is meant by a right to education in a society which today, even more than a few years ago, questions universal entitlements to have most basic needs met, including food, clothing, shelter, and health care. (See, for example, Charlotte Towle, *Common Human Needs*, which has become a classic in social work since its publication in 1945.) Therefore, it has probably never been more urgent than now to examine and clarify the purposes of education for older adults in the United States.

A decade ago, H.R. Moody, one of the few U.S. gerontologists who has explored philosophical questions related to education of older adults, called attention to the lack of understanding about why older adults should be educated. "[A]s educators, we have no clear idea of why older adults should be educated, and this absence of fundamental philosophical reflection is ultimately dangerous for the whole enterprise" (Moody, 1976, 14). Without a clear understanding about why older adults should be educated it is difficult not only to develop long-range educational goals but also to defend against short-sighted dismantlings of program components, particularly in a political climate of perceived fiscal austerity. It is essential to know what, if any, priority education for older adults should have among national goals in general and of social welfare in particular.

Stages of Educational Policy

In an attempt to develop a philosophical framework for understanding the various reasons societies have for educating the old, Moody (1976) proposes four stages that describe the social values and attitudes about aging which influence social policy generally and, specifically, educational policy: (1) rejection, (2) social services, (3) participation, and (4) self-actualization. The stages represent a social progression from the absence (in the early twentieth century) of educational policy for older adults to Maslow's highest stage of human fulfillment—self-actualization. The delineation of these stages does not resolve the questions about educational purpose, but it helps to reveal some of the underlying reasons why societies do—or do not—educate their older citizens. A summary of Moody's four-stage model provides a useful backdrop for our later discussion about why we should educate older adults.

1) *Rejection,* Moody's first stage, describes the state of educational gerontology in the late nineteenth and early twentieth centuries. Education then was seen as preparation of people (mostly children and youth) for the future, and thus was not considered relevant or appropriate for older adults. "Older students" at that time were those over the age of 22 and usually under 35; they were not over 60, the age at which William Osler, writing in 1905, had declared men to be "useless" (Graebner, 1980). Moody emphasized that this neglect or rejection of older people was not a chance occurrence but rather flowed from the social values and assumptions of industrialization. At its base was the view of education as an investment in human capital, an investment in the future, which for older adults could not be justified on economic grounds.

2) *Social services,* the second stage, was the basis of most current educational activity in which older adults participated from the late 1950s through the mid-1970s. According to Moody, proponents of this view tended to see education as something to be done for or to older adults in the same way that transfer payments and professional social services in the narrower sense were to be provided. Older adults were still isolated in the sense that they were seen as clients with time on their hands who were to be entertained or kept busy with leisure-time pursuits or, as they were called, "leisure-play" (Kaplan, 1958). The early Senior Center movement was imbued particularly with this view. Moody suggested that from this perspective older adults were "human beings who have become something less than human . . . not seriously engaged in projects and demands of life that are validated by the entire community" (Moody, 1976, 6).

With increasing awareness of the growth of an elderly population, the White House Conferences on Aging in 1961 and notably in 1971 gave expression to a new meaning of this social service view. In addition, the confluence of the civil rights and women's movements, the "War on Poverty," and the "Great Society" programs created a political climate in which another set of proponents viewed the aged now as a social problem to be resolved along with other problems defined as "deviating from a normative standard" (Seltzer, Corbett, and Atchley, 1978), the commonly accepted sociological definition of a social problem. All too frequently, prevailing ageist attitudes in a society of the young reinforced the dependent status of older adults and "homogenized" the aged as a segment of the poor. They were viewed as a part of the population generally in need of financial, health, and social assistance. Despite the ascendancy of a politically and socially more liberal outlook in the United States and a move toward a "Welfare State"—albeit a reluctant one, in contrast to most Western industrialized countries—social policy and programs were mostly "residual" rather than "institutional" (Wilensky and Lebeaux, 1965). With the exception of the federal Old Age Insurance, Survivors and Disability Program (OASDI)—enacted as national Title II of the Social Security Act in 1935, during the height of the Depression, (and the subsequent enactment of Title XVIII, Medicare, in 1965)—virtually all other health and social service programs, even those included in the other titles of the Social Security Act and its amendments up to 1984 (e.g., Public Assistance and Medicaid) have been and continue to be administered by individual states, and benefits are distributed on an "as needed" basis. In most other programs, with the exception of Titles II and XVIII, beneficiaries, or clients, (rather than claimants) have to apply for any benefits through a means-test, proving that they are in need. Educational and recreational programs are no exception and in many instances provided an entrée to other benefits for the "needy" aged. The result has been a vast, variegated and paradoxical patchwork of health, educational, and social programs in the United States.

3) *Participation,* Moody's third stage, moved from the segregationist "social problem" assumptions of the earlier two stages to an assumption that older adults should remain active and involved in their communities and in society. Education for second careers and for social activism has arisen out of this set of assumptions.

By the mid-1970s, many older people and their families, as well as professionals in gerontology, social work, nursing, allied health professions, nutrition, medicine, theology, and so on, had become aware of the heterogeneity of the aging population and the varied processes of aging which eventually affect nearly everyone in the population. No longer could aging or the aged be seen merely as a time-limited social problem, although many older adults have faced and continue to face severe social and economic difficulties. Older adults were and would always be part of a population that was getting older as-a-whole. They were to be part of this society regardless of attempts to segregate and isolate them as a surplus population.

Organizations of elder groups emerged, governmental agencies proliferated, private associations were formed in towns, counties, cities, and states. The Gray Panthers, the American Association of Retired Persons, the Caucus of Black Aged, to name a few, demanded a voice in policies affecting older adults (Binstock, 1972, 1981; Hudson and Strate, 1985); a politicization process grew from grass roots organization, and the 1981 White House Conference on Aging witnessed publicly the emergence of "gray power." This phenomenon was gradually communicated to the general public by the media as well as by organizations of older and younger adults. Many educational programs developed in the late 1970s and early 1980s have stressed this need for participation of older persons in the mainstream of society, a theme which was repeated at the 1981 White House Conference on Aging through its emphasis on "Creating an Age-Integrated Society." The goals of stage three are at "the cutting edge of social reform" in educational programs for older adults (Moody, 1976, 8).

4) Moody projects a stage beyond participation which he considers the ultimate goal of education in the later years. Drawing on Maslow's (1968) hierarchy of needs, Moody adopts the term *self-actualization* to describe the highest goal of education for older adults: the search for meaning. In suggesting this higher level of educational activity, Moody seeks to identify that which is "uniquely possible in old age that is only available at this point in the life cycle" (Moody, 1976, 9). Such education is based on the assumption that there are levels of understanding that may not be possible except in old age or as one approaches death and that these may be explored through a study of liberal arts and humanities. For Moody, this educational search for meaning, is the only stage "worthy of the last stage of life" (Moody, 1978, 47).

Leopold Rosenmayr's thesis in *Die Späte Freiheit* (*The Late Freedom,* 1983) affirms that people are autonomous individuals rather than mere victims of circumstance. As they grow and develop through their lifespans, they can learn to shape their later years as well. Rosenmayr's "life goals" emphasize a search for meaning; he is concerned, therefore, with creating and utilizing opportunities for education in the later years. Rosenmayr affirms that learning is to be oriented toward exchanging life-experiences and advancing social communication. Educational objectives should be geared "to develop capacities toward both a search for meaning of life and a comprehension of one's place in one's culture," a view also expressed by Bubolz and Petzold (1976).

What distinguishes us as humans from other creatures is not our ability to work but our ability to think and feel, our awareness of self and others, and our understanding of the world around us. The capacity to learn, while not unique to humans is certainly more highly developed in homo sapiens. It is this recognition of the uniqueness of the human mind which leads Moody, Rosenmayr, Bubolz-Lutz, and Petzold to argue for the pursuit of higher levels of consciousness as a valued end in itself.

The value of better understanding ourselves as individuals in relation to self and others is, in fact, broader than mere self-actualization. It may prove to be essential to advance our national interest that we learn to better understand ourselves as individuals, as members of our various groups, as a nation, and as members of the human race. We may thus learn how to address the complex problems facing us now and in the future. As Fisher emphasized more than half a century ago, broadening our intellectual horizons individually may improve our collective understanding and decision-making.

Definitions

In many countries other than the United States, education as a social institution is considered part of the *social welfare system*. Varying with the country, the full social welfare system can comprise (1) income maintenance (including social security as well as public assistance or "social relief"), (2) health programs (except those that are private), (3) public housing, (4) employment programs, and (5) public education (Kahn, 1979). To be part of the social welfare system the main criterion is the collective social decision by a country to guarantee a program, a facility, a right, because it is part of a communally conceived minimum service or is believed to fulfill "a broader public purpose so important that individual access should not be determined by adequacy of one's personal income and decisions made in the market place" (Kahn, 1979, 19). The inconsistency among nations about what is to be considered part of the social welfare system can be observed, for example, in the social welfare budget figures compiled by the United Nations Social and Economic Council, where education is included for some countries and not for others, thus making comparisons of international data rather difficult. Depending on the country, the full social welfare sector list would include many different activities, ranging from recreational and cultural activity to public transportation, from area rehabilitation efforts to mass indoctrination as preparation for technological, managerial, or social modernization.

Cultural, ethnic, historical, and sociological factors have significant influences upon the boundaries of social definitions. What we generally refer to as "social services" in this country—services to assist individuals, families, and groups to cope with problems arising from conditions in daily living situations or environmental circumstances—are referred to in Great Britain as "personal social services" (they call this the 6th social service), a label based on the assumption that the other services listed above (including public education) are all part of the social service system (Barclay, 1982). The term "social work service" is used in several first and third world countries to refer to this group of services, a name which recognizes the chief occupational group involved in providing and coordinating these services.

Why is it that education is included in a social welfare system in one country and not in another? Kahn offers a historical explanation: he says that only since the past three or four decades has the idea taken hold that diverse kinds of programs for children, elderly, handicapped, the poor, and so on, be considered components of a system of "social services." Previously, undifferentiated charitable programs for the unfortunate and disabled existed separately. With the advent of industrialization, education was no longer considered a special service but a necessary function valid for all members of a society. For this reason, the more industrialized and technologically advanced societies established education as a separate social institution with all its attributes, professionalizing it and keeping it distinct from the service or helping fields commonly associated with social welfare (Kahn, 1979, 82). This view became most advanced in the United States, where even the tenuous administrative links of a U.S. cabinet Department of Health, Education and Welfare (established as late as 1953) were severed with the creation in 1979 of two separate departments, the U.S. Department of Health and Human Services and the U.S. Department of Education.

Given the circumstances and conventions in the United States, we will conform to the prevailing *modus* and regard education as a distinct social institution. However, as appropriate, we will also discuss linkages with other parts of the broader social welfare system, linkages related to social policies and to the profession of social work.

The term *education* in the United States has been used to signify both a broad and a narrow range of activities. Some (e.g., Johnstone and Rivera, 1965; Hiemstra, 1976; Tough, 1978) extend the concept to all activities in which learning takes place, from formal classrooms to any life experience which contributes to one's understanding or maturity. Others confine their usage to formal education (Harris, 1975, 1981) or to liberal education (Paterson, 1979). Education needs to be distinguished from learning, from training, and from schooling, although in common usage these terms are often used interchangeably. For our purposes, the definition chosen by David Peterson (1985) seems most useful. He defines education as "planned learning that occurs apart from maturation and that is seriously undertaken. . . . Education is distinct [from learning] in that the change [in knowledge, attitudes or behavior] is identified beforehand by the teacher, or the student, or both" (p. 1). The emphasis is thus on education as a systematic, planned activity in which educational goals are established and serve as a basis of later evaluation.

A brief etymological excursion is quite revealing. *Skolé* in Greek means leisure, a connection which refers to the learning and teaching of the upper (leisure) class in their leisure facilities or in the groves of academe. Our use of the word *school* derives from this Greek terminology. *Educare* in Latin refers to training and development in the sense of "leading-out," i.e. leading the mind out of the darkness of ignorance into the light of knowledge. In German, two terms are used: *Erziehen* (training, actually bringing up) and *Bildung* (formation); the former refers to the members of the lower classes who needed to be "trained" (brought up) and the latter to the members of the upper classes who were to be "shaped" to become the nation's leaders. Interestingly, for adult education the Germans have always used the term Erwachsenen*bildung* and not Erwachsenen*erziehung*. The French speak of this shaping or formation as well (*formation continué* and *formation permanente*), essentially pointing to creative shaping. The tendency to view education of or for adults is linguistically embedded in the liberal arts traditions of these Western cultures. (Recently the French have also used the term *éducation permanente*.)

Presently, German-speaking countries employ Greek derivatives: *Pädagogik* (pedagogy), to designate what English-speaking countries call the art or method of teaching. Indeed, social work in Germany and parts of Switzerland is still divided into *Sozialarbeit* and *Sozialpädagogik,* presumably to differentiate between the therapeutic, curative aspect and the cultural, educational aspect of social work, although it has now become increasingly recognized in Germany that the distinction has more traditional, historical, and sociological justifications than practical reasons. Pfaffenberger states that this convergence has been externally validated since the 1971 educational school reform, when educational institutions for the training of *Sozialarbeiter* and *Sozialpädagogen* were given one term: *Schulen für Sozialwesen* (Schools for Social Affairs). He further points out that *Sozialarbeiterische* and *Sozialpädagogische* activities have to be conceived as a unitary, functional social system which provides assistance and learning to people in society. The "convergence theory"* has by now found fairly widespread cognitive acceptance, though there is still a lag in practical acceptance (Lowy, 1983a).

With the further development of adult education in German-speaking countries (e.g., Germany, Austria, Switzerland), the term *Andragogik* has found its way into the literature (the root *andra* meaning "man" as opposed to *peda* meaning "boy" or "child") and with further differentiation of education accelerating in the later years, the term *Geragogik* has been coined, though by no means universally accepted (Bubolz-Lutz, 1984). Unquestionably, the movement to find a special terminology in other Western European countries (e.g., the Netherlands, Scandinavia, France, Belgium, Italy) points to a belief that education in the later years is quite different from adult education.

In the United States, the expression *educational gerontology* has been used to encompass all phases of education about aging and education for older adults (Peterson, 1983). The term *gerontological education* has come to

---

*The "convergence theory" orginiated with H. Tuggener, University of Zürich.

be used as a subset of educational gerontology, that is, educational programs about aging. There is as yet, however, no term in commonly accepted use, which describes only education *of* and/or *for* older adults, although the terms *geragogy* and *eldergogy* have also been suggested by writers in this country (Lebel, 1978; Yeo, 1982).

The focus of this book is on this latter aspect of educational gerontology: education of older adults (including that provided by older adults). In the context of this book, the expression *educational gerontology* is used solely in reference to education in which older adults participate. (This is also the sense in which the expression is used in Great Britain). To the extent that older adults participate in education directed toward professionals or lay persons providing care or services to older adults, such material will certainly not be excluded; nevertheless, the scope of this work does not specifically deal with the education or training of gerontological personnel.

Education is being viewed increasingly as a continuous process of *lifelong learning* rather than as being restricted to the early stages of life. Education over the entire life span, especially in the middle and later years, is expected more and more to be considered a normal phenomenon in many societies. *Life-cycle education* differs from lifelong learning. Butler (1975, 389) refers to the former type of education as that "in which different psychological, personal, familial, occupational and other tasks related to specific processes and stages of life are taught." Life-cycle education is an important factor in preparing for and coping with developmental tasks and the transitions which a person must make from time to time throughout the span of life. Preparing for marriage, career, retirement, loss of family members, are illustrations of such nodal events. As Butler states: "We need to understand the general processes of life and the various rites of passage which come along—sex, marital choice, early marriage, parenthood—and how to handle disability, illness and finally death" (p. 389). And as we experience longer life spans, we need to understand also how to handle grandparenthood (or lack thereof), leisure, boredom, aloneness, widowhood, economic and filial dependency, group-living, new technological and cultural experiences, as well as significant events on the national and world stage.

Finally, the age-related concepts addressed in this book must be clarified. Aging has been depicted as "a continuous process whose cumulative effects are manifested at a later stage in the life cycle" (Lowy, 1985b, 2). Aging is thus seen as a process of growth and adaptation to changes in our bodies, in our minds, in our emotions, in our social contexts, and in the world around us—in short, all of us are aging. Old age is viewed as a normal developmental stage which is being experienced by larger numbers of individuals than has been true in the entire history of mankind. For the first time, nearly every person in the United States has a real chance to live to be an old person. However, we have to be clear that despite scientific and technological progress, biologic life spans for all living organisms have not changed. Life expectancy is not the same as life span, which is the maximum number of years for which an organism is biologically programmed. (Scientists estimate that the expected life span for human beings is 100 years). It is life expectancy, a person's chances of reaching a certain age, not life span, which has changed. Obviously, the odds of reaching the biologic life span are affected by genetics (including sex and race) as well as by a host of environmental factors.

Aging of our whole society stands in remarkable contrast to our own history. The later years may be a period of growth and fulfillment or a period of loss and frustration, and most likely they are a mixture of both. However, it is the view of the authors that the outcome is to a large extent affected by our social policies, programs and attitudes about aging and old age.

It would be simple but also simplistic to accord numerical descriptors for terms like *old, aged,* and *older adult.* However, such descriptors are irrelevant if used without recognizing the heterogeneity of a population whose birthdates span several decades, whose health conditions cover the entire human spectrum, whose mental abilities are as diverse as those of the population at large. Bernice Neugarten (1982) has decried the tendency to attach age-ranges to a distinction between the young–old and the old–old, a distinction which she specifically designed to reflect the substantive differences between the healthy, active older adults and those who are less active due to chronic and acute health conditions.

Nevertheless, given the distortion in the literature of adult education about who older students are, there is some value in using age categories to suggest who is not included in our definition of older adult students. An older student is not simply anyone over the age of 22 or 25, as is still commonly assumed in reports of "older," nontraditional students. Nor does our definition of older students include those between the ages of 35 and 50—another common classification. The older students, or learners, who are the subject of this analysis are chronologically at least aged 50; more often by individual program definitions they are over 55, 60, or 65, and they include individuals who are in their 70s, 80s, 90s, and beyond. Other labels which may be used to describe this older population include seniors, senior citizens, elders, elderly, aged; while these terms will occasionally be used in reference to specific programs, the terms *older adults, older people, older students,* or *persons in their later years* are preferred by the authors because they offer a nonpatronizing, nonjudgmental description of the population under discussion.

Conceptual Analysis

The lack of a philosophical framework for educational gerontology has been true for all of adult education until recently. Not until Elias and Merriam's (1980) *Philosophical Foundations of Adult Education* had the range of philosophical perspectives been described and analyzed. Malcolm Knowles (1980), in the preface to their volume, describes the anticipation with which he awaited the book due to the void which it was proposed to fulfill. This unravelling of the philosophical dimensions of adult education in the United States is an important contribution to the field of adult education and has important implications for our own analysis.

In the book, Elias and Merriam present a conceptual analysis of five schools of educational thought, along with a description of the role of analytical philosophy in adult education. Unfortunately, some confusion is created by the failure of the authors to make a clear distinction between the five philosophical *theories* under discussion and the chapter on conceptual analysis which describes a *method* of philosophical analysis. Despite this flaw, their discussion emphasizes the importance of examining the fundamental philosophical issues involved in educational policy for older adults.

Conceptual analysis, the analysis of fundamental philosophical concepts, is the starting point of philosophical reasoning (Nielsen, 1971). Through the elimination of vagueness and ambiguity in the language, conceptual analysts provide a common language through which the normative questions of philosophy can be debated. Linguistic clarity is particularly essential to those who apply such fundamental concepts in the policymaking arena. However, pure conceptual analysis does not tell us what we *ought* to do. Normative decisions must be based on criteria which are external to, although influenced by, the definitions of concepts.

And yet there is a sense in which conceptual analysis does influence normative judgments and policy decisions. The definition and explication of a concept may include or exclude elements which are disputable. The choice of one definition over another is in itself normative, and may have significant implications as the concept is used in philosophic or policy debate. Elias and Merriam provide an excellent example of this problem in discussing Paterson's (1979) analysis of education. Although Paterson analyzes various aspects of adult education, liberal, vocational, role education, and education for leisure, he concludes that the designation "education" should be applied only to liberal arts education: "Most of the teaching and learning in which men and women find themselves engaging forms no part of anything that could remotely be called 'education'" (Paterson, 1979, 179). In doing so, he narrows the meaning of the concept, thus restricting the scope of his discussion (and in the case of those who follow his analysis, all future discussions) to education in the liberal arts. As Elias and Merriam point out, this restriction biases future discussions in favor of what tends to be the most elitist form of education and runs counter to ordinary use of the term *education* in our language. The result can create more confusion than clarity.

It becomes obvious that although Paterson uses the tools of conceptual analysis, he is also an advocate for the liberal arts philosophy and is not free of bias. Understanding his fundamental philosophical principles is as important as appreciating his use of conceptual analysis to defend those principles. The case provides a vivid example of the importance of understanding the underlying philosophical positions before making value judgments about, for instance, why we should educate older adults. This discussion of conceptual analysis should lead the reader back to our original definitions. In accepting a broad definition of education ("planned learning that occurs apart from maturation and that is seriously undertaken"), we have begun to formulate a philosophical position. This definition will, no doubt, influence the direction of our arguments.

Elias and Merriam have explicated the various philosophical positions regarding education for adults. There seems little reason to assume that this range of possibilities is different for older adults, although some will argue that the range is or should be more restricted. It is not the purpose of this discussion to replicate the analysis of Elias and Merriam in the context of older learners; rather, it is one of our major intents to develop a philosophical position to justify the education of older adults in our society. It is hoped that this focus on older learners will not only shed light on policy decisions affecting older learners but will have implications also for the field of education in general.

2
Philosophies of Adult Education

Five Philosophies of Education

In their analysis, Elias and Merriam (1980) present five philosophies of education which are relevant to the education of adults. Their analysis seeks to uncover the roots of each educational theory, to critique it, and to explain its specific relevance in current adult educational practice. Although they do not address specifically the education of older adults, their work has direct application to the search for fundamental purposes to which we have already alluded. Thus, a review of their analysis is appropriate here.

1. Liberal Adult Education

Reaching back to Socrates, Plato, and Aristotle, Elias and Merriam describe the "liberal arts" tradition as the earliest school of educational philosophy. With its emphasis on the study of logic, philosophy, history, literature, rhetoric, and the natural sciences, the goal of liberal education was "to produce the good and virtuous man." (Alas, *men* indeed were the only targets.) Preferring to emphasize more recent trends in liberal education, Elias and Merriam devote only brief space to the contributions of the Greek masters; nevertheless, they acknowledge the profound contributions of the Greeks to an approach that has remained viable in the twentieth century.

Liberal education is conceived in four phases. The foundation is a rational, or intellectual, understanding of the world. This phase involves the collection of information, synthesis of that information to form a base of knowledge, and application or contemplation of that knowledge to achieve wisdom (p. 23). Such intellectual education forms a base for the next phase—moral education. Moral education is directed toward the development of values: prudence, temperance, fortitude (Aristotle), justice (Plato and Aristotle), faith, hope, love, and humility (St. Augustine).

Moral education leads directly to spiritual or religious education, the search for that which is beyond human understanding. Elias and Merriam note the influence of Christian theology on the development of liberal arts from St. Augustine to the present day, but they are also careful to note that not all proponents of the liberal arts identify themselves with a religious or spiritual dimension. Finally, the liberal arts include the search for beauty, the development of the aesthetic sense. Perhaps the search for truth and beauty best symbolizes the goals of this type of education.

Often contrasted with the vocational education developed as part of the progressive education movement in the United States, liberal arts emphasizes the training of minds for their own sakes rather than training for careers. The educational process is conceptual or theoretical rather than practical or pragmatic, and it draws on intuition and contemplation. The concept of learning over a lifetime fits more naturally with the study of liberal arts, which calls for such depth and quantity of reading that true liberal education can only be achieved over a long lifetime.

Elias and Merriam note that the most serious criticism made against liberal arts education is its perceived elitist character. This they attribute to its Western origins in Athens and Rome as education for a leadership class (the only citizens) and its perpetuation as the education of the privileged classes through the feudal, preindustrial, and industrial eras, mostly in Europe. They note that the critiques of liberal education as elitist have served to liberate liberal education, enabling it to overcome some of its historical bias.

Acknowledging that liberal arts education in the United States since the Civil War has received a lower priority due to a different historical and sociological tradition—except for the South, there was no feudal period—its greater emphases on vocational and behavioral education, Elias and Merriam nevertheless state that liberal education continues to be "a potent force" in adult education.

2. Progressive Adult Education

Although Elias and Merriam suggest that the progressive movement in education can be traced back to the sixteenth century, its most dramatic impact can be seen in the rise of industrialization in the nineteenth and early twentieth centuries. Largely a product of English utilitarianism and American pragmatism, the movement combined a strong emphasis on scientific reasoning, with a belief in the potential for education to solve social problems. This led to the development of vocational programs and education as a tool to promote and preserve democracy.

Progressive education has been linked to the adult education movement which followed a parallel course in this country. In 1862, the Morrill Act established land grant colleges to provide agricultural education for farmers. Toward the end of the century, evening colleges and programs were developed for young adults who wanted to continue their education while still working (Knowles, 1969). At the same time, settlement houses became adult learning centers to foster the assimilation of the immigrant population (Friedlander and Apte, 1974; Cohen, 1958). Just after the turn of the century, universities began to develop a role as a "service agency" (Knowles, 1969), a role which can be viewed within the "social welfare" concept referred to earlier.

Through these developments, adult education and progressive ideas joined forces. Courses tended to be more practical in orientation. Training in agriculture and industry was prominent in these programs, as was an emphasis on education for democracy, with courses available in citizenship, democratic principles, and social reforms. Elias and Merriam quote from Knowles to show the link between the goals of adult education and progressivism.

> The general character of adult educational content shifted from general knowledge to several pin-pointed areas of emphasis—vocational education, citizenship and Americanization, the education of women, civic and social reforms, public affairs, leisure time activity and health. Adult education was clearly in tune with the needs of this era of industrialization, immigration, emancipation, urbanization, and national maturation. (Knowles, 1977, p. 75)

The progressive movement represented a broadening of the view of education to include practical skills along with intellectual development. John Dewey became a major advocate for these ideas, espousing a view of education that was lifelong and varied. He argued for a meshing of the liberal and the practical, and a greater focus on the learner as the center of the educational activity. Jane Addams, Eduard C. Lindeman, Florence Kelley, Philip Stokes, Lillian Wald, Robert Woods, among others, represented these positions as social workers in advocating social change through the settlement movement (Axinn and Levin, 1980).

While there is emphasis on influencing social change in the theory of progressive education, particularly in the link with social group work, this aspect of progressivism remained relatively limited in its impact on the broader social scene because it emphasized incremental change via group and intergroup work in the neighborhood, mostly via settlement houses in the urban centers of America. (The original idea of the settlement house came from Toynbee Hall in London, England, established by a churchman, Samuel Barnett, in 1884.) From an educational point of view, a more serious emphasis on social change was to be seen in the radical philosophy of education espoused by the contemporary Latin American scholar Paulo Freire.

Elias and Merriam (1980) indicate that while the progressive movement in education has quite significantly influenced the character of education in this country, it is in fact "a theory of the past" (p. 73). The movement suffered from too much optimism and too much faith in positivism, which dominated sociological and philosophical thinking at the time. In expanding the influence of the sciences and vocational subjects in formal educational programming, the movement has often diminished the influence of the arts and humanities, leading to a tendency to measure educational achievement in practical terms, in terms of productivity and human resource enhancement, not out-of-tune with the Puritan capitalistic ethics flourishing in the United States.

3. Behaviorist Adult Education

In the United States, the name B.F. Skinner is virtually synonymous with the concept of behaviorism owing to the wide appeal of books like *Beyond Freedom and Dignity*. Although not the founder of behaviorist theory (John B. Watson is widely regarded as its founder.), B.F. Skinner has been greatly responsible for much of the development and popularization of this theory of human behavior.

Based on the assumption that all behavior is conditioned by life experiences, this theory assumes that all human behavior can be understood and controlled as a combination of reflexes and conditioned responses. Human experience is thus presumed to be determined by biology and psychology.

As a philosophy of education, Elias and Merriam indicate that behaviorism aims at the conditioning of individuals to ensure the survival of the species. Contrary to the competitiveness feared by those who objected to the Darwinian concept of "survival of the fittest," modern behaviorists emphasize the need for cooperation and interdependence in order to assure the survival of the society and the species.

In this view of education, the role of the instructor is central in determining which responses are to be reinforced and which are to be discouraged. The learner is also expected to be active, exhibiting outward signs of learning so that the instructor can measure and evaluate their appropriateness. Key emphasis is placed on measurable results, on evaluation and accountability, because behaviorists believe that the results of education are not only measurable but also malleable. The emphasis on competency-based education, programmed instruction in which learning goals, objectives, and criteria for evaluation are established in advance of the learning experience, is a product of such thinking. Elias and Merriam note that the principles of competency-based instruction have been widely applied in adult vocational and professional education and training in the acquisition of a variety of complex skills.

This competency-focused approach has been particularly influential in programs which attempt to individualize instruction or to allow the learner to work at his or her own pace. Granting of high school degrees based on the mastery of certain skills and subject matter, waiving course requirements, or allowing credits for life experiences are examples of the assumptions of behaviorism put into practice. In this way, the behaviorist theory of education has recognized and encouraged lifelong learners of all ages.

Most critics of behaviorist education fault it for a mechanistic view of human behavior which suggests that individuals are unable to act through free choice or to be creative. While behaviorist concepts, such as reinforcement and conditioning, have had important influences on educational theory, they are often seen as manipulative and reductionist—considering human achievement as a sum of positive and negative forces. Of the various philosophical theories of education, the behaviorist's is least optimistic about the creativity and growth potential of human beings.

4. Radical Adult Education

In the view of radical thinkers, most public education is simply a tool for reinforcing the values and institutions that perpetuate the status quo. Following the fundamental philosophical tenets of Karl Marx, most advocates of radical social change have deemphasized the role of institutionalized education because of its potential to be influenced and controlled by the dominant economic and social class.

Elias and Merriam point to Paulo Freire as the most significant influence on contemporary adult education from the political left. From his work in education for literacy in Brazil, Freire developed a "liberating" theory of education for the oppressed which he called *Pedagogy of the Oppressed* (1970). Freire criticized the traditional forms of education for "banking" knowledge, dispensing education as a gift from teacher to pupil rather than enhancing the freedom and autonomy of the student. He saw this form of education as paternalistic and authoritarian, harmful in its tendency to convert thinking individuals into passive receptacles of information.

The solution to this "banking" approach was, according to Freire, to design and implement education which developed a historical and social consciousness of oppression and which linked this consciousness to political and social activity. Using methods which drew the material of learning from the students' existing knowledge, he advocated the teaching of literacy through discussions of the conditions of oppression—a technique which merges the goals of basic education with political consciousness-raising. It was assumed that once conscious of the forces responsible for their oppression, individuals would unite to fight for equality.

Many educators are afraid that such consciousness-raising discussions will lead also to indoctrination. Yet, radicals contend that all education is indoctrination of a different sort anyway, or at least it is not value-neutral. Freire himself warned against this dangerous tendency toward indoctrination:

Unfortunately, however, in their desire to obtain the support of the people for revolutionary action, revolutionary leaders often fall for the banking line of planning program content from the top down. . . . They forget that their fundamental objective is to fight alongside the people for the recovery of the people's stolen humanity, not to "win the people over" to their side. Such a phrase does not belong in the vocabulary of revolutionary leaders . . . (Freire, 1984, 83–84)

However, radical educators—from the right or the left of the political spectrum—tend to be more willing than non-radicals to admit to shaping the political beliefs of their students; indeed, they assert that "politicization of education" is an important tool of all dominant groups in a society and thus should also be used as a tool for the liberation of the oppressed.

Other influences of the radical philosophy of education are revealed by Elias and Merriam, most notably the "Deschooling Movement" which was revived in the 1960s. Emphasizing the inability of formal educational institutions to support anything but the status quo and differentiating *schooling* from *education*, critics like Ivan Illich advocated a total decentralization of educational activity and the establishment of "learning networks" rather than schools. (The present U.S. Secretary of Education, William Bennett argues for decentralization through a voucher-system, a "capitalistic" radical device.)

The techniques of Freire are evident in current practices for tutoring adults in basic skills. The Literacy Volunteers of America, Inc., a nonprofit organization with state and local affiliates, uses techniques similar to Freire's in training its volunteers to provide tutoring in basic reading and writing skills. For example, the organization publishes a manual *TUTOR* (Colvin and Root, 1984) which stresses the use of the "experience story," narrated by the student, as a basic source of reading material for adults who are learning to read. The technique draws on the student's own language and interests, calling on students to indicate words that they want to learn and to build a reading vocabulary from these. There is no reference in *TUTOR* to Freire's political ideas, no suggestion that experience stories should specifically focus on consciousness-raising. Yet, the technique of drawing from and building on the student's own vocabulary and choices of which words to learn has been a basic part of the literacy programs which Freire developed and described in his writings.

Elias and Merriam suggest that while the radical philosophers of education have made important contributions to educational thought, the overall impact of this philosophy has been minimal: "Radical thought has not greatly influenced the practice of adult education" (Elias and Merriam, 1980, 170). They suggest that the radical view that human potential is unlimited is utopian, and contend that the major failure of radical education is the lack of recognition of the existence of pluralism, especially in the United States.

Radical thinkers would likely reject this charge, arguing instead that pluralism is a myth perpetuated by the dominant class to encourage the oppressed to feel that they have influence in the political system. The ideology is disputable, but the inability of a major socialist or Marxist movement to gain sufficient popularity in this country to play a powerful political role is something that even their advocates cannot dispute. Several theorists trace this phenomenon to an absence of feudalism in U.S. history on a national scale.

5. Humanistic Education

Tracing its roots back as early as the roots of liberal studies, Elias and Merriam explain that the first major development of the humanist philosophy was in the Italian Renaissance of the fifteenth century. Taking its name from the word *humanista,* teacher of the humanities, humanism stressed the dignity and autonomy of every human being. The course of study drew much from the liberal arts philosophy and stressed the study of the classics of antiquity, history, philosophy, ethics, and science. Their maxim was Menander's dictum: "Homo sum, nihil humani alienum est—I am a human being; nothing human is alien to me."

Humanistic education differs from liberal arts education perhaps more in its practice than in its philosophy. While both are concerned with the growth of the individual, liberal education has tended to place a greater emphasis on the subject matter under study and the need to master a range of subjects; humanistic education has maintained a focus on the individual as the learner, emphasizing the "social, emotional, spiritual, and intellectual development" of the learner (Elias and Merriam, 1980, 112).

In more recent times, humanism was revived as a reaction against the mechanistic view of human behavior supported by the behaviorists. In psychology the humanists charged that the behaviorists painted an incomplete picture of human nature, ignoring the creative potential and freedom which humanists considered the unique characteristics of men and women.

Five basic elements comprising modern humanism are described by Elias and Merriam:

1. belief that human behavior is not totally determined; there is freedom and autonomy;

2. respect for the uniqueness and potential of all human beings;

3. attention to individual growth and self-actualization;

4. belief that the individual's perception of reality is in fact the reality upon which he or she acts; thus empathy is necessary to understand and change individual behavior;

5. emphasis on social responsibility as the fulfillment of individual potential.

In its application to education, humanistic philosophy embodies many of the ideals that a majority of adult educators have advocated. The assumption is that a teacher is both a facilitator and a learner who participates actively in shaping the learning experience. Motivation to learn comes from within the learner, who is assumed to know best what his or her learning needs are. The experience, personality, and values of the learner are drawn upon to facilitate a mutual learning process.

Although attempting to approach the various models objectively, Elias and Merriam weigh favorably toward humanism as the philosophy of choice for adult education. They find nothing to criticize in humanism as they do in the other philosophies, and one of their criticisms against both the radical and the progressive philosophies—that the view of human nature is overly optimistic and fails to account for the evil and weak side of human nature—is not laid against the humanistic philosophy of education. While there is much to commend it, humanism—like the radical and progressive philosophies— must also defend itself against charges of optimism and idealism. Advocates of a humanistic philosophy of education must demonstrate that they have a realistic view of human nature which embodies positive *and* negative attributes.

Four Fundamental Questions

If we assume that the range of philosophical positions outlined by Elias and Merriam encompasses the major philosophical possibilities for education of older adults (admittedly a daring assumption but one which, barring any evidence to the contrary, we will accept for now), there remain four important philosophical questions: 1) Is there anything special about the later years or old age which either makes this period more conducive to certain kinds of education or less worthy of individual and societal investment? 2) Is there any one of these philosophies of education which is more appropriate to educational gerontology? 3) Should we educate older people? 4) And if we should, why should we?

Moody (1985) suggests a creative method for approaching the first question by encouraging us to imagine the "age-irrelevant society," an approach also taken by Neugarten. In Moody's hypothetical society, individuals do not know their birthdates but do know the dates of their upcoming deaths. Thus, time is measured, not in years accumulated, but rather in years remaining. This perspective, Moody suggests, leads individuals to think differently about how they use their time and, in particular, how they approach continuing learning.

Moody then argues that this view of time as "what's left" is indeed the perspective of the old in our own as in the hypothetical society. He explains that persons in their seventies understand the likelihood that they probably do not have more than 10 to 15 years of life to look forward to, or that, given family history, health, and other factors they are capable of a rough measure of years till death. This view of time, Moody contends, dramatically influences educational goals and must be considered seriously in developing a philosophy of education for older adults.

Our second question asks whether any one of the educational philosophies articulated by Elias and Merriam is to be preferred for the education of older adults. It may not be necessary to make such a choice, and others may argue that to force a choice of educational philosophies only for older adults suggests an inherent age bias. However, in attempting to understand and explain the importance of education for older adults, we have found ourselves embracing an educational philosophy that is fundamentally humanistic. We have found ourselves echoing the arguments that have been made in favor of humanistic education in the past and have come to believe that the education of older adults gives new force to the importance of a humanistic philosophy of education for persons of all ages.

In developing this philosophy of education, we have attempted to address three central philosophical questions which, according to Moody (1985), require answers as part of a development of an educational philosophy:

1. What is to be learned (epistemology)
2. What purpose supports such education (ethics)
3. What is the role of society in supporting such education (social philosophy)

Moody began to address these questions by indicating what was needed to answer them. He emphasized, however, the need for further development of a philosophy of educational gerontology to adequately address his questions. The later chapters of the present book seek to provide justification for our choice of a humanistic educational philosophy.

Our third question, "Should we educate the old," is not a rhetorical question, but for now we will give it an affirmative, albeit only a rhetorical response. A more complete response will emerge after we have demonstrated that the conditions necessary for the education of older adults do prevail and as we attempt to present sufficient justification for an investment in such education. This justification coincides with our answer to the fourth question, "Why should we educate older persons," and is linked closely to Moody's questions about epistemology, ethics, and social philosophy. These, then, are the central questions of our present analysis and a sound argument will require a detailed analysis.

In a much earlier attempt to explore aspects of these questions by examining the links between social group work and adult education, Louis Lowy discussed the purposes of adult education in his book, *Adult Education and Group Work* (1955). Three basic objectives were identified then:

Development of citizen participation in a democracy;

Growth opportunities for the individual and the group;

Acquisition of knowledge and skills and development of attitudes.

(Lowy, 1955, 28)

Despite many major developments which have occurred in the thirty years since these observations were made, it is surprising to find that no recantation is necessary and that, indeed, what is still needed is a fuller development of the thesis that guided that work. Relationships with the various educational philosophies identified by Elias and Merriam (1980) can be seen in this simple statement of educational philosophy. Influences of the liberal arts and progressive schools are mixed in an educational philosophy that is ultimately humanistic. It is this foundation from which we begin to evolve a philosophy of educational gerontology.

There has been much disillusionment about the power of education as a tool of social reform. After many failures of social reforms in the past, we have come to wonder whether indeed "education and progress are inter-related" (Lowy, 1955, 23). We seek long-range solutions to problems of poverty, oppression, and the threat of nuclear catastrophe. Education is clearly not enough to avert these major social problems, calamities, and threats. However, if Fisher is right, the potential of education to change "the quality of any national thinking" is an important key to long-term resolutions of major social problems.

We must look realistically at the place and purpose of education in our individual lives and in our society; we must consider whether, if, and how age influences that place and/or purpose. It will not help us to rhetorically affirm or exaggerate the importance or priority of educational endeavors for the old, the middle-aged, or the young, but neither can we afford to negate or under-estimate the potential contributions to a society of continuing, life-long learners.

As mentioned already, education is one of the parts of the mosaic of *social welfare* in a broader (non-American) definition. This mosaic consists of economic, social, and educational components which interconnect. They are parts of a fabric which is designed to assure a basic level of economic, health, social service, and educational provisions in order to enhance communal, social living and personal functioning, to facilitate access to human services and social institutions generally, to intervene beneficiently and creatively when needed, to help when needs for assistance arise, and to prevent the deterioration of worthy living conditions. They are parts of a fabric to promote the optimal well-being of people, the growth and development of themselves, their families, neighbors, and peers, as well as their physical surroundings. Various efforts and activities are needed by professionals in many occupations, by organizations and institutions, by persons of all ages who can contribute their internal and external resources in "leading us out of the darkness of ignorance into the light of knowledge" to improve the quality of our own lives and the lives of those who follow us.

Part II
The State of Education for People in the Later Years

We stand in need of a revolution of the mind—not a mere exchange of power-groups—before an economic revolution can transform industry into a cooperative enterprise, before "power *over*" is transposed into "power *with*" in industry.

—Eduard C. Lindeman, *The Meaning of Adult Education,* 1926

Prelude

In public policy debate, as in philosophical argument, it is important to establish both the necessary and sufficient conditions in order to defend a position. *Necessary* conditions are those essential elements of a case without which it is impossible to make a good argument, but which, in and of themselves, are not enough to prove one's point. In logic, they are those propositions which must be true in order that a conclusion be valid. Yet, if the conditions are only necessary (not also sufficient), the conclusion cannot be deduced from the propositions; the conditions are necessary but not sufficient to make a valid argument. They are important but not enough to defend a particular public policy choice.

Sufficient conditions are those elements which are enough to effect the desired result, but they may or may not be necessary. There may be two or more sets of conditions, either of which is sufficient to demonstrate a point. The conditions may be adequate to support a conclusion, but they may not be the only arguments to be used. To develop a valid and convincing argument, both the necessary and the sufficient conditions which pertain must be established.

One of Aesop's fables illustrates this point simply and clearly. A crow, desperately searching for a drink, stumbled on a pitcher which contained water. Unfortunately, the vital fluid was too deep in the pitcher for the crow to be able to take a drink. It had the necessary element—the water—but this was not sufficient to enable the crow to quench its thirst. The crow was also physically unable to pour water out of the container. Not eager to die of thirst, the clever bird found some small pebbles nearby and, dropping them one by one into the pitcher, gradually raised the water level until it could take a drink. The crow thus met the necessary and sufficient conditions for achieving its goal.

It is important to note that finding water was the only necessary condition that the crow had to meet. It was unnecessary that the water be in a pitcher. Indeed, if the water had been in a bowl, a cup, a puddle, or a lake it would have been more convenient to the bird; however, none of these specific conditions was necessary for the crow to meet its objective. Neither was it necessary that the water assume its pure liquid form. Lemonade might not taste as good to a bird, but it could have saved it from dehydration; snow would eventually have satisfied the same need.

Moreover, raising the water level in the pitcher with stones was a sufficient but not a necessary solution. Perhaps another creature could have been enlisted to help overturn the pitcher; perhaps a straw could have been fashioned out of reeds (we have a clever crow, remember). The point is that there might have been more than one condition sufficient to enable the crow to drink the water. As long as there was another option, no single condition was necessary. In order to quench its thirst, the crow had to meet both the necessary and the sufficient conditions. For our purposes, that will serve as the moral of the story.

Incidentally, there is also another set of conditions called *contributory* conditions. As the name suggests, these conditions contribute to an argument (or a defense of public policy); however, they are neither necessary nor sufficient. An example in the fable is the crow's physical condition, its proximity to death by dehydration. Because the crow was quite weak from thirst, it was unable to fly much further in search of another source of water. This condition, then, contributed to its discovery of a clever solution to the problem (i.e., raising the water level with pebbles). Nevertheless, this condition was neither necessary nor sufficient.

To establish a policy of lifelong learning it is necessary that older adults be able to learn, that they be willing to learn, and that barriers to their involvement in educational programs be removable. Projections about demographic trends can contribute to an understanding of the need for increased educational opportunities for older adults, especially given expectations that future generations will be better educated and more likely to seek educational opportunities in the later years. Political and economic realities can encourage or discourage lifelong learning policies as well as determine the types and levels of involvement which are appropriate or possible, given a set of assumptions about the nature of a particular society.

Such conditions, however, though necessary and contributory, may not be sufficient to convince political leaders and policymakers to appropriate resources for educational programs; yet, it is important to establish the necessary and contributory conditions for the education of older adults before arguing why we should invest in such education or discussing the merits of specific policy options. This is the focus of Part II of this book; Part III returns to the philosophical questions raised earlier, in an attempt to provide sufficient evidence to support educational policies for the later years.

3
Demographic Change and Educational Participation: Implications of an Aging Population

Demography is producing many changes in this country and indeed in the world. The publication *Periodical on Aging* of the United Nations Department of International and Economic Affairs (1985) provides a demographic overview of major world regions and supports the contention that the population is graying in every part of this earth. This U.N. report offers the following summary data for comparison: the 60-plus population of the world has increased from 200 million in 1950 to 350 million in 1975 and is projected to amount to 1.1 billion in 2025. The percentage of people over 60 on our globe forty years from today will be approximately 13.7, as compared to 8.5 percent in 1975. Persons over age 80 will rise proportionately higher than the rest of the over 60 group, and what is more, the groups of nations usually referred to as "less developed" already have the bulk of the 60-plus population and their rate of increase will take them far beyond the more developed regions within the near future.

How has this come about? The United Nations Report cites three major reasons: control, in many regions of the world, of prenatal and infant mortality; a decline in birthrate; and improvement in nutrition, basic health care, and the control of many infectious diseases.

The projected growth of the older adult population will have an impact on the educational system in this country, as well as on all other institutions and systems. Without any other changes, educational institutions can expect to find greater proportions of older adult students taking courses at the turn

---

An earlier version of this chapter was presented by Dr. Louis Lowy at the 1985 Professional Symposium, National Association of Social Workers (NASW), November 8, 1985, Chicago, Illinois.

The demographic data and projections reported here are compiled largely from the following sources:
Aging America: Trends and Projections, American Association of Retired Persons and U.S. Senate Special Committee on Aging, Washington, D.C., 1985–86 edition.
America in Transition: An Aging Society, 1984–85 edition, Special Committee on Aging, United States Senate, Washington, D.C., June 1985, Serial No. 99B.
Chartbook on Aging in America, 1981 White House Conference on Aging, Washington, D.C.

of the century simply because of the dramatic increase in their numbers. More important than the mere rise in the population of older adults, however, is the increase in educational level. The median number of school years completed by persons over the age of 65 has been gradually rising. This increase in educational attainment by older adults can be expected to have a profound effect on the educational expectations of future generations of older adults.

This chapter reviews major demographic changes related to the aging of the U.S. population. Following what may seem a lengthy excursion into a wilderness of detail, an examination of the significance of these developments—for families, for social welfare policy in general and for educational policy in particular—attempts to focus attention on the broader implications of these trends.

A Changing United States

In the United States, the changes have been equally profound. By 1900, there were 3 million older Americans—65 and over—comprising 4 percent of the total population, or every twenty-fifth American. As of mid-1975, 22.4 million older persons made up better than 10 percent of the over 213 million total civilian resident population—or every tenth American.

Census Bureau data indicate that in 1982 there were 26.8 million older Americans (11.6 percent of the population, or every ninth American). By the year 2000, 35 million Americans will exceed age 65, comprising 13.1 percent of the population, or every eighth American; and by the year 2050, 67 million Americans, or 21.7 percent of the population will account for every fifth American!

The ratio of women to men at ages 65 to 74 is 131 to 100 and at age 85 + it is 229 to 110. Obviously, single-status older women will be the predominant group of elderly, with many, many social, economic, and cultural implications.

Marital Status. In 1983, older men were twice as likely to be married as older women (79 percent men, 40 percent women). Half of the older women were widows. There were over five times as many widows (7.7 million) as widowers (1.4 million). Although divorced older persons represented only 4 percent of all older persons in 1983, their numbers (nearly 1 million) had increased four times as fast as the older population as a whole in the preceding 20 years (2.7 times for men, 5.4 times for women).

Race and Ethnicity. In 1980, the nonwhite population was 16.8 percent of the total population, but only 10.2 percent of those 65 years of age and older. There is a difference in life expectancy between the white and non-white populations.

Blacks. The number of blacks 65 years of age and older will increase because their standard of living, medical care, and nutrition is improving, though very slowly. The number reported in 1980 was 2,086,000. Most were females (57.6 percent), most resided in the South (60.8 percent), and 66 percent lived in metropolitan areas. Although comprising more than 16.8 percent of the total population, black people make up only 10.2 percent of the older age group. The effects of institutionalized racism fall most heavily on black men, their life expectancy of 65.0 years is 4.5 years less than that of white men.

East Asian-Americans. The majority of East Asian-Americans (primarily Japanese, Chinese, Filipino, Korean, and Samoan) live in California and Hawaii as a result of immigration directly to those areas. Immigration policies have profoundly affected the lives of elderly Asian-Americans, particularly with regard to family life and male-female sex ratios. Males outnumber females by 30 percent, reflecting pre–World War II immigration laws that prohibited women and children from accompanying men to the United States.

In 1980, 8 percent of the total Japanese-American population were over 65 years of age. With four men for every three women, the proportion of elderly living with a spouse was 68 percent.

American Indians. The 1980 Census estimated that 418,000 persons 65 + accounted for 5.3 percent of Native Americans with an average life expectancy of 44 years, one third shorter than the national average. The U.S. government has, to a limited degree, recognized the severe plight and unique needs of Native Americans. A separate title was established under the Older Americans Act Amendments of 1978 (and reauthorized in 1984) to provide Indian tribes and tribal organizations with direct funding for social and nutritional services. These monies are not always available to urban Indians, however, due to requirements that populations be "clustered" rather than dispersed throughout the metropolitan area.

Mexican-Americans. 1978 data indicate the elderly constitute 3.7 percent of the Mexican-American population. About 86 percent live in urban areas, primarily in five southwestern states—Arizona, California, Colorado, New Mexico, and Texas. The elderly make up an estimated 4 percent of the Mexican-American population. Mexican-Americans, due to segregation and several other factors, have retained much of their culture and language. An estimated 58 percent of the Mexican-American population was born in Mex-

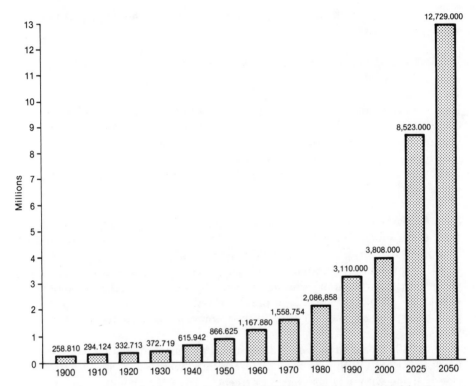

Source: U.S. Bureau of the Census, Population Projections Division, compiled by Gregory Spencer.

Figure 3–1. Actual and Projected Nonwhite Population 65 Years and Older, 1900–2050

ico, and 42 percent are second- and third-generation Americans, most of whom were born and still live in one of the southwestern states. Although Mexican-Americans cling to the ideal of extended family living, young urban Mexican-Americans are often unable to care for their elders in the traditional way.

Income and Poverty. Older persons have half the income of their younger counterparts. In 1980, half of the 9.2 million families headed by an older person had incomes of less than $12,900 ($22,600 for families with under-65 heads); the median income of 8 million older persons living alone or with nonrelatives was $5,095 ($10,526 for younger unrelated individuals). Some 3.9 million, or approximately 15 percent of the elderly, lived in households with incomes below the official poverty threshold for that kind of household. This is some improvement over the 4.7 million, or a quarter of the elderly, in 1970 and results primarily from the increases in Social Security benefits. Women and minority aged are heavily overrepresented among the aged poor. Many of the aged poor became poor after reaching old age because of a half to two-thirds cut in income from earnings that results from retirement from the labor force. Regardless of previous means and socioeconomic status, one may be thrown into poverty for the first time in old age. In addition to those older people who become poor, there are poor people who become old. In absolute numbers, more whites than blacks are elderly poor, but in 1980, proportional to the total black and white populations, almost three times more elderly blacks lived in poverty than elderly whites.

Older people are still hurt by inflation, despite its decreasing rate since the early 1980s, as many live on fixed incomes and Social Security benefits. Although these are adjusted to the inflated dollar in COLA, they still do not absorb previous higher costs of living. In addition, most private pension plans are not indexed to inflation rates. Although in 1980 only one out of five men and one in twelve women 65 years of age and older worked, employ-

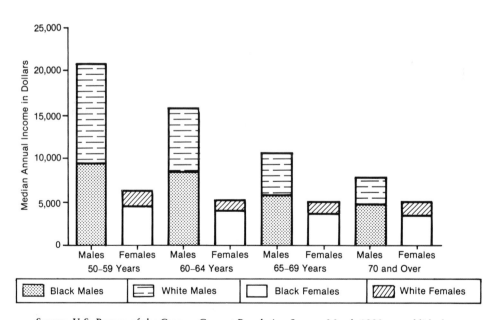

Source: U.S. Bureau of the Census, Current Population Survey, March 1982, unpublished.

Figure 3–2. Median Annual Income, Persons 65 Years and Older by Age, Race, and Sex, 1981

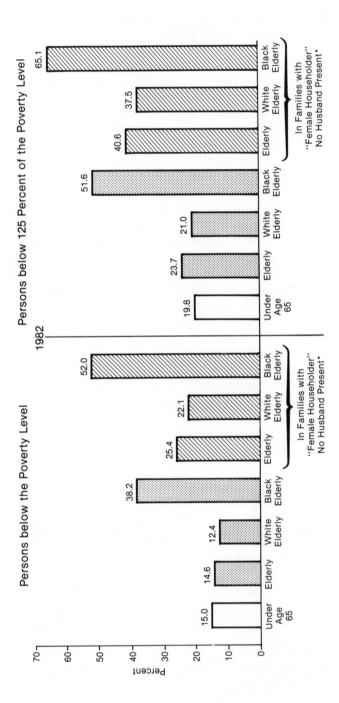

*Includes female "unrelated individuals."

Source: U.S. Bureau of the Census. Money Income and Poverty Status of Families and Persons in the United States: 1982. Current Population Reports, Series P-60, No. 140.

Figure 3–3. Poverty Levels, 1982

ment was the second largest source of income, accounting for 23 percent of the aggregate income of American elderly. Social Security income accounted for the greatest chunk of their income (approximately 40 percent), other retirement income and pensions make up 20 percent, and investments accounted for 17 percent. In 1981, 91 percent of all aged 65 + received income from Social Security (providing in most cases at least 45 percent of their income), and most recipients had at least one additional source of income.

Employment. The working elderly make up approximately 3.0 percent of the total work force in the United States while they represent 11.6 percent of the total population and a greater percentage of the total adult population. More than 2.9 million (11 percent) of our older people were working in 1983. Slightly more than 19 percent of the older men (1.9 million) and about 8 percent of the older women (1.1 million) are in the labor force. The average retirement age is now pegged at 62.

In 1900, there were about 7 elderly persons for every 100 persons 18 to 64 years. By 1982 that ratio was almost 19 per 100 persons of working age and in 2000 the ratio is expected to increase to 21 per 100 persons. The "support ratio" has been changing dramatically.

Housing and Living Arrangements. In 1980, approximately 16 million, or one-fifth, of all American households were headed by persons 65 + . One factor contributing to this trend has been an increase in single-person households, particularly those made up of widows and other older women who live alone. Data from 1980 show that more than seven out of every ten household heads who are 65 + own their own homes, 84 percent of which are mortgage-free. Even mortgage-free homes incur high costs for elderly homeowners, however. Taxes, utilities, and repairs require older homeowners to spend a greater proportion of their income on housing. The same holds true for older renters whose incomes are lower than younger renters.

In 1980, 83 percent of older men, but only 57 percent of older women lived in family settings; the others lived alone or with nonrelatives, except for the less than one in twenty who lived in an institution (which jumps to one in five in the group 85 and over). About three-quarters of the older men lived in families that included the wife, but only 38 percent of the older women lived in families that included the husband. Four out of ten older women lived alone. Almost four times as many older women lived alone or with nonrelatives than did older men.

Place of Residence. In 1980, a somewhat smaller population of older than of younger persons lived in metropolitan areas (64 percent versus 68 percent). Within the metropolitan areas, however, more than half of older people

(53 percent) lived in the suburbs. These figures are based on the total population; patterns for white and black elderly differ fundamentally. Older blacks are much more concentrated in metropolitan areas than are whites, and more than 75 percent of the older blacks in metropolitan areas live in the central city. Twenty-one percent or almost 5 million of the persons then 65 and over had moved from one residence to another in the five-year period since 1975. Some 57 percent moved within the same county, 22 percent moved to a different county in the same state, and 20 percent moved across a state line. The extent of interstate movement seems larger because such migration tends to flow mainly toward Florida, Arizona, and Nevada. Although differing on proportions, older movers follow a pattern quite similar to that of movers of all ages.

Transportation. Transportation means mobility and therefore is a major factor in providing meaning and preventing isolation for elders. In a 1981 report by Louis Harris and Associates, 14 percent of the nation's 65 + population surveyed said that "getting transportation to stores, to doctors, to places of recreation, and so forth" was a "very serious problem" for them. Inadequate transportation is especially serious for those elders who reside in the suburbs or rural areas where community services may be accessible only to those with automobiles. In urban areas, elderly are often fearful of public transportation or may live too far from the nearest transportation to avail themselves of it.

Health Status of Older Persons. Chronic conditions are more prevalent among older persons than young people; 45 percent of older persons reported limitations in their major activity (e.g., working or keeping house) due to such conditions. The utilization of hospitals increases significantly with advancing age. The hospitalization rate for persons 65 + is 2.5 times greater than that for younger persons. In addition to a higher incidence of hospital admissions, older people stay in the hospital longer than younger persons and account for a disproportionate percentage of medical procedures. It is important to note, however, that most persons 65 + are not hospitalized in any given year. Fewer than two out of every ten persons 65 + are hospitalized as compared with one in ten in the under-65 population. It is estimated that, like the population as a whole, between 15 percent and 25 percent of all persons 65 + *may* have significant symptoms of mental illness, especially depression. However, older people use mental health services at about half the rate of the general population.

The increasing reported incidences of Alzheimer's disease have enormous implications for its victims, family members, and care-givers. The symptoms of memory lapses, confusion, and dementia worsen as the disease progresses, and there is no known cure. It is by far the leading cause of mental deterioration among the elderly. Alzheimer's disease affects between 5 and 10 percent of all people over 65. Alzheimer victims constitute 50 to 60 percent of the 1.3 million people in nursing homes, accounting for more than half of the $25 billion spent annually on such care. The disease will become more common and take an even greater toll as the population begins to age. On July 1, 1985, the United States had, for the first time, more Americans over 65 (27.4 million) than teenagers (26.5 million).

Heart disease, cancer, stroke, and Alzheimer's disease cause 80 percent of the deaths of older people. Diseases of the heart are still the primary cause of death among people of all ages.

Nursing-Home Population. The U.S. nursing-home population has increased markedly during the last two decades. From 1963 to 1977 the number grew from 505,000 to 1.3 million, an increase of 150 percent. The 1977 figure, it must be noted however, represents less than 5 percent of the elderly population, but 20 percent will spend some time in a nursing home during a given year. The likelihood of nursing home residence climbs with age to more than one out of every five persons in the 85 + category. More than 70 percent of nursing-home residents are unmarried women, and whites represent 93 percent of the 65 + residents. Projections by Manton and Liu (1985) predict that between 1985 and 2000 the nursing-home population will increase by 47 percent, from 1.5 to 2.1 million.

Involvement in the Community. A majority of older Americans are active, involved members of society. This is illustrated by several facts: e.g., the elderly are better represented at the voting booth than any other group of the population; 22 percent of the elderly in the United States are currently engaged in volunteer work, and another 10 percent who do not now volunteer are interested in doing so; persons 65 + are the heaviest subscribers to daily newspapers and have the highest rates of regular TV news viewership of any age group in the population. Whether this is primarily a middle-class phenomenon remains to be studied.

Tomorrow's Older People in the United States. A profile of older people in the year 2000 must be undertaken cautiously for unexpected trends could change predictions radically. Yet, it seems likely that the future older person will differ from today's by being better educated, having a higher income, and probably experiencing better health. With the continuing trend to early retirement and a probability that life expectancy will somewhat increase, tomorrow's older people could spend as much as a third of their life in "retirement." Estimates now range from 23 million to 45 million for the number of persons aged 65 and older by the year 2000. The most common prognostication, however, is around 35 million—8 million more than there are today.

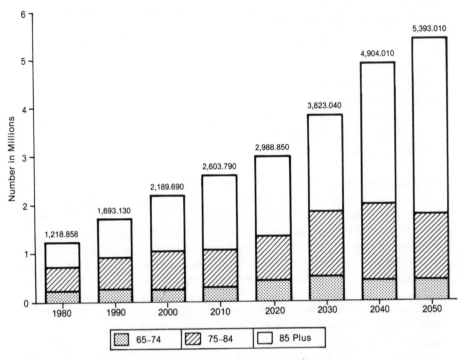

Source: Based on most recent revised estimates of the 1977 population base, Series P-25 #917-1977 estimated, Bureau of the Census; Projections of the Population of the United States: 1982 to 2050 (Advance Report), Current Population Reports, Series P-25, No. 922, October, 1982, Middle Series Projections; and the National Nursing Home Survey (1977); National Center for Health Statistics.

Note: Projections are based on the most recent data available on nursing home utilization and U.S. Bureau of the Census population projections without making assumptions about future changes in nursing home usage.

Figure 3–4. Nursing-Home Population Projections, Persons 65 Years and Older, by Age Group, 1980–2050

Today, most older Americans are younger than 75, but only 2.5 million, about 9 percent, of older Americans are 85 or older. By 2000, there is likely to be a larger percentage of aged persons at the upper end of the age spectrum. Nearly 50 percent of older Americans, or 17 million persons, will be over the age of 75.

Most older persons are women. This trend is expected to accelerate in the years ahead. Today there are approximately 150 women 65 and over for every 100 men. By 2000, this ratio is expected to increase to 155 for every 100. Three viewpoints emerge with regard to life expectancy. One school of thought maintains that life expectancy for adults who reach age 65 will not be much higher than it is today—approximately 13 years for men, 16 years for women, and 15 years on the average. Others contend, however, that if there are major breakthroughs in cures for cancer, stroke, heart disease, and other ailments associated with advancing age, it is conceivable that the average life expectancy at age 65 might be increased to 31 years—more than double what it is today. A third group holds that changing life-styles of people, different nutrition, exercise, reduction of stress, and improved ecological factors could improve health more significantly and thus lengthen life, albeit at the price of increasing chronicity of illnesses and considerable stresses placed on family members and other care providers, who have to deal with these chronic conditions physically, emotionally, and socially.

Educational Participation of Older Adults

The educational attainment of the current population of older adults is much lower than that of younger generations. Older adults are much less likely to have a high school education than younger adults of any age. Figure 3–5 illustrates this point vividly: not quite half of those over 65 had graduated from high school, compared with about 75 percent of those over the age of 25. But this fact is changing. Figure 3–6 indicates that the median number of years of schooling for persons over the age of 65 was 8.1 years in 1940; by 1980 the median had increased to 10.2 years.

When those over aged 55–64 are included, the increase is even more dramatic, rising from 8.2 years in 1940 to 11.9 years in 1979 (1981 White House Conference on Aging, based on Census data). Moreover, the generation of middle-aged adults (those between the ages of 35 and 54) has an even higher rate of participation, with a median of 12.5 years in 1979. As the population shifts in just this decade, the median number of school years is expected to rise to 11.9 years for those over age 65—not much different from the median 12.6 years for the total adult population over the age of 25 (Ventura and Worthy, 1982, 4).

This rise in educational level is particularly significant because prior experience has shown that individuals with higher levels of education are more inclined to enroll in educational programs when they retire (Johnstone and Rivera, 1965; U.S. White House Conference, 1981). For this reason, we can expect increased participation by older adults in educational programs in the future, whether or not special incentives are provided.

The rising participation of older adults in educational activities is already apparent. Table 3–1 reveals that although 3.1 percent of those persons aged 65 and over actually participated in educational activities in 1981, this was a significant increase from the 2.4 percent of the over-65 population who

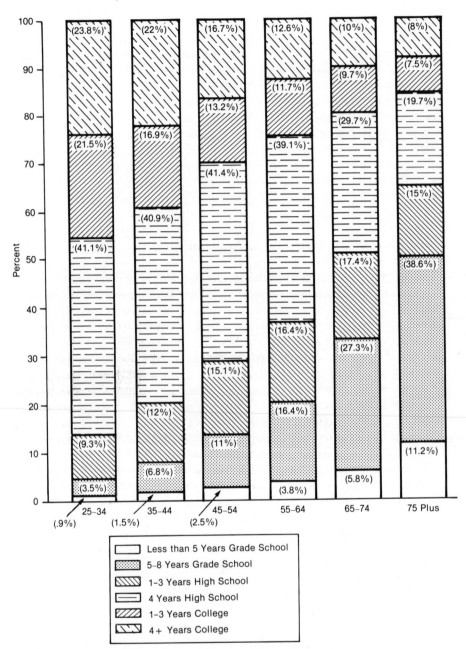

Source: U.S. Bureau of the Census, Current Population Survey, March 1982, unpublished.

Figure 3–5. Educational Attainment by Age, 1981

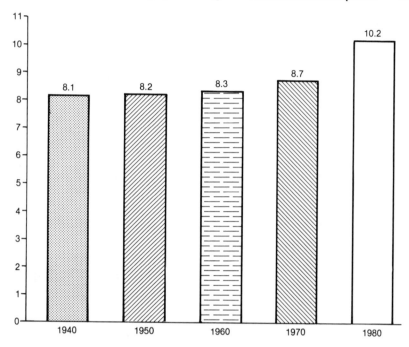

Source: U.S. Bureau of the Census; 1940 Census of the Population Vol. 4, Part 1; 1960 Census of the Population Vol. 1; 1970 Census of the Population Vol. 1, Part 1; 1980 Current Population Survey, unpublished.

Figure 3–6. Median Years of School Completed, Persons 65 Years and Older, 1940–1980

participated just three years before. The older adult population represented the fastest growing age-group of participants in adult education, growing at a rate of 29 percent (Pisko, et al, 1983, 156). Figure 3–7 reflects the dramatic increase in participation in adult education by all adults; indeed, participation in adult education rose faster than the population for all groups except those aged 25–34.

This optimistic picture of increasing educational participation on behalf of older adults must be qualified, however, by recognizing the variation among different groups of older adults. While two-thirds of white persons aged 60 to 74 (half of those over 75) attended high school, this was true for only 40 percent of blacks. (Only 25 percent of blacks over 75 attended high school.) The statistics for higher levels of educational attainment are even more dismal: 33 percent of aged whites graduated from high school, only 16 percent of blacks reached the same level; 10 percent of elderly whites completed four or more years of college; only 3 percent of blacks did the same (Chartbook, 1981).

Table 3-1
Age Distribution of Participants in Adult Education Compared with Population 17 Years Old and Over: Years Ending May 1978 and 1981

Item	Total Population		Participants in Adult Education			Percent Change in Participation Rate From 1978
	Number in Thousands	Percentage Distribution	Number in Thousands	Percentage Distribution	Participants as Percent of Population	
1978						
Total	154,496	100.0	18,197	100.0	11.8	—
17 to 24 years old	31,730	20.3	3,563	19.6	11.2	—
25 to 34 years old	32,881	21.3	6,596	36.2	20.1	—
35 to 54 years old	46,787	30.3	6,091	33.4	13.0	—
55 to 64 years old	20,391	13.2	1,395	7.7	6.8	—
65 years old and over	22,707	14.7	551	3.0	2.4	—
1981						
Total	165,830	100.0	21,252	100.0	12.8	8.5
17 to 24 years old	33,073	19.9	3,941	18.5	11.9	6.3
25 to 34 years old	37,714	22.7	7,509	35.5	19.9	-1.0
35 to 54 years old	48,568	29.3	7,333	34.5	15.1	16.2
55 to 64 years old	21,722	13.1	1,702	8.0	7.8	14.7
65 years old and over	24,753	14.9	768	3.6	3.1	29.2

Source: U.S. Department of Education, National Center for Education Statistics, *Participation in Adult Education, Final Report, 1978* and *1981 Survey of Participation in Adult Education*, unpublished tabulations (November 1982).

Note: Adult education includes all courses and organized educational activities, excluding those taken by full-time students in programs leading to a high school diploma or an academic degree, and other than courses taken as part of occupational training programs of 6 months or more duration. Full-time students who were also engaged in part-time adult education activities were included as participants.

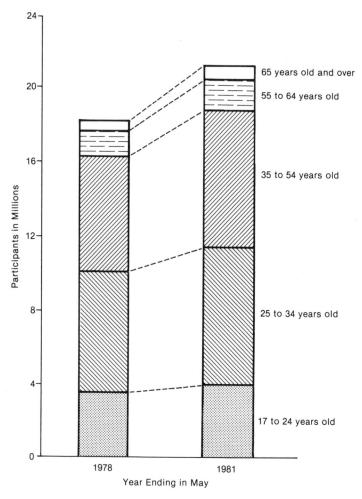

Source: U.S. Department of Education, National Center for Education Statistics, *The Condition of Education,* 1983 edition.

Figure 3–7. Participants in Adult Education, by Age Group, 1978 and 1981

Table 3–2 demonstrates that gaps in educational attainment may be directly related to current rates of participation in adult education. Although the actual numbers and percentages of participants in adult education rose for all groups from 1978 to 1981, participation among whites was almost double (13.8 percent) the percentage for blacks (7.5 percent) for all age groups. For those aged 65 and over, the percentages were 3.3 percent for whites, 1.2 percent for blacks, and 2.1 percent for Hispanics. Notably for nearly all groups, women outnumber men as participants in adult education both in real numbers as well as in proportion to their population.

Table 3-2
Participants in Adult Education, by Sex, Age Group, and Racial/Ethnic Group: Years Ending May 1978 and 1981

Sex and Racial/Ethnic Group	Total	Participants in 1981, by Age Group						Participants in 1978
		17–24 Years	25–34 Years	35–44 Years	45–54 Years	55–64 Years	64 Years and Over	
				Number, in Thousands				
Total	21,252	3,941	7,509	4,512	2,821	1,702	768	18,197
White non-Hispanic	18,674	3,369	6,494	4,010	2,505	1,574	723	16,350
Black non-Hispanic	1,298	283	510	250	158	73	25	900
Hispanic	770	192	300	147	92	25	12	613
Other	510	96	204	105	67	31	8	334
Male	9,358	1,640	3,385	2,075	1,240	739	278	7,820
White non-Hispanic	8,279	1,412	2,935	1,870	1,104	697	261	7,094
Black non-Hispanic	1,505	104	214	98	64	16	10	338
Hispanic	333	78	137	58	48	7	4	260
Other	242	46	98	49	25	20	3	128
Female	11,893	2,300	4,123	2,437	1,581	962	490	10,377
White non-Hispanic	10,395	1,957	3,559	2,140	1,401	877	462	9,255
Black non-Hispanic	793	179	296	152	94	57	15	562
Hispanic	437	114	163	89	44	18	8	353
Other	269	50	106	56	42	11	5	207

Participants as Percent of Population Subgroup

Total	12.8	11.9	19.9	11.0	12.6	7.8	3.1	11.8
White non-Hispanic	13.8	13.2	21.8	19.0	13.5	8.4	3.3	12.7
Black non-Hispanic	7.5	6.6	12.1	9.3	7.1	3.8	1.2	5.7
Hispanic	8.6	7.9	11.9	9.3	8.3	3.5	2.1	8.3
Other	13.4	10.6	18.6	15.0	14.2	9.2	2.7	12.8
Male	12.0	10.2	18.4	16.4	11.5	7.3	2.7	10.7
White non-Hispanic	12.9	11.3	19.8	18.0	12.2	7.9	2.9	11.6
Black non-Hispanic	6.6	5.3	11.4	8.2	6.4	1.9	1.2	4.8
Hispanic	7.7	6.3	11.2	7.9	9.1	2.1	1.6	7.4
Other	13.3	10.0	20.5	14.1	11.4	12.4	2.2	10.8
Female	13.6	13.6	21.4	18.1	13.6	8.3	3.4	12.7
White non-Hispanic	14.6	15.1	23.7	19.9	14.7	8.8	3.6	13.7
Black non-Hispanic	8.2	7.7	12.6	10.1	7.6	5.4	1.2	6.4
Hispanic	9.4	9.6	12.5	10.5	7.5	4.8	2.5	9.2
Other	13.5	11.3	17.1	15.8	16.7	6.2	3.2	14.6

Source: U.S. Department of Education, National Center for Education Statistics, *Participation in Adult Education, May 1981*, and unpublished tabulations (June 1982).

Note: Data refer to participants in courses and organized educational activities, excluding those taken by full-time students in programs leading to a high school diploma or an academic degree, and other than courses taken as part of occupational training programs of 6 months or more duration. Full-time students who were also engaged in part-time adult education activities were included as participants.

Details may not add to totals because of rounding.

The members of the Technical Committee on Education for the 1981 White House Conference on Aging warned that the proportion of older adults participating in formal education was small and "relatively advantaged." They noted that "to merely extend the scale of present efforts would have little impact on the educational needs of older people whose level of educational attainment is low, who are members of minority groups, who are physically handicapped, and who are poor" (U.S. White House Conference, 1981, 36). In its recommendations to the Conference delegates, the members of the Technical Committee argued for a range of actions aimed at expanding opportunities for all older adults to participate in educational activities at all levels. Those recommendations will be reviewed in later chapters.

What Are the Implications of These Demographic Characteristics?

To put it dramatically at the outset, our society faces two radical options: either to prepare ourselves for an increasing lifespan for a large segment of our population by curtailing the present standard of living in the younger and middle years of middle- and higher-income class groups (via public and private sector arrangements, such as paying higher taxes and higher Social Security premiums and instituting national health-care financing mechanisms geared toward preventive, chronic, *and* acute health care on a continuum), or to cut off the older segment of our population from societal benefits by curtailing health-care measures, decreasing public and private pensions (including Social Security) and social services, limiting educational opportunities, depriving them of voting rights, and so on—in effect to devise a policy of exclusion, if not outright elimination, of an older population. There are major ethical, moral, political, economic, and social (including educational) issues at stake. These options are posed deliberately as dichotomies in order to highlight their significance and to generate serious public policy dialogues. (A suggestion to disenfranchise the elderly was made by T. Stewart in the middle fifties in an article in *The New Republic.*)

Making the assumption, however, that we will choose option number one and move toward a society that is inclusive of older persons and which considers them a part of its total fabric—a society of the young, middle-aged, and elderly—there are a host of issues that have to be considered, such as our outlook on the meaning of life in general, the intergenerational distribution of national resources, the uses and structuring of time, the structure of lifelong education, a variety of arrangements for health care, the functions of religion, the roles of the young, the middle-aged and the aging cohorts living at the same time in history.

Let's single out some specific implications for a brief analysis: 1) implications for the family; 2) implications for social welfare in general; and 3) implications for educational policy.

1. *Implications for the Family*

America's trend toward an older population has already changed the nature of our family structure. Three- and four-generation families have become increasingly common, with an estimated one third of all persons 65 + having at least one grandchild and one fourth of persons 58–59 having one or more surviving parents. Neither is it uncommon for elderly to outlive their adult offspring. The Family Service Administration (1985) study, "The State of Families," has highlighted several of these trends.

Traditionally, middle-aged offspring, in most cases women, have taken care of their aging parents. Today, many more of these daughters are in the work force or going to school and/or struggling with supporting and educating their own offspring at the same time. More of their parents live into old age today, many of them suffering chronic illnesses that necessitate ongoing care. Also, middle-aged adults are increasingly placed in the position of supporting their adult offspring for longer than ever before. The question arises, therefore, of just how long the "sandwich generation" can stand the squeeze. It becomes obvious how critical this question is when one realizes that 80 percent of the care given to our elders is given by their families (National Center for Health Statistics, 1984; Brody, 1981).

Presently, an estimated 75 percent of the old remain in independent living situations cared for by spouses of either sex, while 18 percent live with an adult child. There are relatively few living in isolation; statistically, 80 percent of older people see a close relative every week (Shanas, 1968; *The Older We Get . . . An Action Guide to Social Change,* 1985). Because of the increase among older people who are dependent upon health and social care supports, the prospect is of an aging population in which the old will be caring for the very old—with all the emotional and financial strains which that implies. Right now, at least 5 million Americans are caring for a parent on any given day and, for all their dedication to the task, they experience considerable stress in the process. What is needed is orchestration of assistance to the elderly and to the care-givers to alleviate this stress. For example, those families who have to care for persons suffering from Alzheimer's disease may greatly benefit by joining the numerous mutual aid/self-help and educational groups (Simmons, Ivry and Seltzer, 1985; Mace and Rabins, 1982).

Family relationships of older persons are maintained through an exchange of resources and services. Help is provided across generations by older persons receiving as well as giving help. The majority of elders also help their spouses, children, and grandchildren. They also receive help from their spouses and children, such as assistance with home repairs, housework, babysitting, care in illness and various kinds of gifts. Many older people function as contributing members of the family. They not only take needed resources from their children, they also reciprocate as much as their means allow. Adult children and grandchildren benefit from their parents' contributions at the same time that the elderly themselves gain from the help they receive from their children. Aluma Motenko, in her forthcoming dissertation, investigates the role of husbands as care-providers; so far she has found support for one of her hypotheses—that care-giving by retired men increases their sense of self-esteem and provides a time structure in their lives. The ability of older persons to give as well as to receive within the family is an important contribution to the self-esteem of the elderly.

The most important function in providing care is care-management (still referred to as "case-management"). The first step is to arrive at an assessment. Family members must be alert to the daily functioning of their spouse, parents, or grandparents. They must listen carefully without being intrusive, evaluate the strengths and resources by observing the older person's behavior to conduct activities of daily living and communicate with their older parent or spouse. Families who have a close, warm relationship, visit frequently, and engage in activities together will be better able to have fuller knowledge of the elder's daily patterns and preferences than families who are not as close physically and emotionally. Long-distance managing not only takes time and money, it is emotionally exhausting as well. Not being close at hand for a parent breeds anxieties and guilt (see, for instance, Kane and Lebow, 1984).

The second step is to find out what professional and lay health, social, and educational services are available and accessible in the community and at the same time acceptable to the older person. Public media—newspapers, magazines, radio, TV—have a responsibility to teach, to portray aging as a normal aspect of human development. The fear of growing old and prejudices against aging and the aged have to be combated. All of us professionals and citizens have to let local, state, and federal officials know that aging is here to stay and that the population as a whole is growing older.

2. Implications for Social Welfare Policy in General

The inspiration for creating a system of social insurance came from Germany, where in 1884 Chancellor Bismarck set up a comprehensive program of "state socialism" for the country's working class. The program, which included accident-, medical-, and old-age insurance, and a limited program of factory inspections, was the first such state-run, state-subsidized insurance system in Europe. Today, most major industrial countries have comprehensive old-age and medical-insurance programs in place and, as Henry Steele Commager (1985, 31) observes, the United States "is still 40 years behind" because of its failure to enact a national health-insurance plan for all its citizens.

The social-insurance system that has grown up in this country since 1935 was a major new departure—financial as well as philosophical—committing the federal government to care for its most vulnerable citizens. In 1986 the total benefits from these programs inches toward the $200 million mark. For the first 15 years there were few changes in the Social Security Act. In the years since, Congress has enacted major new benefits programs, including disability insurance in 1956 and supplemental-security income (SSI) in 1972, providing a minimum floor of financial protection for the poor, elderly, blind and disabled. The growth in federal transfer payments to the elderly is the primary reason for a decline in the poverty rate among the elderly. "Medicare" has seen its budget grow from $5.8 billion in 1970 to an estimated $71.8 billion today. Thirty million elderly and disabled people now take part in the federally financed health-insurance program.

Because of its soaring costs, "Medicare" in particular has become a prime target of the Reagan Administration's budget cutters; between 1981 and 1985, Congress has agreed to cutbacks worth more than $18 billion through a series of changes aimed at hospitals, doctors, and beneficiaries alike. Pressure for further cuts in Medicare spending has been intensified by reports of looming bankruptcy of the program's hospital-insurance trust fund. Despite the reforms of 1983, the "date of doom" has merely been pushed back from the late 1980s to the late 1990s (Commager, 1985, 32–34).

The Social Security program is an "intergenerational transfer program," by which the younger generation takes care of the older generation through a national administrative mechanism (Lowy, 1982, 3–4). Though opinions differ as to why, the consensus is that Social Security will survive the fiscally conservative climate of the 1980s. The main reason is that it meets different needs and has public and political support, because as a social-insurance program it provides a predictable retirement income benefit, while at the same time respecting the dignity of the individual beneficiary.

We are moving toward abolishing mandatory retirement, but the key in the future is to adjust our Social Security system to create options to establish "flexible retirement" patterns and equitablity for men and women. The "Older Americans Act," in existence since 1965, is the only federal piece of legislation exclusively directed to the social care of the elderly; however, it needs to be strengthened, fiscally and programmatically (Lowy, 1980, 36–41).

3. *Implications for Education*

The increasing ratio of older to younger people has its implications for education and their institutions as well. On the one hand we are going to see a longer, if not necessarily better educated, generation emerging with expectations for opportunities in traditional settings, schools, colleges, and in multiservice centers, and so on; on the other hand we are going to experience a search for occupations of available time other than through and outside the marketplace. Whether unoccupied time can be called "leisure" is of more than semantic interest, as we associate leisure with "time off from work." Once a person is no longer in the workforce, he/she cannot be a member of the "leisure class" by definition. And here lies the rub: retirement systems—whether flexible or mandatory—are still oriented toward retirement, but to what and where? To be sure, many women and men are kept busy taking care of their families, their health, and their finances worrying about the next day, week, month or year. Others are kept busy going, rushing, traveling, visiting, volunteering, working, and just plain doing.

Increasingly the caretaking functions assumed by family members, peers, friends, and neighbors call for skills—training, and practical education of these care-providers and collaborative partnerships between professionals and non-professionals of any age will become necessary in the community as well as in nursing homes and similar institutions. A good illustration is a project recently developed jointly by Boston University School of Social Work and the Jewish Family Service of Greater Boston:

The Family-Centered Community Care for the Elderly project included 202 clients and their families who were referred to the agency between January 1982 and December 1983. The agency training program drew upon the social worker's practice, skill, and experience to provide individualized training in case management to families. The specific instructions and strategies used to assist an individual family member to perform case management tasks related directly to and emerged from the case management needs of that family member's elderly relative. Problems which were encountered in the performance of case management activities and family members' responses to these problems shaped the individualized training provided to each individual. Specifically, the agency training program consisted of: 1. The expectation that the participating family member identified by the elderly client, would assume responsibility for the performance of at least one new case management task, dictated by the needs of the elderly client, during the course of agency service. 2. Collaboration between the social worker and family member on the development of a service plan for the elderly client, including allocation of case management tasks between family member and social worker. 3. Provision to the family member of information on community resources and entitlements. Family members received the following five training booklets specifically developed for the project: Guide to In-Home Services; Guide to Housing; Day Care, Respite Care and Nursing Homes; Guide to Transportation and Social Opportunities; Guide to Financial Entitlements and Legal

Protective Services; Guide to Advocacy. 4. Regular contact with family members via telephone or in-person interview. The objectives of systematic contact between the caseworker and the family member were to enhance family case management skill; to provide individualized consultation on how to perform assigned case management tasks; to monitor case management performance; to provide supportive counseling; and to ensure ongoing assessment of client needs . . .

Preliminary analyses indicate that experimental group families performed more case management tasks on behalf of their elderly relatives than did control families. Interestingly, no differences appeared between the two groups with respect to the number of case management tasks performed by the social workers. Furthermore, experimental group cases were, on the average, of shorter duration than control group cases, suggesting that, when families join in partnership with the agency, more service can be provided to the elderly client in a shorter period of time than is ordinarily the case. A full-scale analysis of data is currently underway . . . (Simmons, Ivry and Seltzer, 1985, 345)

Similar projects are on-going in Massachusetts, as well as in other parts of the country.

Nevertheless, the idea of a certain period in life free from societal obligations with time available for the development of one's own wants, desires, dreams, and self-assumed tasks is tantalizing as well as frightening to many. Is the "late freedom," as Rosenmayr (1983) terms it, myth or reality? Can education be one of the options to give meaning to our lives though at a later stage? Can education deliver what is promised in its name? The data in this section compel us to look at learning and teaching, at experiencing and absorbing, at claiming time and using time.

4
Margins of Power

Much has been written to prove that older adults can indeed learn, possibly as well as people in younger years, that they have a wide range of educational needs and wants, and that there are specific experiences which can enhance or discourage learning. Canestrari (1963), Eisdorfer (1963), Axelrod and Eisdorfer (1961), Hulicka and Weiss (1965) investigated learning capacities of older people and found that with more time available to them than to younger persons, they could solve cognitive problems just as well. "The more time available to aging persons, the more capable of mastering intellectual tasks" (Eisdorfer, 1967).

This chapter will review what we know about learning abilities, motivations, problems, needs, and opportunities of older adults. The following can only hope to give the reader new to the field a preliminary understanding of the extent of research in educational gerontology to date and to provide evidence that conditions necessary for the education of older adults do prevail. (For more information, see bibliographic note 1 at the end of this chapter.)

Learning Abilities of Older Adults

Research in the early part of this century suggested that learning ability, particularly in the cognitive realm, peaked in youth and declined steadily thereafter. Studies by Thorndike (1928), Miles and Miles (1932), and Jones and Conrad (1933), among others, all confirmed a learning peak at around the age of 20 with significant decline in the later years. Myths and clichés about mental decline in old age were thus reinforced by scientific studies. Major revisions in scholarly thinking about learning have provided a much more optimistic picture of adult learners; nevertheless, many old stereotypes continue to influence public thinking.

Because the early studies of learning ability compared young people with old people, many biases in these studies were later discovered. The older test subjects tended to have fewer years of educational training than their younger counterparts, and this was found to influence test results. More important was the recognition that the timed nature of the tests had biased the results in favor of youth by measuring speed of response rather than quality of response. Irving Lorge (1955) was one of the first to isolate the effect of speed of response on performance. After testing adults under timed and untimed conditions, he argued that there was a noticeable decline in the speed of response but not necessarily a decline in the power to react.

Building on this question about speed of response, Canestrari (1963) attempted to isolate the effects of pacing on the performance of older adults. Using three levels of pacing—fast, medium, and self-pacing—he compared the performance of a group of young (aged 17–35) and old (aged 60–69) persons. Canestrari found that although the younger respondents performed better than the old on all the tests, the older subjects improved much more than the young when they were allowed to pace themselves. The results were a major breakthrough which had practical implications for those teaching older adults.

In addition to concerns about pacing, studies in the 1950s began to look at data over time, attempting to capture differences in individual performance that were influenced by the aging process as opposed to those influenced by external factors. A group of young men who had taken the Army Alpha test upon entering Iowa State College were contacted thirty years later for a follow-up test. At age 50, the men improved their test scores. And in a subsequent test, when the same men were about age 60, their scores still did not decrease (Owens, 1966). This research revealed that adults could improve, or at least retain, their cognitive learning abilities over time. Similar results were discovered in other longitudinal studies (Terman and Oden, 1955; Duncan and Barrett, 1961; Eisdorfer, 1963). The results pointed to the need to integrate cross-sectional data with longitudinal data in order to gain a truer picture of the learning abilities of older adults.

Increased attention to adult learning abilities led to the development of various theories of intelligence and memory. Horn and Catell (1966) hypothesized that there were two kinds of intelligence: fluid and crystallized. Fluid intelligence was presumed to consist of the ability to perceive complex relations, engage in short-term memory, form and shape concepts and engage in abstract reasoning. Because it was tied to short-term memory, fluid intelligence was relatively easy to measure in standard memory tests—recalling strings of numbers, letters, and so on.

Crystallized intelligence was the ability to perceive relations and to engage in formal reasoning and abstraction based on a familiarity with knowledge of the intellectual and cultural heritage of society. It involved long-term memory and was cumulative. It was based on learning that required a previous foundation to be built on—as, for example, learning about cooking a new recipe when one already knew how to cook. Together, these two kinds of intelligence covered many of the learning tasks confronted by adults, contributing to the global capacity to learn, to reason, and solve problems. Combined, they formed what is commonly understood by "intelligence."

The two kinds of intelligence were presumed to increase during childhood and into adolescence. However, with the slowing of the maturation process, the lifelong accumulation of injury to neural structures, fluid intelligence tended to peak during adolescence and decline gradually during adulthood; crystallized intelligence, on the other hand, continued to increase gradually throughout adulthood (Fozard, 1972). General learning ability remained relatively stable, but, to quote (Knox, 1977, 421), "the older person tends to increasingly compensate for the loss of fluid intelligence by greater reliance on crystallized intelligence, to substitute wisdom for brilliance."

Continued growth of crystallized intelligence depends on continuing accumulation through information-seeking and educational activity (Knox, 1977, 604). This is why older persons may be able to enhance their learning and problem-solving abilities through actively applying accumulated wisdom gained through life experiences; opportunities for doing so are necessary to facilitate this process and reinforce learning.

Other theorists have focused on the process of storing and retrieving information in memory. Arenberg and Robertson (1974), major architects of this "information processing" approach to learning, developed a theoretical model which they then related to various empirical studies of memory. They proposed a three-part system for cognitive functioning consisting of a sensory register, primary memory, and secondary memory.

The first level of information processing, the sensory register, was assumed to store information briefly (measured in fractions of a second) so that the mind could select and discard those bits of information which were not useful. All information not transferred immediately to primary memory was thus discarded. Information transferred to primary memory was retained for longer periods (measured in minutes), but the storage capacity in primary memory was assumed to be quite limited. Trying to remember a list of unrelated words gives an indication of the limited capacity of primary memory. Finally, secondary memory was the long-term storage mechanism (time measured in hours, days, or years). Information to be retained for these longer periods would, according to this theory, be transferred from primary to secondary memory.

The power of the theory rested not simply in its ability to categorize various components of the cognitive process but in suggesting an explanation for some of the age differences found in test situations. Arenberg and Robertson suggested that the effect of pacing on learning for older adults was related to the recall of information stored in secondary memory. Studies found that slowing the pacing in test situations improved the subject's ability to remember earlier information (e.g., items presented early on a list—presumably stored in secondary memory), but had no effect on the ability to remember the most recent information presumed to be retained in primary memory. Recall from primary memory was virtually automatic; recall from secondary memory seemed to involve a separate process, which was enhanced by increased time and the ability to practice or rehearse information.

This model of information processing suggested that the brain behaved somewhat like a computer, taking longer to retrieve information as the volume of information in storage increased. In addition to supporting the need for older learners to have more time for recall of information, it called attention to the retrieval process, stating that if the information stored in secondary memory were well-organized, it might be easier to retrieve in memory exercises and in real life. Hulicka and Grossman (1967) tested this among young and old adults. They found that if the older subjects were not specifically instructed to use cues for remembering paired items, they tended to use cues much less often than the younger subjects. However, when all subjects were encouraged to use such memory devices to help them organize the information for storage, the older subjects showed greater improvement than the younger ones.

Similar results were found by others (Schonfield and Robertson, 1966; Laurence, 1967; Rabbit, 1968; Hultsch, 1969). It became clear that the performance of older adults in testing situations could be significantly improved through the use of memory aids and models for organizing information to be presented.

Increasingly, learning theorists have recognized that learning is a composite of cognitive (information–knowledge), emotional (attitudes), and skill (motor–behavioral) processes. J. Bruner, N.L. Gage, W.J. McKeachie, R.W. Tyler, and A.N. Whitehead, among others, were the leading lights in establishing the trichotomy of attitudinal–knowledge–skill development, postulating integration of learning and teaching (Bruner, 1961; Dressel, 1960) that takes on a Gestalt quality. Incidentally, they go back to Plato's discovery in *Phaedro* and *The Republic,* in which he speaks of a hierarchy of "shadows, images, models and ideas," and to Aristotle's philosophy, in which the hierarchy starts with "sensation," moves on to "experience," "practical and recreational arts," and "productive and theoretical sciences," eventually leading to "wisdom."

Research on learning abilities since the mid-1970s has begun again to focus on the total environment in which learning takes place. Hultsch (1977) calls this a "contextual" approach which considers the total learning context. Thus the cognitive processes—learning, memory, intelligence, and problem-solving skills—may be influenced by noncognitive factors, including not only pacing but also other environmental factors, such as the meaningfulness of the learning activity, attitudes and motivations of the learner, over- or under-arousal. In developing the theory of noncognitive influences on learning, Botwinick (1973) emphasized the difference between learning itself and performance on various tests. The former is an internal process which cannot be seen by an outside observer; the latter is what is measured in so-called tests of learning ability, but it is subject to interruption by various noncognitive factors. Clearly, if an older person's hearing or vision is poor, he or she may have difficulty in receiving and thus relaying information. To suggest that this is a deficit in learning ability is not only a disservice to the older learner but also ignores information which can be used to improve the learning environment for that person by eliminating distracting noise, improving lighting, using audio and/or visual aids.

Attention to noncognitive factors has raised questions about the effect of attitudes on learning and performance. Many researchers have reported the failure of older adults to perform well in learning tests which are not meaningful to them (Hulicka, 1967; Woodruff and Walsh, 1975; Calhoun and Gounard, 1979). In a test in which elders were asked to remember paired associates which had no relation to one another, 80 percent of the older subjects (aged 65–80) refused to complete the exercises. When the tasks were made more meaningful, the older subjects were willing to cooperate (Hulicka, 1967). It is often not possible to measure the extent to which lack of interest may lead older adults to achieve poor results in testing situations, but here was a measurable effect.

Many older adults may have accepted the stereotypical adage that "you can't teach an old dog new tricks." Although a myth, this negative stereotype has affected attitudes of the general public and of educators and has restricted older adults from taking advantage of learning opportunities. Also, depression and anxiety, common among older adults, may diminish motivation to learn. Such motivational problems may distract the learner from the work at hand and may thus inhibit performance in testing situations in greater proportions for older adults than for younger adults (Hayslip and Kennelly, 1985).

It is of interest to note that research has also demonstrated that being highly motivated can also become a disadvantage in a learning situation. Powell, Eisdorfer and Bogdonoff (1964) found that older persons tended to be more nervous or excited in laboratory tests than younger subjects. This "overarousal" was later found to interfere with the learning experience for the older test subjects. When Eisendorfer, Nowlin and Wilkie (1970) gave the test subjects medication to prevent such overarousal of the nervous system, the older adults achieved better results on the tests.

Many factors seem to combine to disadvantage older adults in testing situations: fast pacing, lack of experience with standardized testing, relatively low educational background (see demographic data in chapter 2 for elaboration on this point), lack of motivation to learn trivial bits of information, overstimulation, and sensory deficits (especially hearing and vision). While tests will often attempt to control for one of these factors—e.g., by allowing self-pacing—they usually allow another disadvantage to creep in, as, for example, by testing meaningless paired associates. One study (Friend and Zubek, 1958) attempted to assess the critical thinking ability of older adults using the Watson Glaser Critical Thinking Appraisal Test and found older adults to be less objective and flexible than the younger persons in the study. However, while this test did not pose trivial questions and allowed self-pacing, problems of different degrees of experience with standardized tests, lower levels of education and fatigue could have accounted for the results.

Consequently, older adults have continued to perform less well in testing situations than younger adults. Yet, it is important to keep in mind Botwinick's distinction between learning and performance, along with the different composites of learning: cognitive, emotional, and behavioral. What we are currently able to measure may fail to capture the true composite learning abilities of older adults; we may find that older adults have important strengths which assist them in any or all these differential composites of learning.

Riegel and Riegel (1972) have suggested that the declines in performance which have been noted among older adults may be related to approaching death rather than aging itself. According to their findings, there is a tendency for IQ scores to decline among those who are very close to death. Called "terminal drop," this phenomenon may provide yet another explanation for the lower test scores of older adults when compared with younger adults, since more of the older adults in samples may be presumed to be nearer to death. Whether this is true of younger people with terminal illnesses or those who are "death-oriented" or feel themselves to be near death remains an important question for investigation. By the way, this would fit in with Moody's (1985) assumptions that the older people get, the more they are oriented toward the time left to live rather than toward the time of their birth. Further studies on the dying process (Kübler-Ross, 1969; Kastenbaum, 1981; Kalish, 1984, 1985; Feifel, 1959) may shed more light on this aspect of learning, if learning abilities and motivations are used as dependent variables. Recent empirical work in Sweden has supported the theory of terminal decline and learning (Berg, 1985).

As stated, the theory of crystallized intelligence suggests the possibility that accumulated knowledge and experience is a strength which compensates for the losses in speed of response. Unfortunately, there have been no empirical studies as yet to determine to what extent such crystallized knowledge is a strength as opposed to a weakness involving the need to correct misinformation or to learn different lessons from experience. However, there is certainly room for optimism that much of what one learned in the past can at least inform the present.

In a related search for the strengths of older learners, Woodruff and

Walsh (1975) indicate that the greater self-awareness of older adults may enhance their learning abilities. Hypothesizing that older persons have a greater "internal awareness" as a result of the longer time and experience with their own bodies, Woodruff and Walsh suggest that this bodily self-awareness may enhance the ability of older adults to learn adaptations to such physical conditions as hypertension. They propose testing their hypothesis with biofeedback studies, hypothesizing that since old people can learn to produce more fast brain waves, it may be possible to affect their capacity to process information" (Woodruff and Walsh, 1975, 429). In a similar vein, Ager and her colleagues (1981–82) identified three factors necessary to enhance creative processes during the later years: (1) development of an attitude of exploration in the learner, (2) exercise of body and mind as well as exercise of choice and responsibility, (3) planning ahead. These studies reflect the important relationships between physical and mental capacities.

Many have questioned the validity of laboratory studies and have emphasized the need for realistic test settings (Hartley et al., 1980; Hultsch and Hickey, 1978; Hayslip and Kennelly, 1985). Since most tests of learning ability have been performed in the laboratory, there is a need for evidence to demonstrate whether and in what situations older adults might perform better or worse than younger adults in real-life situations.

Although studies have not shown older adults to be superior to younger students, there is ample evidence that older adults can indeed learn and often at much the same level as their younger counterparts when environmental and situational factors have been better equalized. Minimizing the factors which may interfere with learning has come to be seen as a major task of educators of older adults.

Barriers to Education

Various barriers to education of older adults have been identified in the literature. Identification of certain barriers will depend on which types of elders are being asked, what their backgrounds are, and what educational activity is being considered. Numerous studies shed useful light on the diversity of barriers which may restrict older adults from participation in educational activity.

A relatively early study, *Volunteers for Learning* (Johnstone and Rivera, 1965) reported that older adults themselves found costs, lack of time, and lack of energy to be the major barriers to educational participation, more so than for the younger adults surveyed. This is particularly interesting because Johnstone and Rivera's study was not simply one of participation in formal courses; their survey defined educational activity as "all activities consciously and systematically organized for purposes of acquiring new knowledge, information, or skills" (p. 1). Indeed, the older adults in their study tended more often than not to pursue their educational endeavors outside of formal classes. Older adults also frequently reported feeling "too old to learn." This barrier, however, was peculiar to persons from lower socioeconomic backgrounds. This stereotype about learning in old age may in fact have reflected negative attitudes about learning in general and also may be reflected in the very low participation in educational activities among those in the lower socioeconomic class in the study.

Other surveys of older adults have yielded similar results. Explaining why they were not taking courses or enrolled in an educational institution, older adults (aged 65 +) in a Harris (1975) study reported the following reasons for nonparticipation in order of priority; not interested, too old, poor health, not enough time, don't know of any courses for me, none available, too expensive. Only 2 percent of the older adults in this survey were participating in courses.

In attempting to establish a framework for understanding the various educational barriers faced by adults, Patricia Cross (1979) suggested three types of barriers: situational, dispositional, and institutional.

Situational barriers are those restrictions on educational activity which arise because of the circumstances of the individual's life situation. These may include costs, need for transportation, and restrictions because of physical handicaps or poor health. Lack of time, energy, and financial resources are among the situational barriers identified by the elders in the studies cited above.

Dispositional barriers are attitudinal restrictions on activity, particularly lack of interest or feeling too old to learn. These feature prominently among the reasons given by older adults for failure to engage in educational activity, but Johnstone and Rivera (1965) suggest that reports may actually understate the influence of dispositional barriers. They note that cost, lack of time, or other situational barriers may be perceived as more socially acceptable reasons for avoiding educational activities and thus may be given as reasons instead of just saying "I'm not interested." Attitudes of educators themselves may also present dispositional barriers (U.S. White House Conference on Aging, 1981). Educators who believe that older adults cannot or should not engage in educational activities can convey this message in rather subtle ways and thus discourage future participants. As C. Bolton (1985, 436) points out in a recent book review essay, "unless they [educators] recognize that gerontologists can contribute to their endeavors, their practices will reflect what has been a general experience in the past: older learners will stay away in droves."

Finally, *institutional barriers* were identified by Cross (1979) as a third factor restricting participation of older adults. These are barriers which result from the tendency of institutions to have inflexible operating procedures which have not been developed with older adults in mind. These include conditions reported by older adults themselves—lack of knowledge about courses available to them (a sign that marketing and outreach activities have not been targeted to them)—as well as inconvenient scheduling and registration procedures, inaccessible buildings, and lack of counseling and financial aid.

Because of the different types of barriers to educational activity, overcoming the institutional barriers is by no means a simple task. Educational institutions which have sought to include older adults have found that scheduling classes during the day in accessible locations is not enough. Special outreach efforts are often needed, and this may include having the registration and the actual educational activity take place in an environment familiar to the prospective older student. Multiservice senior centers, libraries, churches, and elder housing complexes are sites which may be more desirable for many older learners (Glickman, 1975). Also, consideration should be given to controlling some of the environmental factors which can make the learning experience a negative one, i.e., by making sure the room is well-lighted and quiet, has comfortable seating, is close to restrooms and refreshment areas, and is accessible by wheelchair.

Overcoming the situational barriers can also be accomplished by making transportation available and reducing personal expenses incurred for those who enroll. Many colleges and universities have reduced costs for older adults who choose to attend their programs by offering free or reduced tuition; such tuition waiver programs are now available in all fifty states (Timmerman, 1981). This directly removes one situational barrier, but it is not without its own costs. Because institutions generally receive no reimbursement for older students whose tuition is waived (Romaniuk, 1982), there may be little incentive for colleges and universities to change other institutional or situational barriers. Moreover, because such tuition waiver programs usually allow older adults to register for classes after tuition-paying students have registered, they may create a category of second-class students, as Weinstock has warned (1978). Even measures like these which seem to have no, or minimal, costs, may have other social costs which discourage their use. Nevertheless, like overcoming institutional barriers, overcoming situational barriers is relatively straightforward.

It is the dispositional (attitudinal) barriers which are most insidious and difficult to overcome. Because they are based on individual attitudes formed over many years, these restrictions on the participation of older adults are much more deeply rooted. Creating a climate for learning can go a long way toward changing these dispositional barriers. This involves paying attention to spatial and time arrangements, as well as to social-psychological dimensions, such as genuinely according feelings of respect to people's opinions, interests, and capacities. Older persons need to participate in planning, shaping, and carrying out the educational enterprise. A non-threatening atmosphere that allows for give and take, instructors who make use of the cumulative experience of older adults, these help to encourage such participation and to promote active rather than passive learning by older adults. If elders find out that their peers experience such a welcome atmosphere, they may be more inclined to participate. In research on helping relationships and creating a welcoming climate for learning and helping, Carkhuff (1973) and Truax (1967) found that four qualities have to be present and communicated: empathy, acceptance, unconditional positive regard for others, and genuineness.

Elimination of these barriers to educational participation of older adults involves a concerted societal effort to convince older people now and in the future not only that they can learn but that they themselves have educational needs, educational capacities and opportunities, and above all that there is a value to education in the later years, to themselves, their social world, and to society. It is therefore essential that those involved in educating older adults become not only familiar with, but more and more knowledgeable about, those special factors that may affect learning for older students. Educational facilitators can help older learners to improve the efficiency of their learning by compensating for difficulties in storing and retrieving information in long-term memory, declines in vision and hearing, poor health, and barriers caused by motivation.

Marginal Theory of Power

In developing the background material on education for the 1971 White House Conference on Aging, McClusky (1971) developed a "theory of margin" to depict the struggle that adults face in attempting to maintain a minimum level of autonomy in their lives. The marginal level of energy required for the individual to maintain autonomy was represented by a balance between what McClusky called the individual's load. i.e., the demands made on the individual—and the individual's power—i.e., the resources which she/he possessed to control the load. The desired state of autonomy was represented by a state in which the individual's power was at least marginally greater than his or her load.

McClusky theorized that older individuals frequently faced a disruption in their sense of autonomy because of an increase in their load (e.g., increased expenses, new caregiving responsibilities, illness) and/or decreases in power (e.g., role losses, reduced income, decreased energy). Gaining a sufficient level of power to maintain a sense of autonomy could be achieved by decreasing the load or increasing the power, for it was not the total amount of the load that mattered but its relationship to the individual's personal power. McClusky saw education as "a major force in the achievement of . . . margins of power for the attainment and maintenance of well-being, and continuing growth toward self-fulfillment" (p. 2).

Attention to individual and collective power has been a major focus of social welfare advocates in the 1980s. Empowerment has become a rallying cry for many minority groups, for homeless people, the mentally ill, abused women and elders, along with many other groups which have experienced continuing oppression in our society. The Gray Panthers have adopted the term *empowerment,* as have the Older Women's League and various other advocacy groups. A special funding source, the Villers Foundation, was established in 1981 with a goal of "nurturing a movement of empowerment among elders" (Villers Foundation brochure).

Empowerment is a process of helping others to take control of the decisions that affect their lives. "Empowerment focuses on increasing the capacity of people to function on their own behalf" (Akins, 1985). It is a "mechanism by which people, organizations, and communities gain mastery over their lives" (Rappaport, 1984). This is not power which seeks to dominate or control others but rather a personal sense of power which enables individuals to exercise control over their own lives, to experience a sense of autonomy and mastery.

Viewed in this context, McClusky's marginal theory of power can be seen as a forerunner of the empowerment movement which even in Reagan's era has been acknowledged as a significant political fact, despite attempts to question its validity. McClusky's theory illuminates how empowerment works by elevating education in its broadest sense to a primary tool of empowerment to achieve social welfare goals. By enabling individuals to better understand themselves and the world around them, education can increase their ability to control those aspects of their loads which can be controlled. Education can thus tip the scales in favor of individual autonomy, growth, and fulfillment (certain shades of Paulo Freire's notions are visible) and arrive at a healthier balance of life situations.

Educational Needs

McClusky (1971) did not further elaborate his marginal theory of power but rather went on to discuss the various needs that older adults had for educational experiences. Presumably, optimal fulfillment of these needs would translate into increases in the marginal power of older adults through learning ways in which to decrease their loads or to increase their power.

All people have needs. The term *needs* has a variety of meanings. It can either be a condition marked by the lack of something requisite, or a requirement for survival, growth, health, social acceptance, and so on. Needs are socially molded and defined but individually felt and expressed, interfacing with norms, expectations, and demands by society. In order to satisfy these needs, people rely on inner resources, that is, they make use of their personal motivations, capacities, ego strengths, as well as external resources, i.e., social measures. Such measures include social supports, programs, services, and education. The degree of equilibrium that exists at any time in the life span of people in this interface determines how well they cope and what kinds of changes—whether on individual or social levels, or on both—are necessary to achieve better personal functioning and a better functioning social order that moves toward achieving more equitable conditions of social justice.

Developmental theorists (e.g., Erikson, Gould, Levinson, Lowenthal, Neugarten, Peck, Vaillant) hold that people at any stage in their life cycle must meet bio-psycho-social tasks that are incumbent upon them during this phase of their lives. In the later years, these tasks include coming to terms with physical limitations resulting from biophysiological changes, with changing social roles resulting largely from re-definitions by society, with changing time perceptions, and with the prospect and meaning of death. It further means coming to terms with new values and goals for one's life within a social milieu characterized by incremental losses on the one hand and potentials for continued participation, growth, and development on the other, with a newly evolving identity born of new criteria for self-evaluation in the light of these changes and, ultimately, finding new ways to fulfill one's needs (Lowy, 1962).

The educational needs of older adults were eventually grouped by McClusky (1974) into five categories: coping needs, expressive needs, contributive needs, influence needs, and transcendental needs. Although McClusky indicated that the categories were ranked in order from the most to the least essential, all were considered important in meeting the educational needs of older adults, in helping them to maintain a sense of autonomy. We maintain that the order is less important and may vary with individual differences in personality and maturity. Yet the categories do suggest that the range of learning needs for older adults is no more limited than that of their younger colleagues.

Coping Needs

In keeping with Maslow's (1968) hierarchy of human needs, McClusky (1974) placed the basic needs for survival and security—the coping needs—first in order of importance. The basic skills of reading, writing, and computation were emphasized, while needs for other coping skills—education on good nutrition, health care, income security, and family adjustment—were not far behind. The evidence that older persons (over the age of 65) lacked basic coping skills was presented in terms of literacy rates. It was stated that the literacy rates for older members of the population (those over 65) was lower than those for younger people (Kasworm, 1981). Evidence was also cited to show that older adults (over the age of 65) had fewer years of schooling than people under age 65. In 1970 older adults had 8.7 years and in 1980 9.7 years of schooling in contrast to 12 years of school attendance of persons 25 years and over (Current Population Reports, NCoA, 1980). For those without such coping skills, learning to read, write, add, and subtract could significantly increase their marginal power and sense of autonomy, particularly in an increasingly bureaucratized society in which filling out forms and complying with regulations—whether for obtaining social and health services or following prescriptions on medications—is essential for survival.

Practical life skills such as general and functional literacy can be bolstered. Despite the fact that most older people have already demonstrated their ability to cope, many do need these types of skills to solve specific problems. Education for physical fitness, consumer training, skills in accessing the aging network, identifying and promoting personal needs and interests, as well as recognizing and seizing opportunities to improve their lives can result in older adults' learning vital empowerment strategies.

Costs to society of paying for retirement are increasing; employers are in need of skilled workers and older persons are expressing interest in full- or part-time employment to support themselves or to supplement their income, to remain productive as members of the labor force. Education can help meet these needs by assisting older persons to learn career development and job-search techniques, to acquire new and marketable skills or retool old ones, and to explore new options for earning money. Older persons entering the workforce can use not only technical training but can also benefit from counseling and techniques to bolster confidence and self-image. However, we must keep in mind that according to *Aging America: Trends and Projections* (1985–86 edition) three quarters of the labor force would prefer to continue some kind of part-time work after retirement. In 1984, of persons over age 65 who were working in non-agricultural jobs, 46 percent of the men and 61 percent of the women were on part-time schedules. Unemployment creates serious problems, however, as older workers who love their jobs stay unemployed longer than younger workers and are more likely to give up looking for another job (*Aging America,* 1985–86, 3).

Contributory Needs

The need to contribute to the well-being of others is clearly a necessary element of a person's social existence, as McClusky (1974) aptly pointed out. Older people face constant threats to their sense of being useful. The loss of family members and close friends, coupled with the loss of productive roles through mandatory or voluntary retirement, growth of children, failing eyesight, or diminished energy can create a sense of uselessness and social isolation. Education which encourages and equips older adults to find new ways to make contributions and exert influence can fill an important need, can increase the power and autonomy of older adults. As Butler (1975) put it, leaving a "legacy," contributing to the heritage of culture and civilization, is important to elders and a major function of the aged in any society.

Education for community participation not only offers older persons an opportunity to learn specific skills, it also empowers them to help their communities cope with mounting social and economic problems, and by learning to persuade institutions to be responsive to human needs, their own as well as those of others. The National Retired Teacher's Association/American Association of Retired Persons (NRTA/AARP), for example, trains widowed persons as peer counselors to help other recently widowed persons cope with grief, share experiences, and seek help, by referral, in financial or health-related matters. Older persons can receive training as tax counselors to help their peers complete and file government income tax returns; the Internal Revenue Service works cooperatively with NRTA/AARP to conduct such training. ACTION, a federal governmental agency, sponsors the "Foster Grandparents Program"; in 1977, more than 15,000 older persons with low income received forty hours of orientation and training in providing care to children in institutions, such as schools for retarded or disturbed children, infant homes, temporary care centers and hospitals. The "grandparents" offer a service to the children and the community; at the same time they gain psychologically and emotionally from the experience of being of service to others and being engaged with children.

Listening to lectures or developing expertise of a self-enriching nature appeals to some older persons. Others are more interested in planning their own self-directed learning programs, leading their own discussion groups, or training themselves for paid or volunteer work. Many social welfare agencies, private and public, such as daycare and multiservice or recreational senior centers, counseling agencies, councils on aging, area agencies, multiservice programs, YM/YWCAs, Jewish community centers, churches, synagogues and temples, provide service programs to elderly and non-elderly, staffed by older adults. The Senior Aids Service Corps, Volunteers in Service to America (VISTA), and the Peace Corps offer eloquent testimony to the service ideal of older people.

Intergenerational programs have become more generally accepted as many people begin to recognize that aging is everybody's affair and that contacts not only within but between generations are essential to reduce gaps and tensions and to provide role models to the young as they add years to their lives. The "Intergenerational Service-Learning Project," a demonstration project during 1978–1981 involved thirteen colleges and universities in seven states. In its preliminary findings, it concluded: "Intergenerational service-learning is feasible and adaptable to a multiplicity of disciplines" (Firman and

Ventura, 1981, 35). A variety of learning projects were reviewed in an attempt to identify the most effective roles for students (mostly young adults) in service-related projects. It was determined that:

> students were most effective in two roles: working directly with older persons on a one-to-one basis and developing and implementing special projects. The existence of a single contact person strengthened and, in some cases, significantly improved relationships between community agencies and the participating college. Although the centers were effective in developing exemplary self-sustaining projects, lack of funds prevents most from continuing. (Firman and Ventura, 1981, 36)

Finally, an educational project which matches individuals seeking to fulfill their contributive needs with others who are seeking to develop coping skills is the tutoring program sponsored by Literacy Volunteers of America, Inc. Founded in 1962, the organization provides coordination and training for volunteers willing to tutor adults of all ages in basic reading and writing skills. Recently, the National Council on the Aging has worked with Literacy Volunteers of America to develop a unique tutoring program in which older adult volunteers learn to be tutors for other older adults who want to learn how to read. The National Council on the Aging has selected twenty-five demonstration sites across the country to develop this Literacy Education for the Elderly Project (LEEP), and has provided technical assistance to the participating organizations in setting up this special tutoring program.

Influencing Needs

All people need to exert some degree of influence on the various aspects of their lives. Feelings of powerlessness have been associated with alienation among the poor (Haggstrom, 1969). Mental health professionals have identified such feelings of alienation in their clients as contributing to a diminishing sense of autonomy in people at every stage of their existence. Just at the time when people grow older, their influence on conditions that affect them is weakening. All too often their voices are ignored; they are more done to than done with in a society geared to material productivity and consumption that bestows power on those who are identified with fulfilling these goals: the young. Older people have generally not fared too well in the halls of power. But "less powerful" does not mean powerless; many elderly do have influence, individually and collectively. Even residents in institutions can demonstrate influence, as several studies have concluded (Brody, 1979a; Getzel, 1983; Weiss, 1985). An organization in Massachusetts called Living is for the Elderly (LIFE) has assisted nursing-home residents in organizing to advocate for their own needs (Benoit, 1982). Through the help of LIFE, nursing-home residents in the state have successfully lobbied for legislated reforms which have given them added privacy and security (for example, a security bill which guarantees that every resident has a locked space for personal possessions). The experiences of the Gray Panthers have similarly given proof that with proper leadership, older persons (in this case in league with younger persons) can exert appreciable influence on social institutions and on lawmakers.

The 1981 White House Conference on Aging has provided telling evidence that older people are determined to participate actively in shaping events which affect their lives. Many organizations of older adults (e.g., AARP) have learned to behave in the political arena like a number of other interest groups in the United States, following the lobbying principle of American politics. AARP now has 20 million members, and one of their major goals is to lobby on behalf of their members, claiming to be spokespersons for "the aged" as a whole. Changes in the politics of aging has led many older persons to seek out opportunities to express their need for influence and become agents of social change for personal as well as for altruistic reasons. However, it is important to keep in mind that older adults do not constitute a single political interest group; politically, as in most other ways, older adults have diverse interests (Binstock, 1972).

Originally, activities that addressed the need for a sense of mastery and autonomy were mostly the province of social agencies and community organizations. Recently, educational institutions have developed training programs in social action and advocacy. For example, at the New York City Community College, the course "Leadership Training for Social Action" was initiated in 1975 and has flourished ever since. Peer help, peer service, and/or peer assistance emerged as the identifying style.

Government agencies have awarded grants to train older people to conduct energy audits in private homes to increase heating efficiency. And in some locations, older persons have been trained as ombudspersons to monitor conditions in nursing homes and other long-term care facilities and to help form patient advocacy groups. "Silver-Haired Legislatures" have been held in a number of states, following the success of the original one in Florida. These events provide examples of first-hand experiences in learning about political processes and decision-making, ultimately aimed at developing leadership abilities among older people for transfer to other organizations (not necessarily for elders) and to serve in the public arena in general.

Expressive, Contemplative, and Transcendental Needs

The needs of older adults for growth and fulfillment may range from expressive to contemplative to transcendental. These need not be seen in a hierarchical relationship among themselves or in relation to the other needs, although some forms of education cannot take place until some of the coping needs are met (i.e., ability to read is a prerequisite to doing more advanced educational work). Individuals do find fulfillment in learning to paint for example, for its own sake, while remaining functionally illiterate. They may find greater value in reflection of their past and present lives rather than in attending classes about nutrition. Setting priorities regarding individual needs must be a matter of individual choice.

The *expressive need* encourages the individual to engage in an activity for its own sake—learning for the pure joy of learning. There has been an age-old search for self-expression, for beauty, for the aesthetic, since human history has been recorded. Human beings have pursued this quest through the study of the arts and humanities since ancient times in Egypt, Babylonia, Mesopotamia, Ancient Israel, China, India, Greece, and Rome. McClusky (1974) has argued that older adults in particular can find great possibilities for life enrichment in the pursuit of such expressive activities.

Contemplative needs may be seen as an outgrowth of expressive needs, moving from the understanding and growth of individual expressive activity to a more systematic need on the part of older adults to reflect on and reexamine their lives, to assess accomplishments and failures, and to redefine priorities. The fulfillment of this need can be best seen in "life review," a process which has been described by Butler as

> the progressive return to consciousness of past experiences, in particular the resurgence of unresolved conflicts which can now be surveyed and reintegrated. The old are not only taking stock of themselves as they review their lives, they are trying to think and feel through what they will do with the time that is left and with whatever emotional and material legacies they may have to give to others. (Butler, 1975, 412)

Education which encourages such contemplation, and in its more intensive form, "life review therapy," can increase an older adult's marginal level of power by enabling the individual to resolve old conflicts and to recognize a new significance in his or her life.

While all these needs are relevant in one form or another at any stage of life, allowing for particular developmental tasks, the one need which is perhaps uniquely relevant and connected to the later stages in the life-cycle of the older person is the need to *transcend* the physical experience of life, to reach a higher level of human understanding, beyond any other level of our earthly existence.

> The need for transcendence rather than preoccupation with continued ego-involvement . . . appears to be a most profound need as one reaches the later years of one's life. What have I done with my life? (Erikson) Has it been invested with meaning? (Frankl) What legacy do I leave? (Butler) To age

successfully, indeed, means to come to terms with body-transcendence and to achieve a "sense of integrity" when completing the only life cycle available to any of us. (Lowy, 1982)

Drawing from Robert Peck's concept of ego-transcendence, McClusky (1974, 337) argues that the need "to rise above and beyond the limitation of declining physical powers and of diminishing life expectancy" is an essential task of the final period of life. Recognition of the finiteness of life makes the time remaining all the more important; the focus of attention often turns to those family members, friends, and associates who will be left behind and who can carry forth one's legacy. Like Moody, McClusky considers this capacity for self-transcendence "uniquely relevant" for older adults (1974).

Assessment of Needs and Interests

How can human needs be identified in order to be met? There is need for educators to become aware of and knowledgeable about human needs and developmental tasks throughout the life-cycle. While some needs, whether defined as educational or emotional, will be dominant in certain individuals, an educational policy which seeks to serve older adults must address the full range of developmental needs from survival to mastery, self-expression, contemplation, power, and transcendence.

Economist John Kenneth Galbraith (1958) differentiated between private wants and public needs; he pointed out that *wants* imply a desire, a wish to be satisfied, while *needs* point to a lack of something or somebody that requires relief or fulfillment. He argued that the economic value system in the United States encouraged the satisfaction of wants, particularly in the private sector and neglected the meeting of needs, notably in the public sector. "Private opulence and public squalor" characterizes our society even better today than at the time Galbraith first coined the phrase at the end of the Eisenhower era.

Peterson (1983) also makes this distinction between wants and needs in the educational realm, noting that what older people want may vary significantly from what educational planners decide the elderly need. He notes that those who develop educational programs for older adults often fail to consider the desires of their prospective clientele, assuming that these are equivalent to their needs. Peterson notes that a series of factors, such as educational level, occupation, and various influences on the life experiences of particular generations will affect educational needs and wants, but these influences may be contradictory. Lack of early education or poor experiences with prior learning may leave individuals in need of basic skills (like reading or manual skills) which can greatly affect their ability to cope with life problems; on the other hand, negative experiences with early education may have depressed their interest in educational programs designed to provide such skills, resulting in lack of participation among the groups who are most in need of continuing education. This is a serious problem, reflected in reports of low participation in educational activities among older adults (Johnstone and Rivera, 1965; Cross, 1979; Harris, 1975, 1981).

Merriam and Lumsden (1985) also support the distinction between educational needs and wants. They distinguish between *needs* and *interests* and emphasize the importance of creative assessment in determining priorities based on both the needs and interests of older adults. The typical needs assessment (so-called) is really an assessment of the desires of older adults, their educational wants or interests. It is important that this be recognized, because regardless of their "true" educational needs, if these needs are not perceived by the older adults themselves, their participation in programs developed to fulfill these needs is likely to be low. As Peterson (1983) emphasizes, it is necessary to design educational programs which balance the educational needs with the stated desires of older adults. This way, optimum educational participation can be encouraged and anticipated.

The educational desires which older adults identify to others will vary depending on how questions are asked. Given a list of options to choose from, individuals may indicate their relative preferences among the various items. This was the method selected by Wasserman (1976). Results revealed that hobby and craft courses were most preferred by older adults (34.4 percent were interested), with humanities (20.9 percent) and social science courses (20.5 percent) also ranking high. Least preferred, according to his study, were business courses (10.8 percent were interested), science (12.0 percent), and courses on health and family matters (14.0 percent).

This method of determining needs and interests is useful if an institution is attempting to set priorities from among its variegated offerings and to target certain offerings to older students. It suggests that if crafts programs are offered, they will get a larger response from older adults than if business courses are offered. However, the drawback to this method is that respondents may feel constrained to support some of the options whether or not those options have any relevance to their own needs and interests. Moreover, such a survey does not indicate whether the individuals would actually be willing to participate or become involved in such activities, which, after all, is the ultimate test of interest.

An alternative method involves a more open-ended format. Such was employed by Green and Enderline (1980) in attempting to assess the needs of older adults. They found that educational needs varied according to socioeconomic class, with one group—upper-middle-class white women—seeking book clubs, discussion groups, and other more "expressive" activities, while those in lower socioeconomic groups sought coping skills, particularly in relation to personal safety from harassment and crime. While this approach is likely to reveal more immediate concerns of the respondents, it is also flawed. Respondents may not think to discuss some interests which are nonetheless important to them. Nor is there any more assurance that the persons questioned will actually participate in educational activities related to those interests they have identified.

Londoner (1978) advises a three-pronged approach to needs assessment which involves getting information from experts, prospective clients, and educational planners. Expert sources of information can include research reports, a panel of judges, interviews with professionals, advisory councils, and consultants; information from clients or potential clients can be gathered through interviews, surveys, and questionnaires; similarly, information from educational planners can be gathered from interviews, observations, questionnaires and advisory committees. Londoner emphasizes that "no one source of information is adequate for program planning" (p. 108). When combined, the three sources of information for needs assessment can complement one another.

Programs and Approaches

Improvements in education can help to raise the standard of living and the quality of life for older people (Cohen, 1974). In the decade since Wilbur Cohen made this assertion, a whole array of new educational programs have been developed, and our knowledge of the needs of older students has expanded considerably. We have learned that special educational programs targeted at older adults must take into account the psychological and social characteristics of the prospective students in order to facilitate their learning (Mackay and Hickson, 1977). Because older adults are diverse in their physical, social, cultural, intellectual, and psychological characteristics we have come to realize the importance of recognizing the uniqueness of the individual learner, especially in educational programs for older adults. For this reason, Wass and West (1977) encourage a humanistic design for educational programs which more than anything else emphasizes the strength and dignity of the older learner. An even greater need for personalized instruction thus becomes important to assure that education is relevant to the individual needs of older students (Bass, 1978).

Although the participation of older adults in educational activities remains low, relative to that of younger populations, the overall number and proportion of elders involved in education has been gradually increasing. A study by the National Center on Educational Statistics (1981) found that 768,000 persons aged 65 and over (3.1 percent of that population) were engaged in educational activities in 1981; a similar survey by Louis Harris

(1981) found that 5 percent of older adults had taken a course in the previous year. In an earlier study, with a different cohort, the proportion had been less than half of that with only 2 percent of elders involved (Harris, 1975). The number of older adults participating in educational activities had more than doubled in a short period.

The range of educational options available to older adults since the 1970s has also increased dramatically. Of the traditional educational institutions, community colleges have been the fastest to respond to the needs and demands of older adults. Yet programs in elementary schools, high schools, and four-year colleges have also grown dramatically. Nontraditional providers have, however, continued to outperform the traditional educational institutions. About three-fifths of the courses in which older adults were enrolled were provided by nontraditional institutions or organizations, including employers, government agencies, community organizations and professional associations (Ventura 1982).

The descriptions that follow are intended merely to give a sense of the range of options currently available and to demonstrate the vast potential that exists in developing educational opportunities for older adults. (For further detail, see the bibliographic note at the end of this chapter.) Obviously, not all programs are available in all geographic areas or to all subgroups of older adults any more than health and social service programs are. It has been noted that minority groups have made little use of such programs for many reasons other than simple lack of interest. Institutional racism, expressed in attitudes and in lack of special outreach to the victims of long-term oppression, account to a great extent for the failure to enlist the interest of minority groups in these programs.

There is a great deal that remains to be done to meet the educational needs and wants of older adults of all racial, class, ethnic, and religious backgrounds, to increase their marginal levels of power "for the attainment and maintenance of well-being, and continuing growth toward self-fulfillment" (McClusky, 1971). The sample of programs described below merely serves to indicate the diversity of efforts that have been undertaken and, it is hoped, suggest what is possible in the near future to develop education for older adults.

1. Nontraditional Programs

Basic literacy and high school competencies are the focus of the **Senior Citizen Adult Education Program for Monroe County** in Monroe, Michigan (Ventura, 1982). Developed through cooperation between the local senior center and the public school system, the program provides educational programs at convenient sites in the community, including senior centers, elder housing complexes, and nursing homes. The program serves about 600 individuals annually, most of whom are aged 60–80. Half of the students have not completed high school, and many of those enrolled are striving to complete this level of competency. However, a wide range of continuing education opportunities are available, and participants are able to study creative writing, crafts, gerontology, advocacy, and nutrition, among other subjects. A companion intergenerational program enables participants to tutor children in the local schools. This program thus addresses a range of needs from coping to expressive to contributive.

A program especially well known to directors of senior centers is the National Council on Aging's (NCOA) **Senior Center Humanities Program.** Developed in 1976, the program was designed to provide life enrichment and self-discovery through the humanities. The program is organized around discussion groups which are initiated in local communities by local elders. Materials, including course books, guides, tapes, posters, and diplomas are available from NCOA at no charge, but beyond that the groups are self-directing. Topics explore expressive and transcendental needs and include such subjects as "Images of Aging," "The Remembered Past," "The Search for Meaning," "Words and Music," and "Exploring Values." NCOA estimates that over 80,000 older adults have participated in the program since its inception, with approximately 25,000 participants annually (Ventura, 1982).

An interesting variation of the Senior Center Humanities Program (also described by Ventura) was developed by the University of Kansas in 1981. Called **Home Humanities,** the program attempts to extend the NCOA program to older adults in nursing homes and those who are otherwise unable to read the written materials. Through the use of closed circuit radio, the university broadcasts the NCOA tapes to residents. Discussions can then be scheduled at convenient times at the affiliated nursing homes.

A program similar in format to the NCOA Senior Center Humanities Program is sponsored by the National Retired Teachers Association (NRTA) and the American Association for Retired Persons (AARP). **The Institute of Lifelong Learning** attempts to stimulate discussion groups by publishing "minicourse" articles in NRTA/AARP's monthly magazine, *Modern Maturity.* This learning situation allows individuals to explore new topics independently or in groups. For those who choose the latter approach, NRTA/AARP provides bibliographies, self-tests, and discussion questions to further enhance the learning experience (Timmerman, 1981).

Demonstrating that the sponsorship of educational programs is virtually unlimited, the American Federation of State, County and Municipal Employees (AFSCME) of New York City developed the **District Council 37 Retirees Educational Program** (Ventura, 1982). Designed for the retired members of the city's largest unions, the program attempts to meet the needs of a diverse group of retirees. Between 1500 and 2000 individuals participated in the program in 1981. Unlike most educational programs, the District Council 37 Retirees Educational Program serves a large minority population; 29 percent of the participants are black, 1 percent are Hispanic. Subjects range from literature and history to vocational education and self-help programs.

The **Center for Understanding Aging,** located at Framingham State College in Massachusetts but national in scope, offers the field of aging education a "talent pool" consisting of leaders in such varied professions and fields of practice as gerontology, education, elder services, youth services, religion, arts and humanities, media and public relations, social sciences, health services, recreation, intergenerational programming, and various academic subjects. This network plans to build closer ties between young and older persons.

Preparation for retirement has become popular as of late, and numerous corporations, universities, nonprofit agencies (governmental and nongovernmental) elder organizations (e.g., AARP) have run series of courses, workshops, sessions to prepare employees, workers, and already retired men (fewer women) for "retirement." The entire phenomenon of retirement has become a political and behavioral issue. It is political because of the changes in mandatory retirement laws and provisions; it is behavioral because retirement is viewed as a process rather than an act (Atchley et al., 1985), and many studies have been conducted analyzing data of retirees-to-be, those who are retiring, and the post-retirement process.

Helen Dennis, in *Retirement Preparation: What Retirement Specialists Need to Know* (1984), devotes one chapter to the educational process of retirement preparation. She delineates methods of instructing retirees how to learn about psychological and social aspects of retirement, retirement within special groupings, and resources available. The author makes use of her knowledge of adult behavior development and adult learning principles, involving learners in trying to change outlook and behavior.

Unquestionably, learning how to negotiate the later events in the lifecycle, such as retirement, is an important objective of adult education. This requires the preparation of teachers as much as any instructional enterprise does. The teacher's skill in using group-sharing methods, dealing with the personal and interpersonal emotional up and down sides before (remote and near phases), during, and after retirement is particularly crucial here. The deployment of several specialists in subject and attitudinal matters and their coordination requires careful judgment and monitoring. Reports by former retirees about how they have managed their problems are valuable learning tools. What effect does retirement have on family and friends? "Self-inventories for planning" are as welcome as references to audio-visual aids, printed resources telling where and when to turn for emotional help. Here is a good illustration of how various learning orientations can, together, meet coping, influencing, and contributive needs to enable people to deal with inevitable life situations that have been defined as "normal" crises (Banfield and Morgan, 1969; Riley and Foner, 1968; Karp, 1985/86).

2. Traditional Education

Colleges and universities have been notoriously slow to respond to the needs of older adults. Tuition waivers, which began to allow older adults to participate in college courses at reduced or no cost, have had limited success in attracting older students into traditional classrooms. Although the waivers are now available in all fifty states, relatively few older adults have taken advantage of them (Kingston, 1982). Nevertheless, recent developments in institutions of higher education have been more promising.

Community colleges have been the leaders in adult education, and this has been true of education for older adults as well. This is often a function of their greater mission to serve the whole community and to respond to the community's needs.

An example of such responsiveness can be seen in the development of **North Henepin Community College** in Minnesota. In 1970, there were no special programs available for older adults in the area, and when the community college offered a training session about aging for local professionals, the local elders protested the lack of consultation with older adults. An advisory committee was quickly established, and the North Henepin Seniors on Campus Program was formed to provide a variety of educational experiences to meet the needs identified by the community's older adults (Glickman, 1975). Educational programs consisted of: courses for enrichment, advocacy, retirement planning, and planning for second careers. Other activities have included film festivals, choral music, and an exercise program. Traditional education frequently leaves individuals feeling inadequate, but the North Henepin Seniors on Campus Program clearly did not. Rather than being merely the recipients of information, the older adults in the community were the educational planners as well. Such learning can be an empowering experience, something which is all too rare for older adults.

A Gerontology Program at the **College of Public and Community Service, University of Massachusetts, Boston,** has found a different way of enhancing the self-confidence of its older students, who are able to have direct influence on their own lives and/or the lives of their age-peers. Each incoming class works on a project commissioned by a state or local agency, a project which addresses a concrete area of public policy. In the short history of the program, students have influenced legislators, public officials, and service-providers with studies of fuel assistance, home care and nursing-home services. The program is career-oriented and has demonstrated success in placing older graduates in meaningful paid and unpaid employment (Morris and Bass, 1986). Thus older students are able to fulfill their coping, contributive, and influencing needs.

A program which translates the concept of empowerment of older people (albeit empowerment of middle-class elders) to a very high degree is the retirement institute concept developed by the New School for Social Research. There, the **Institute for Retired Professionals** is staffed by individuals who have retired from professional work. Individuals participate in the program as both students and teachers; all members are expected to contribute in both capacities. The maximum number of participants in a given year is 625, and the program consistently runs at capacity. In addition to academic courses, the retired professionals can contribute to the Institute's literary journal or display creative work in art exhibits and shows. Nearly three fourths of the participants are over the age of 70, and because many participants remain in the program year after year, the average age has been gradually rising. In contrast to the Senior Citizen Adult Education Program for Monroe County, 85 percent of the participants are college graduates (half hold advanced degrees (Ventura, 1982).

Traditional educational programs for older adults are also offered through local public school systems. For example, the **Newton School Department** in Newton, Massachusetts, offers a combination of weekly courses of regular academic content plus weekly political forums, talent-presentations by older persons for persons of any age group. These programs are provided on a specific day each week from September through May.

Of course, no description of educational programs for older adults would be complete without mentioning **Elderhostel,** the program which engages older adults in week-long sessions during the vacation periods of regular colleges and universities in the United States and around the world. Focusing on the expressive and, in some cases, transcendental, needs of its students, the program stresses a liberal arts curriculum in a setting which is away from the normal daily routines (elderhostelers typically live in college dormitories during their week of studies) which allows the students to be fully engaged in stimulating intellectual pursuits. The program's growth rate—from 200 to over 100,000 participants in just over ten years—indicates that it fills an apparent void for such learning experiences among older adults.

The different learning needs and interests of older adults call for greater flexibility in roles and opportunities for all adults in our society. The role of "student" is a relatively new one for a great number of older people, many of whom themselves have accepted the social stereotype that older adults cannot or should not learn. Covey (1980) suggests that this lack of familiarity with the student role may be part of an explanation why few but the well-educated older adults participate in educational activities. He suggests that those who have previously adapted well to the student role in their lives may be better able to incorporate this role into their later years.

The **Universities of the Third Age** (L'Universités du Troisième Age), a concept first developed in Toulouse, France, in the early 1970s, emphasize the value and acceptability of the student role in later life. There are now some 120 universities of the third age in Europe, Latin America, and Japan.

About 50 of these are in France. Studies so far indicate that the primary motivation for enrolling is "for intellectual and cultural stimulation and to increase opportunities for socialization. Many of the students see their participation as a form of work rather than leisure and are willing to devote more than one day a week to their studies," (*Aging International,* 1981, 5). The Secretary General of the French Association of Universities of the Third Age indicates that perhaps one of the most important motivators behind participation is that it gives older people an important new role with status in society, namely that of student.

Interest in "self-directed learning" is now growing; retirees may emphasize individual projects, such as renovating one's house, experimenting with new technologies, and so on. Dozens of "Universities of the Third Age" are establishing branches in small towns and many of these universities have television studios where documentaries are being written, acted, and produced by older people (*Aging International,* 1986, 14).

In addition, universities themselves expect to reap benefits, as Phillips University in Marburg (West Germany) makes clear in its statement of goals: "To overcome its isolation from the community, to improve the skills of professors to discuss problems associated with aging, to bring life experiences to bear on academic instruction and research, to encourage a leadership in working with older people" (*Aging International,* 1981, 6). In this country, programs at San Diego State University and Boston University, among others, have been modeled after the *third age* concept.

For instance, the **Evergreen Program** launched in 1980 at Boston University, offers hundreds of courses for persons aged 60 and older, on a non-credit basis at a registration fee of $10 per course. More than 800 people participate each year. In addition, there are a number of "Campus Series," which meet two times per week, consisting of lecture and discussion sessions focusing on a particular topic, such as "Making Boston Work."

Cyril O. Houle (*Patterns of Learning: New Perspective on the Life-span,* 1984) describes the intellectual lives of several historical figures such as M.E. de Montaigne, Alexander Pope, and Henry D. Thoreau, exploring how they used "patterns of learning methods to facilitate their own education" (Peterson, 1985b). Houle illustrates the way that "scholarly companionship, reading, travel, involvement in affairs of state," self-examination, (experiential methods) and tutoring, self-directed study, observation of nature, small group discussion, spoken discourse, use of journals, libraries (cognitive method), as well as teacher-student relationships, interpersonal learning, have been applied. Studying this approach, Houle "discovered that people tend to use multiple and segmented methods, rather than limiting themselves to one approach." Therefore, he points out that the value of independent learning lies in using its patterns rather than concentrating on one method. Four hundred years covered by his examples give Houle ammunition to stress that variety over time yields more results in learning than getting fixated on one or the other learning or teaching method.

While he mostly addresses adulthood, Houle also speaks of older learners, and his insights regarding the learning approach of eminent figures in history offers interesting vistas to educational avenues in the education of older persons. Obviously, these figures had extraordinary discipline, material success, and personal gifts to avail themselves of such opportunities when they were quite rare to come by for ordinary mortals. This begs the question, however: how can a multiplicity of unorthodox, nontraditional, and traditional educational opportunities (i.e., patterns of study) be made accessible to a majority of aging persons in the lower and middle classes, of different racial, ethnic, and religious backgrounds? Herein lies another major challenge for educational gerontology.

One of the goals of educational gerontology may be to encourage the development of what has been called the "fluid society," a society which provides opportunities for persons of all ages to enter new careers, to become involved in new learning opportunities, to take on new roles and to discard old ones. (Unlearning habits of a lifetime may prove to be the hardest learning objectives to be achieved.) If we expand opportunities for individuals to mix work and education over their lifetimes, we may find that the whole society benefits from the increased human potential released through the new opportunities for individual growth.

Bibliographical Notes

1. It is impossible to do justice to the wealth of information available on this vast subject. Readers who would like more depth in any of these areas are directed to several selected texts. Of the recent texts in educational gerontology, David Peterson's (1983) *Facilitating Education for Older Learners* is likely to become a major classic in the field, organizing as it does a mass of detail into a readable text which is particularly useful to educational planners and practitioners. A collection of essays edited by Ronald Sherron and D. Barry Lumsden (1978, revised 1985) *Introduction to Educational Gerontology* is also an excellent basic text, with each chapter covering a different aspect of the field; a similar text edited by Lumsden (1985) has further reported on the state-of-the-art in educational gerontology. A new text by Moody, (in press), *The Abundance of Life: Human Development Policies for an Aging Society* promises also to make a major contribution in this area.

Moreover, earlier texts should not be avoided simply because of their early publications. McClusky's (1971) background paper for the 1971 White House Conference on Aging is a seminal piece and provides a good review of the early literature on learning abilities from which we have drawn in compiling our own review; Wilma Donahue's (1955) *Education for Later Maturity* is also well worth reading. It is surprising to realize that what we now have confirmed about education in the later years was intuitively known and presented nearly thirty years ago by Sheats, Jayne, and Spence (1953), Kidd (*How Adults Learn,* 1959), and Diekhoff (*Schooling for Maturity,* 1955), among others.

2. Unfortunately, there is no one source that contains descriptions of all educational programs available for older adults. A good sampling can be found in *Education for Older Adults: A Catalogue of Program Profiles,* published by the National Center on Education, Leisure and Continuing Opportunities for Older Americans and the National Council on the Aging, Inc. (Ventura, 1982). This guide describes sixteen programs, all quite different from one another, and provides detailed information on program objectives, educational activities, staffing, costs, enrollment figures and future plans. A similar catalogue containing only profiles of programs in the arts and humanities is also available (Cahill, 1981). Descriptions of community college programs can be found in *Community Colleges Respond to Elders: A Sourcebook for Program Development* (Glickman, et al., 1975) and *Older Americans and Community Colleges: A Guide for Program Implementation* (Korim, 1974).

5
Transformation of Education by Older Adults

Adults, even older adults, have never been specifically excluded from educational opportunities in this country. A variety of movements have focused on expanding such opportunities: the Junto discussion groups, started in 1727 by Benjamin Franklin, were open to persons of all ages, as are the "Great Books Clubs," an outgrowth of Franklin's idea, developed by Mortimer Adler largely for "middle-class" adults. The Lyceum lecture series, originating in the nineteenth century, also reached some older adults, although its target audience was the younger adult; and the Chautauqua movement, founded in 1874 and still continuing over one hundred years later, has enriched the lives of many older adults with stimulating discussions, lectures, and programs in the arts (Peterson, 1983).

University education also included adults beyond the "traditional" college age. The development of land-grant colleges through the Morrill Act (1862) and the subsequent development of evening colleges and evening programs within regular universities contributed to the opportunities for adults as did the evolution of the community service role in universities just after the turn of the century (Knowles, 1969).

Despite these early developments, greater commitment to lifelong learning has been largely a twentieth-century phenomenon in the United States, one which has only begun to assume importance in the past few decades. This recent "discovery" of adult education has led to an infectious scholarly discourse on educational theory, educational goals and tasks, which is evident in the ongoing debates about theories of education for adults and older adults. The debates have both confused and illuminated issues of educational philosophy, theory, and practice.

The debate, "Why education?", had basically settled on responding to three goals rather than on a single philosophy: to create good and effective citizens; to provide individuals with the possibility of upward mobility; and to prepare prospective workers for jobs. All these goals are related to the quality of life (Lauer, 1985). The tasks and purposes, as well as theories of education, were originally concentrated on educating the young. Education of adults—young, middle, and older—has not been in the mainstream of these debates until more recent times.

The increased participation of younger and older adults in a wider range of educational experiences, along with the increased awareness of their presence, has been referred to as *revolutionary* (Knowles, 1969; Apps, 1981). Optimistic predictions suggest that this increased pressure from older learners can even transform our educational institutions. The following analysis of pedagogical, andragogical, and geragogical theories provides some insight into the potential contributions of older learners to a new approach to education; the experiences of other Western countries provides further testimony of this potential impact. Whether such transformation of education for all ages will indeed occur is, of course, an open question at this time.

Andragogy versus Pedagogy

In chronicling the andragogy debate, Davenport and Davenport (1985) note that the term "andragogy" was first identified in 1833 by Alexander Kapp, a German educator who invented the term by combining the Greek roots *andr* (meaning "man") and *agogos* (meaning "learning"). The term was used by Kapp to describe Plato's educational theory and the use of dialogues by both Socrates and Plato. After some criticism, the term quickly went out of fashion, although it was carried to this country in 1927 by Anderson and Lindeman (Davenport and Davenport, 1983).

Eduard C. Lindeman (1885–1953) was a philosopher, scholar, social reformer and one of the most significant leaders in the field of social work. He, together with Mary Parker Follett, had an important influence on the role of social work in bringing about social reform by utilizing educational methods, primarily through small-group and inter-group activities. His philosophy can be summarized as follows: Democratic ideals must permeate means as well as ends; values must be validated in action (G. Konopka, 1958). Lindeman's philosophical thoughts and activities effected a linkage between the educational and activist approaches of adult education in social group-work and community organization. A further linkage of the therapeutic, clinical stance in social casework with the educational component of group-work and community organization enabled social work to move toward a generic and more unitary base. As Max Siporin (1975, 36) quoted Gaywell Hawkins: "It is the educational forces in social work which give it internal unity." And Siporin continues: "Social workers carry out these educational activities not only in individualized work with people, but also in community programs, in family life and consumer education, in the training of citizen volunteers in community service" (p. 36). Thus a social worker is also a "social educator," a model guide in the teaching-learning process. It is in this context that Lindeman used the term *andragogy* to reflect the special educational role of the social worker.

Andragogy, as a term, was not revived in this country until the late 1960s when Malcolm Knowles became acquainted with the concept. Knowles had already begun to formulate a theoretical approach to adult education, indeed had long since published *Informal Adult Education* (1950) when the old label entered his thinking. Andragogy had already become a somewhat familiar concept in Europe, and when an adult educator from Yugoslavia attended one of Knowles's classes in the summer of 1967, Knowles learned that there was a name for what he had been teaching, a label that referred to "the art and science of helping adults learn." Knowles reports that he began using *andragogy* in his own publications the following year (Knowles, 1984, 6).

Knowles became the primary transmitter of andragogical theory in this country with the publication in 1970 of *The Modern Practice of Adult Education,* notably subtitled *Andragogy versus Pedagogy.* There followed a rash of articles in scholarly educational and social welfare journals, alternately criticizing and defending andragogy as a distinctive theory of education for adults. Much of the criticism focused on the use of the word *versus* in setting up a dichotomy between andragogy and pedagogy although, ironically, Knowles himself had emphasized the applicability of his technique to the education of children and youth:

> But I believe that andragogy means more than just helping adults learn; I believe it means helping human beings learn, and that it therefore has implications for the education of children and youth. . . . For I believe that the process of maturing toward adulthood begins early in a child's life and that as he matures he takes on more and more of the characteristics of the adult on which andragogy is based. (Knowles, 1970, 38–39)

Knowles wrote an entry in the *Encyclopedia of Social Work* of 1977 on "adult education," which began: "Adult education is a complex field of social practice" (p. 52). To differentiate this new theory, he wrote, "from traditional theories of youth education subsumed under the label 'pedagogy,' it is being given the label 'andragogy' " (p. 54). In social work practice, "andragogical principles and methods" have found greatest acceptance in the field of "family life education" (Wooten, 1977). In the *Journal of Social Work Education,* several articles by Knowles were published throughout the 1970s and 1980s applying andragogical approaches to the professional education of social workers on the undergraduate and graduate levels as well as in continuing education for social workers.

Essentially, pedagogy, as depicted by Knowles, focused on subject matter to be learned by individuals who had no previous knowledge and thus had to be instructed and motivated by external influences. It was the education of children, of those who were assumed to be dependent upon outsiders to direct their studies. Of course, this is not a dictionary definition of pedagogy which is usually given as "the art or method of teaching." (Indeed, Freire's concept of the "pedagogy of the oppressed" is more akin to Knowles's concept of andragogy than it is to this more restrictive definition of pedagogy.) Knowles's interpretation came from the Greek root of the word *paida,* meaning boy or child. The undesirable aspects of the concept were reflected in the connotations of a related word, *pedagogue,* which in ancient Greece, referred to the tutor for the privileged class of "citizen." In modern times, the term had come to refer to a teacher who was overly dogmatic, formal or pedantic. Years of study and observation of teaching practice led Knowles to conclude that pedagogy was generally not suited to adults. Andragogy, although originally conceived as the opposite of pedagogy, came to be conceived by Knowles and others, notably in European countries, as a parallel model. Knowles suggested that both models were relevant to persons of all ages; the choice of model was to be determined by which set of assumptions were relevant to the learner's needs, the learning environment and situation (Knowles, 1979).

Nevertheless, the widespread use of the term was almost infectious; the contagion spread through critiques, responses to the critiques, and responses to the responses. It was estimated that within a decade there were approximately 200 publications on *andragogy* in the United States alone (Davenport and Davenport, 1985). In 1979 Knowles conceded that the subsequent dichotomy which he had unintentionally established between andragogy and pedagogy was to be more appropriately conceived as a continuum. He acknowledged the critical contributions of those who had questioned his age-based approach to educational theory and restated his basic assumptions:

> So I am not saying that pedagogy is for children and andragogy is for adults, since some pedagogical assumptions are realistic for adults in some situations, and some andragogical assumptions are realistic for children in some situations. And I am certainly not saying that pedagogy is bad and andragogy is good; each is appropriate given the relevant assumptions. (Knowles, 1979, 52)

Significantly, the revised edition of his text bore the new subtitle *From Pedagogy to Andragogy* (Knowles, 1980).

In a more recent text, Knowles explained again the fundamental differences between the pedagogical model of education and the andragogical model. A summary of this discussion is contained in the following chart adapted from Knowles.

Table 5-1
Comparison of Assumptions between Pedagogy and Andragogy

	Pedagogy	*Andragogy*
Concept of learner	Learner is dependent; teacher makes all decisions	Learner is self-directing
Role of experience	Learner's experience is of little value; experience of teachers and text writers is what matters	Learner is assumed to have valuable experience which is used as a resource
Readiness to learn	Related to age; determined by outside authority	Self-determined when a need to know arises
Orientation to learning	Subject-centered	Life-, task-, or problem-centered
Motivation to learn	Related to external factors (parents, fear of failure)	Related to internal factors (self-esteem, quality of life)

Source: Adapted from Knowles, 1984, 8-12.

From Andragogy to Geragogy to Humanagogy

Some criticized Knowles not for exaggerating age-related differences in learning approaches but for failing to make enough distinctions—specifically for not distinguishing or recognizing the special characteristics of older adult learners. Neither Knowles nor his students and followers made direct references to older adult learners or paid special attention to them as a distinctive age group. Their emphasis on job-related motivations and neglect of attention to special needs of learners with physical disabilities, suggested that it was necessary to go beyond the andragogical analysis in order to relate educational theory to older learners.

Lebel (1978) was the first in this country to advocate the term geragogy in his writing, referring to an educational theory for older adult learners. He acknowledges that M.E. Hartford, a social worker, at that time at the Leonard Davis school of gerontology at the Andrus Center at the University of Southern California, first acquainted him with the term. However, again the term had first appeared in Europe. In 1962, Bollnow, in West Germany, had demanded educational assistance for people as they were aging, coining the term *Gerontogogik* (Bubolz-Lutz, 1984). However, it was Hilarion Petzold in 1965 and H. Mieskes in 1970 who made the term *Geragogik* popular, first in West Germany and later in other countries of Europe. Mieskes (1971) defined *Geragogik* in the broadest sense as "science of 'pedagogical' [!] conditions, consequences, concomitant aspects of the aging process" (Bubolz-Lutz, 1984, 12). E. Eirmbter (1979) pointed out that *Geragogik* encompassed "the systematic study of all aspects which include learning of knowledge, behavior, capacities, abilities and skills and are relevant for the preparation and experiences of the life-phase 'old age' " (p. 12).

The widest possible use of the term leaves almost nothing out as far as learning for, by, and during the later years is concerned. However, Böttcher, Bubolz-Lutz, Brochter, Marcel, Petzold, Pöggeler, Radebold, Schmitz-Scherzer and Siebert (some of the major leadership figures in West Germany), in thinking about *Geragogik*, refer to learning in the *later* years. In contrast to Lebel's brief treatment of the concept of geragogy, Bubolz-Lutz (1984) spells out in greater length and depth the goals of education in the later years:

to enable individuals to avoid the deficits of aging

to assist in coping with socio-emotional developmental tasks

to help individuals achieve a reasonable degree of personal life satisfaction

to consciously avoid "utility" as a goal of education; in fact, to achieve a sense of human worth without proving to be useful

to aid both in socialization as lifelong learning and role adaptations as well as in desocialization when needed for the personal and social good

to help individuals realize greater societal equalities of opportunities based on needs, motivations, and social programs

to assist in coping with changing conditions and needs over time

to enable individuals to achieve competency in interpersonal communications

to enable people to accept external help—informal as well as formal

to help develop an understanding of the meaning of life

to aid in a person's self-realization, in concert with others, of the "gift of life," and

to view life as a wholistic experience

(Bubolz-Lutz, 1984, 31–32)

In this way, life is to be viewed dynamically, a dialectic interplay of individuals and others in the immediate and more remote environment. Life is affected by three interacting "forces": individual existence, existence of other people, and the existence of the world outside of the self.

In fact, this view goes back to Kurt Lewin's (1947) field-theory, which postulates that human behavior is a function of life space, consisting of interacting field-forces between and among person and environment that create and maintain a quasi-stationary equilibrium. Conditions are always in a state of flux and adaptations to ever-changing conditions—particularly in the later years with reduced energy and resources—coping with life conditions (personal, interpersonal, and environmental) becomes a *learning,* not only a *helping,* task. This is in contrast to the more static view of providing one-time learning experiences or learning for preparation for specific conditions that are viewed as time-limited and time-bound, such as retirement from work, becoming a grandparent, adapting to the symptoms of chronic illness, compliance with medication, moving to different housing or geographic areas, and so on. This does not deny that such learning goals have validity; it merely points out that they are static and may therefore lead to a limiting educational perspective of education in the later years. In other words, these events are not single acts but continuing events, processes with antecedants and postcedents. They are circular, not linear.

Lebel admitted that he did not plan to develop a theory of geragogy. He chose instead simply to argue that older adults were sufficiently different from younger adults to deserve a separate educational theory. He called on "those individuals equipped with the necessary research competencies" to develop and test the validity of such a theory for which he chose the label. Ironically, Lebel's label was in dispute before a theory had been developed in this country to support it. An alternate term, "eldergogy" was proposed by Yeo (1982) with no reference to geragogy, with no development of a theory to support "eldergogy," and indeed with an implicit contradiction in the author's protestations that "there is an inherent flaw in attempts to categorize [older people] even for the noblest of purposes" (Yeo, 1982, 6).

The problem of labeling should not be minimized as it can lead to greater clarity or greater confusion in our understanding of educational principles for persons of all ages. Hans Toch (1970) states the problem of labeling succinctly when he points out that "classifying people in life is a grim business which channelizes destinies and determines fate." People become categories; they are processed as such, play their assigned roles and live up to these expectations. In order to avoid this self-fulfilling tendency, it is important to consider just what contribution a theory of *geragogy* or *eldergogy* might make to our understanding of education that is not encompassed in the pedagogy—andragogy continuum.

Martha Tyler John attempts to explain the contribution of geragogy in *Teaching and Loving the Elderly* (1983). She presents a matrix which purports to differentiate between pedagogy, andragogy, and geragogy. While her attempt is well intentioned, there are flaws in her trichotomy. Part of the fault in this characterization lies in her definition of elderly persons as "those who need special assistance in managing their daily lives due to factors that are largely age related" (John, 1983, 5). John chooses this definition because the focus of her text is on techniques for teaching older adults who are living in nursing homes and not the majority of elders living in the community. Yet even the focus on this highly restricted population does not justify the fundamentally ageist assumptions about geragogy. In John's view, the older adult is to be directed as much by the teacher as are children. The educational need is not even determined individually by the teacher as is the case in her version of pedagogy, and certainly not jointly by teacher and student; instead, the universal diagnosis for elders is "general need for stimulation." One finds further evidence of this stereotyping in John's mental status assessment tools, which seem adapted from kindergarten teaching aids. Prospective students of "geragogy" are thus to be asked to name and point to body parts and to identify large sketches of chickens and eggs!

In fairness to John, her efforts do seem sincere. Indeed, at some points in her writing she emphasizes the dignity of every individual and stresses the importance of enhancing the "quality of life."

> In a democracy each individual has worth and should be given the opportunity for self-improvement regardless of race, sex or *age*. It is, in short, our social responsibility to provide learning opportunities for all people. (John, 1983, 12)

John aptly points out an inherent ageism in asking *whether* elders can learn. Yet the search for the distinct features of an educational theory or method for the frail older learner leads her to make assumptions about the education of older adults which are dehumanizing. In *The Aging Enterprise,* Estes criticizes such ageist assumptions in a number of U.S. social welfare and educational programs. She notes that such assumptions lead us to "segregate and stigmatize the aged" (Estes, 1979, 17) and serve primarily to advance the interests of service-providers. (Not very different from latent functions of other professionals and health-care providers than open, undeclared rather than declared intentions.)

Kalish, in "The New Age-ism and the Failure Models: A Polemic" (1979), identifies three groups who perpetuate the "new age-ism," knowingly or unknowingly:

> funding agencies that compete with other agencies by stressing the dire needs of the elderly

> gerontologists and geriatricians who need to keep their programs going and may place a high value on activism,

> the media which provide these two groups and others with what they want to hear.

Instead, Kalish proposes the "personal growth model," which is oriented toward a humanistic philosophy of education.

Denouncing the plague of "gogies," Knudson (1979) added his own strain with a call for a "unifying concept" which he labeled *humanagogy*. For Knudson, humanagogy was "a *human* theory of learning, not a theory of 'child learning,' 'adult learning,' or 'elderly learning.' " Noting that individuals learned differently, according to their experience and its relation to the matter to be learned, Knudson argued against the growing factions among educators, emphasizing instead that his concept of humanagogy "takes into account the differences between people of various ages as well as their similarities" (p. 263).

One might speculate, as Rachal (1983) did, on whether Knudson created the new term for this educational theory with tongue in cheek. Certainly, *humanagogy* is the kind of term which should lead us to wonder "if we have become just a bit too engrossed in our own jargon, perhaps to the detriment of understanding terms in that jargon" (Rachal, 1983, 14). It is as unhelpful (as Rachal argues) as a term like "infantagogy" or "adolescentagogy" would be. Yet the basic idea of Knudson's unifying concept bears thinking about. For if we ask not just how are older adult learners different from those younger or middle-aged, but also how are they alike, we may arrive at some differences in techniques that may be relevant in different ways to various subgroups. If we approach the question from a humanistic perspective, we are more likely to identify the common needs of people to be treated with respect and genuine dignity; we may find educational approaches which value the individual's worth and experience in interaction with the environment, learning and teaching techniques that encourage and develop freedom of inquiry and which empower individuals to control their own learning pace and content, keeping in mind limitations imposed by both the inner and outer worlds. In fact, the by-products of such a process may be that people gain a sense of mastery which they can transfer to other types of situations in their lives. Isn't "transfer of learning" a time-honored concept in educational theory and practice?

The Contribution of Andragogy

In exploring techniques for facilitating education for older adults, Peterson (1983) attempts to look at the similarities and differences between older and younger adult learners. He indicates that older learners will benefit especially from slower pacing and greater organization of course materials. Also, because of their experiences with schooling in the early part of this century, many of the present generation of older adults are likely to associate education with memorization, discipline, and irrelevance; hence encouragement and positive feedback may be especially helpful to them. However, Peterson rejects the idea of establishing a separate theory or methodology for older adults, arguing that geragogy is "neither practical nor necessary" (Peterson,

1983, 149). Instead, he stresses how the concepts of andragogy may be utilized in the education of older adults.

As we pointed out in a previous chapter, the educational philosophy underlying andragogy is basically a humanistic one, focusing on the social individual as the center of learning, and emphasizing the person's freedom, dignity, and potential for continuing creativity. Indeed Elias and Merriam (1980) use Knowles as their chief example of the practitioner of a humanistic philosophy. Through refinements, testing, and retesting of andragogical principles, we can learn much about how to implement a humanistic philosophy of education for older adults.

Knowles lists the following elements as most important in designing a process that facilitates learning for adults:

1. climate setting
2. involving learners in mutual planning
3. involving participants in diagnosing their own needs for learning
4. involving learners in formulating their learning objectives
5. involving learners in designing learning plans
6. helping learners carry out their learning plans
7. involving learners in evaluating their learning.

(Knowles, 1984, 14–18)

Setting the physical and psychological climate for education is one of the most important roles for any educator. This is especially true for those who are facilitating education for older adults. Many of the physical barriers to learning identified in chapter 6 can be eliminated or modified to enhance the learning experience. Adjusting lighting and temperature, eliminating distracting sounds, and arranging seating to promote greater interchange can enhance the learning potential of older learners. Enhancing the psychological climate can be even more important; Knowles emphasizes the necessity of establishing a climate of mutual respect, collaboration, trust, support, openness, and pleasure to enrich the learning atmosphere.

Older learners have had many years of life-experience which taxed their coping abilities, improved them at times, and at other times impaired their ability to meet the challenges which life-situations demanded of them. In other words, they are likely to have experienced all degrees of success and failure over a longer period of time than younger learners. Depending on personality, value orientation, gender, class, ethnic, religious, racial or other background, people at any stage of life will approach life tasks and situations differently. People in the later years however, tend to follow life styles which have developed over time when tackling new tasks. Persistency of coping patterns is by now a well-established finding of research (Clark and Anderson, 1967, Neugarten, 1963, 1979; Treas and Berkman, 1985).

Moreover, we have found that learners at any age have acquired patterns, or styles, of learning. Some learners are more cognitive, affective, or motoric/behavioral; others tend to use different patterns and styles, depending upon the nature of the learning tasks. Some people, for instance, tend to solve problems with an intellectual-cognitive approach; others prefer to learn through experience, by examples, or by illustrations; some are more inductive, others more deductive in attacking problems. Others tend to be at home in the mechanical world and approach learning tasks by *doing* rather than by *reasoning,* and many combine these tendencies, depending on personality and situational variables. At any rate, the longer people live, the more likely it is that they will utilize problem-solving or learning approaches that are ego-syntonic (in accord with their ego structure) rather than ego alien (out-of-tune with their ego structure). The flow of time tends to reinforce such learning patterns.

Much remains to be discovered about teaching and learning. Data clarifying the preferred learning styles of categories of older persons in particular (e.g., young-older versus old-older men or women, those who have been exposed to cognitive learning rather than to experiential learning in the past) would make it possible to plan instruction that would facilitate more effective learning. By selecting instructors who can relate to older persons, and classes in which older students enroll in the regular course offerings of a college or university, we are more likely to attract older students who are more cognitive-oriented than those who are more affective and experientially oriented, as these courses are generally more formal, analytical, and subject-matter oriented. Best learning outcomes can be obtained by providing a choice of learning options, allowing persons to learn either through formal classes or through self-paced instruction.

Humanistic education postulates the premise that the worth and autonomy of the learner is fundamental; therefore, the learner must be involved in every stage of the educational process. Students are to be the central focus of the educational activity, taking part in planning the program, assessing their educational needs at any point in the total process; formulating their purposes or objectives (what it is they want to learn; when and where they want to learn). Obviously, there are always going to be situations that demand adaptations (e.g., weather, health, levels of personal and emotional functioning, travel limitations, time changes, and other conditions). But we are talking here of "general principles" rather than of immutable scientific facts.

For this reason, learners at any age—particularly older learners—must have frequent opportunities to communicate with the facilitator and to adapt, where possible, the educational system to meet their needs. Essentially, education is communication which consists of two major linked components: content and affective relationships. Watzlawick includes in affective relationships, 1) self-revelation (what the sender says about him/herself), 2) the nature of the relationship between the sender and recipient of the message, and 3) the appeal aspect (what the sender wants the recipient of the message to do, think, or feel about the messages overtly or covertly).

Discovering and assessing learning needs and motivations means finding out people's backgrounds, their past experiences, strengths, and limitations, interests, readiness, capacities, and learning styles. It means also tapping latent motivations and transforming these into manifest desires. Two principles are significant here: (1) The "principle of wholeness," postulates that soma and psyche are one, and education must focus on cognitive, affective, and motoric (behavioral) aspects of people at their particular stage of development, allowing for individual and group differences of age, sex, race, ethnicity, socioeconomic class, position, state of health, functional abilities, and social competence. The heterogeneity of older people calls for instructional designs that respond to such differences and which focus on their varied cognitive styles and emotional predispositions. The fear of failure that tends to inhibit the learning processes of persons in their later years more than those who are younger must be alleviated by reducing task-complexities. (2) The "principle of context" alerts us to the fact that older adults—like other people—and educational programs are part of a physical and social environment, located in time and place and inhabited by people. The arena for learning and teaching consists of interacting people and social institutions; in other words, educational programs are operating in social systems.

Achieving an appropriate match of learners and teachers creates a milieu conducive to learning and growth, as does the development of a cohesive group feeling among the older participants to counteract feelings of aloneness and, at times, loneliness. Subsequently, older learners may use these group experiences as points of reference and transfer learning outcomes to new situations by making use of reminiscing. The humanistic educator will assist the learners in meeting their educational needs and goals; he/she is not a teacher in the traditional sense, but a facilitator or enabler.

Steps in Planning Educational Activities

Included in an educational plan are the following five major tasks:

1. Formulation of learning objectives based on the assessment of learning needs and motivations. What is to be accomplished? Which educational program is most likely to meet the needs of coping, expressing, contributing, influencing, and searching for meaning in life?

2. How can motivation be initiated and maintained? Raymond J. Wlodowski (1985), in examining the effects of motivation on the instruction

and learning of older persons, distills the major factors that motivate learning: attitudes and needs of the instructor and learner, stimulation offered to both, affect surrounding the learning situations, competence of learner and teacher, and reinforcements offered by the environment, as well as by the participants in the educational enterprise.

The following hypothesis should be tested: Positive attitudes toward learning and instruction, meeting optimal needs of learners and teachers, providing strong stimulating efforts, creating and maintaining highly affective interpersonal relationships, offering high-level competence, and reinforcing the content of learning and its outcomes are likely to engender and sustain high motivation of people toward learning.

3. How should such a program be organized, arranged, and delivered? What types of educational methods and techniques are best suited to maximize learning on the cognitive-affective and skill levels? Those media, methods, and techniques that are familiar to older persons and to which they have responded best in the past are likely to strike a more responsive chord than those which are unfamiliar to them.

Media are types of educational structures such as institutes, workshops, roundtables, seminars, learning groups, courses, conferences, symposia, colloquia, clinics, etc.

Methods include: lectures, discussion, buzz groups, role-plays, field trips, field work, and so on.

Techniques involve a repertory of asking and answering questions (Socratic method), summarizing, assignments, presenting problems-to-be-solved, critical incidents, use of audio-visual aids, including exhibits, bulletin boards, blackboards, movies, cassettes, slides, portfolios, books, hand-outs, manuals, case-records, use of food, recreation, among others.

Adult education programs of all types employ such media, methods and techniques in an often impromptu fashion, governed by such considerations as: Does it work? Do people come and respond favorably to programs by coming again? The trial-and-error approach, indeed, may still provide the best kind of validation.

4. The actual operation of a plan creates learning experiences that are individually perceived and felt. As stated, to transform an educational plan into an educational experience demands adaptability and restructuring, via feedback. Educational activities become learning experiences when learners are engaged actively rather than passively in the learning process and feel its impact cognitively, affectively, and behaviorally. Learners and teachers share mutual responsibility which, however, must be made explicit. Older persons

are not strangers to such sharing; in fact, they frequently wish to demonstrate their acquired competencies and to be respected for their contributions. They may feel left out or unwanted when not called upon. Such negative motivation may result in withdrawal. On the other hand, feeling wanted can go quite a distance toward maintaining or refurbishing an affirmative self-image.

Much has been written, based on research findings, about methods and techniques in adult education. Peterson's (1983) text is the most effective in applying this research to the learning goals and environmental factors relevant to older learners. It is evident that the societal/social milieu, plus the person in-the-situation, plus the educational goals of the learner and the teacher (as facilitator) at a particular point, must all be considered in developing the appropriate media, methods, and techniques.

5. Peterson (1983, 161) emphasizes that "it is one of the clearest insults to self-sufficiency of the older learner to have the teacher evaluate the student." All learners want and need a reflection of their progress and an assessment of future expectations. However, learning experiences which respect the capacity and autonomy of learners and move them toward greater capacity for self-directed learning cannot be realized with a simple judgment from authority figures. Learners who are striving to reach their optimum potential must be helped to evaluate their own accomplishments, and therefore to become their own evaluators.

There are several aspects to evaluation. To what extent were the educational objectives realized? Or, to put it another way: What was learned as perceived by the learners? To what extent were teaching approaches and methods conducive to achieving or not achieving the expected outcomes? What unintended learning did occur? Were the educational objectives desirable in the first place?

While evaluation is a continuous process, the act of evaluating must be done at specific time intervals, particularly at the end of an educational program. Evaluation should lead to generalization and stabilization of what was learned so that learning can be transferred to new situations. As Peterson repeatedly notes—keeping in mind the "health, perceptual and energy changes" experienced by many older adults—involvement in all aspects of the learning experience is appropriate for older adults as well as for those who are young or middle-aged; certainly, these andragogical principles are necessary and appropriate for older learners.

Transforming Education for All Ages

In *Andragogy in Action* (1984), Knowles has collected three dozen examples of andragogical principles applied in a variety of settings, with diverse subject matter and across a broad age range. The book concludes with several generalizations drawn from the practice of andragogy which are summarized here.

1. *Wholesale or Gradual Change*

Andragogical principles can be applied holistically or incrementally. In developing a new program, it may be best to apply the complete andragogical model; however, in adapting an existing program or institution, Knowles suggests that it is probably best to introduce gradual changes and pilot projects. Change which is an outgrowth of successful experimentation is likely to be resisted less.

2. *Preparation of Participants*

Both the learner and the facilitator need preparation to engage successfully in andragogical methods. Because their expectations are likely to be based on prior experiences with teacher-directed learning, learners may benefit from ongoing teacher orientation and peer support; otherwise, confusion and anxiety may develop. Moreover, because most instructors have only been exposed to pedagogical approaches to education, they need assistance in learning to adapt their skills to this type of education if they want to implement the andragogical methods.

3. *Overcoming Institutional Barriers*

Because institutional policies and practices often conflict with andragogical principles, andragogical innovators need to develop many more creative approaches to grading, attendance requirements, and to removing other barriers to motivations for learning. Practitioners have found that it is possible to make significant changes within pedagogically based systems and to minimize resistance to such changes through involving and informing the relevant parties.

Some would argue that such changes merely reinforce the status quo, that truly fundamental changes cannot be incremental. Yet the range of examples that Knowles presents suggests that many basic assumptions of education for all ages are being challenged in our educational institutions and that these institutions can and will eventually emerge transformed. The proof that this will occur, however, will come only in the future.

International Trends in Educational Reform

While educational techniques do not seem sufficiently unique for older adults that they justify a separate theory, a *geragogy,* still, the experiences of adult educators in various countries have suggested that the involvement of older adults in educational experiences has the potential to transform our assumptions about the very nature of education. It is the changed perspective of time (Moody, 1985) which makes education of the old unique, thus influencing the traditional conceptions of education as future-oriented and related to productivity.

Henri Bergson speaks of subjective and objective time. The passage of time, as it occurs throughout the universe, is measured in units of split seconds, minutes, hours, days, weeks, months, years, decades, centuries, eons. This is objective time. It provides us with a context and a yardstick for our daily lives, with an instrument to place events within a framework of past, present, and future (Butler, 1975, 410).

Subjective time is the passage of time experienced individually by each person, regardless of the impersonal external calendar. One minute, still consisting of the same sixty seconds as the previous or next minute, may appear to be of short or long duration to an individual at a particular time, place, or situation in that person's life history. The life-historical moment has meaning and relevance to the person, and subjective time is therefore as real to the person as is objective time; in fact, the degree of fit, or match, the degree of congruence or noncongruence (fit or nonfit) between objective and subjective time may be an important factor in a person's life at any stage and indicate healthy or non-healthy ego manifestations.

However, as people grow older, subjective time becomes more significant and has to be given major consideration in planning and implementing educational activities in the later years (Butler, 1975).

At the XIII International Congress of Gerontology in 1985, representatives of France, Great Britain, and Canada were invited to comment on the impact of education of older adults on traditional education in those countries. Their observations suggest that the influence of older learners is only just beginning to be felt in traditional educational systems.

Reflecting on the experience of the French Universities of the Third Age, Pierre Brasseul (1985) suggested that older adults had indeed helped to transform educational institutions in France. Responding to the restrictions of the *Formation continué,* laws which confined educational opportunities to those in the active workforce, retirees organized to develop their own unofficial educational opportunities: Universities of the Third Age and Clubs for the Retired. Brasseul suggested that these institutions contributed to a revival of the enjoyment of educational activities:

> Its greatest originality . . . lies in the way in which it brings together the joy of learning with the pleasure of teaching, at a time when official education is characterized by a certain gloominess." (Brasseul, 1985, 2)

Although the Universities of the Third Age were originally intended exclusively for older adults, they soon opened their doors to younger adults who were available to study during the day. Eventually this interaction between the young and the old created a climate in which the retired were able to participate in traditional courses as well. However, their motivations were generally not work-related, and this broadened the scope and purpose of education in France:

> Consequently, education takes on another meaning. It is linked to the person and no longer to production, to the "being" and no longer to the "doing." It is also this which explains why there is no longer a time limit. This type of education goes on throughout a lifetime. (Brasseul, 1985, 5)

According to Brasseul, this revolution was not as new as it might have seemed; it was rather a return to the preindustrial goal of education which, however, was directed at the leisure class. Now, as leisure was becoming a more or less universal experience, education for leisure and education directed at the development of the individual added an important new dimension to the meaning of education for all adults.

Brian Groombridge (1985) argued that the impact of older learners on educational systems in France was in part a result of the restrictive practices which had tended to characterize the educational institutions in continental Europe. Since retired persons were specifically restricted from participation in the French universities, the potential for impact through the creation of the Universities of the Third Age was greater, because opportunities were expanded for a previously excluded group. On the contrary, the universities in Britain had no such restriction of older adults from educational opportunities in the formal settings; thus opportunity was wider, and involving older learners in higher education programs required no such major efforts.

This difference in opportunity reflected a difference in the purpose of the university in continental Europe as compared with Britain, according to Groombridge. He suggested that the basic purposes of universities in continental Europe were to conduct research and to teach young people to carry on the scholarly traditions; the universities in Britain, particularly in recent times, had a further purpose: to make a university contribution to adult education.

Another writer from the United Kingdom has suggested that this change has begun to be fulfilled in Britain:

> The growth and distribution of knowledge is rapidly making traditional models of education obsolete, and new learning technologies are being developed which give greater potential than ever before to the possibilities of

education as an instrument of social change, but only if we change radically our conceptions of education itself and adopt a critical view of the uses to which it could be put. (Champling, 1985)

Nevertheless, Groombridge contended that it was still too early to assess the impact of older learners on the educational institutions in England. He noted that although opportunities had always been available to older learners, only 2–7 percent of elders were involved in educational activities. Thus greater outreach efforts were needed to involve a broader distribution of older learners in educational activities before their influence could be assessed.

Also at the International Congress of Gerontology, David Radcliffe (1985) noted the lack of a basic philosophical justification for adult education, which he saw as "potentially socially devastating" because of the danger that such programs would be the first to be eliminated in times of fiscal austerity. He suggested that education of the old had the potential to influence thinking about our whole attitude regarding education, to help us to learn whether there are different reasons why we educate older adults, reasons which might be used in defense of adult education programs in general.

The potential contribution of older learners to a transformation in our conception about teaching and learning has been widely recognized. Michel Philibert, one who has been at the forefront of the development of Universities of the Third Age in France, emphasizes that the involvement of older adults in university education is likely to have much greater impact on those institutions than has been true of the involvement of younger adults. He explains that young and middle-aged students have done little to transform educational institutions for two reasons: 1) they have been so indoctrinated by pedagogical teaching methods that they cannot imagine any other ways to learn, 2) they are so much interested in getting degrees or improving their job prospects that they are not willing to challenge the system or individuals (teachers) who have such great influence over the material aspects of their lives. Therefore, they learn and repeat back whatever the instructor expects in order to pass their examinations (Philibert, 1984, 55).

Philibert proposes that older learners, being less likely to be motivated by concerns about degrees and promotions, are freer to be creative and to demand educational methods and experiences which treat them as mature learners. He argues that "reinterpretation of their life" is of primary importance to older adults and to all of us who stand to benefit from "whatever light their reinterpretation, their evaluation, their repentance may shed on our own life and history" (Philibert, 1984, 59). Because of their greater freedom to question and challenge existing methods of instruction, Philibert suggests that older adults are "quite able to teach their teachers better ways" (p. 56).

From West Germany, Bubolz-Lutz (1984) proposes the following summary points regarding the influence of older learners on educational institutions: People, during their entire lifetimes, need education (*Bildung*). This is not to be understood as an exclusively externally induced effort to "shape or form" people, but to design active, self-directed, and emancipated activities by individuals in interaction with others. Education in the later years can only be understood as a wholistic entity; it includes all aspects of the human existence: physiological, somatic, psychological, emotional, cognitive, mental contacts and values, social contacts as far as they still exist or get newly established, contacts with the ecological and societal environment. As deficits in the later years are reinforced by societally shaped conditions, it is important for older persons to be able to confront such conditions and work to bring about changes to reduce negative influences. To acquire such capacities is as important as individual growth and development in moving toward "self-realization." Education is not limited to being conducted by or in an educational institution or in a social welfare agency; however, such institutions or agencies have an obligation to make it possible to carry on such educational activities and to make their facilities and organizational apparatus accessible for educational purposes and functions (Bubolz-Lutz, 1984).

In Switzerland, *Erwachsenenbildung* has been developed, nurtured and supported for many years in a decentralized way by the governments of the Kantons (states) as well as by the private sector, notably by Pro-Senectute, a private large-scale organization established at the turn of the century to provide health and social benefits for the older population (Winter, 1984).

In the early 1970s, becoming aware of demographic changes, many additional private organizations (religious and secular) offered expressively and instrumentally oriented (see chapter 8) programs for older adults throughout the land. This was in tune with public social welfare policy changes in favor of increased health care and pension benefits for its aging population.

To promote the idea of education with, by, and for older persons, several privately sponsored health and social service organizations (Pro-Senectute in the forefront), and a number of schools of social work, nursing, and education, became interested in disseminating information on how to start such educational programs and how to "educate the educators." To give an illustration:

A public, privately funded sectarian multipurpose center for older people (including a hospital and a hospice), which at the same time also serves as an adult education, social service and recreation center for children, youth, and middle-aged adults, the "Staffelnhof" in the Kanton of Lucerne, started to conduct a series of "Staffelnhof Seminars" in 1977 which continue until today. Leadership was provided by Swiss and American social workers, physicians, nurses, clergy, and adult educators, including one of the authors (Lowy). For one week in the summer, over 300 adult educators, social workers, physicians, nurses, mental health personnel, family members, older residents of the Center, and clergymen assemble at the Staffelnhof, which is located three miles outside of Lucerne, to present lectures on gerontological and geriatric findings from many parts of the world, to conduct round-table discussions with experts and lay participants—including older people—to review, analyze and assess existing programs in Switzerland. Regular press conferences are held to promote a different, non-stereotypical image of aging and the aged. Subsequently the proceedings of the seminars are published and widely disseminated, not only in Switzerland, but in other adjacent countries of Europe. Since then, the Swiss have coined the term *Betagtenbildung* to differentiate education in the later years from adult education, *Erwachsenenbildung*. They have come to acknowledge increasingly the continuum of social welfare and education as evidenced by the choice of the Staffelnhof themes, contexts of discussion and qualifications of the presenters and participants. One of the most recent themes was: *Bildung & Soziale Sicherheit Kennen Kein Alter* ("Education and Social Security Know No Age," *Staffelnhof Seminar Proceedings,* 1977–1985).

The Staffelnhof model has taken hold. Additional seminars and conferences are being held; officials of the Swiss Federal and Kanton governments, health officers, social welfare personnel, adult educators, members of the clergy of different faiths in the German-, French-, and Italian-speaking parts of the Swiss Confederation are actively engaged in training of personnel and research about the aging process, providing social and health-care programs, notably on the preventive level, and utilizing adult education in making the country aware of the resources of its older citizens. A large proportion of the Swiss aged (estimated at 20 percent) are engaged in learning and teaching activities.

One of the fullest developments of the essential differences which older adults bring to educational experiences is described in a text which, at this time, appears only in its original German. In *The Late Freedom* (*Die Späte Freiheit*), Leopold Rosenmayr (1983) explores the historical and social conditions which shape our views of aging, raising the question of whether these conditions can be reshaped in order to enhance one's fulfillment of life.

Like Moody, Rosenmayr (1983) contends that the proximity of death, the heightened awareness of the finiteness of life, creates a unique perspective for older adults which combines a new sense of freedom *from* work responsibilities, social obligations, and various encumbrances of youth and freedom *to* explore more fundamental questions of meaning in life, to search for fulfillment in the last stages of life.

Rosenmayr argues that education in the later years should be directed toward the creation and further development of new experiences and knowledge to achieve a deeper understanding of oneself. Like Bubolz-Lutz (1984), he suggests that in this regard the goals of therapy and education are more closely related than is commonly assumed; education, counseling, and therapy may thus be seen as constituting a continuum with fluid boundaries. All are elements of the process of coming to terms with oneself as an individual person and developing a social conscience in a societal context. Rosenmayr contends that our present educational models are inadequate to the achievement of the tasks of the "late freedom;" we need rather to create new models of education. Education for this "late freedom" must stretch our creative capacity to make aging an opportunity rather than a burden. Educational institutions must be transformed if they are to enable older adults to fulfill their potential for themselves and for society.

> Without an illusory assumption of future outcomes, education for older people will have to proceed beyond the teleological ethic of traditional education. Without optimistic images of infinite growth, education for older people requires a concept of human development grounded in human finitude but affirming the enduring value of the experience in all its forms. Without assuming that our educational institutions are suitable for everyone, we will have to discover new ways of reaching the potential of the least advantaged groups among the aged. Only in this way can we hope to develop a social philosophy supportive of education for older adults, and based on a vision of the learning society encompassing the entire life span. (Moody, 1985, 46)

Put more simply, Norman Evans suggests that education should be directed toward helping individuals "make sense of themselves." He advocates a *Posteducation Society* in which the transformed educational system places emphasis on "recognizing and using adults' learning" (Evans, 1985, 99).

Neither Rosenmayr nor Moody gives a prescription for educational models which can best serve the needs of those who are experiencing the "late freedom." Evans comes closer to a prescription in describing the transformed educational system as a "democracy of learners" in which the role of the educational system is "to empower individuals to take charge of their own study" (Evans, 1985, 146), by encouraging and recognizing (through credits and degrees) the self-directed learning of adults. Yet we still know very little about what such a "system" would be like for older learners; we know even less about what implications such changes might have for the education of younger adults and for children.

If our educational institutions do not respond to the forces pressing for change, we may have much to lose as individuals, as a nation, as a species.

As individuals, we may lose the possibility of reaching our own highest levels of consciousness, and we may risk experiencing the period of the "late freedom" only as a burden rather than an opportunity. As a nation, we may face the future growth in the aged population without learning how we can make that shift a human benefit rather than a liability. As humans, we may risk the possibility that we will fail to make use of resources that may help us to steer a more hopeful and more humane course for the future of the human race. As Philibert suggests:

> From a world of perspective, at this unique moment in the history of humankind and the spaceship earth, happy will we be if, calling on the aged of today as indispensable partners in our examination of past experience and planning for the future, we may reach truth and wisdom in time to save our species on the planet, instead of falling into our own traps and dying fools. (Philibert, 1981)

6
Who Is Responsible? The Federal Role

Analysis of individuals and organizations responsible for developing a national educational policy is a complex task which must consider all three levels of government, the private sector, and individual responsibilities. Such an analysis would have to take into account political, economic, sociological, cultural, and philosophical factors and forces which influence the education of older adults at all these levels. The magnitude and detail of such an endeavor, however, are beyond the scope of the present volume; for this reason, we confine ourselves to looking at the federal role in order to indicate what remains to be done in order to respond unambiguously to the basic question: Why invest resources in the education of older adults?

Review of the Federal Role in Education of Older Americans

Historically, the federal role in educational policy for persons of all ages has been a distant one. Education in the United States is largely a decentralized operation; direct control rests primarily with local communities and social institutions under statutory and regulatory control by the individual states and territories.

A limited federal role dates to the early history of this country, founded upon a capitalist, Puritan economic system and emphasizing individualism, states rights, and local control of public decision-making.

> The doctrine of local responsibility and community independence (in American education) can be related to our pioneer history without difficulty. Parish and county autonomy in the South, the seventeenth-century independence of New England church congregations, and suspicion of centralized government are among the factors that shaped the present political structure of our school systems in many states. (Conant, 1959, 20)

The federal government was, in de Tocqueville's words, "circumscribed within certain limits and only exercising an exceptional authority over the general interests of the country." Responsibility remained at the state and local level, because education was not constitutionally reserved for the federal government.

> The powers not delegated to the United States by the Constitution, nor prohibited by it to the States, are reserved to the States respectively, or to the people. (10th Amendment to the Constitution)

Since the latter half of the nineteenth century, the federal government has become more and more involved in the support of educational activities, a role that has been defended in the Preamble to the Constitution, which calls for federal responsibility to "provide for the common Defense and general Welfare of the United States." Yet, controversy about the meaning and practical application of the concept of the *general Welfare* has continued ever since. Franklin D. Roosevelt emphasized the constitutional responsibility for the general welfare in introducing the New Deal legislation to Congress in the 1930s in order to justify federal intervention in social programming during the Great Depression (Axinn and Levin, 1980). Yet federal responsibility has continued to be questioned and reconsidered since those days by many political, business, and professional groups. In the 1980s, under the Reagan administration, the new federalist interpretation of the Constitution has made its greatest inroads in practice. It has led to a reassertion of state and local rights, deregulation of economic, social, and legal programs, promotion of private sector initiatives and deemphasis of the role of the federal government in the economic, social, and educational spheres. Debates about the federal role in educational policy, like debates about the federal role in social welfare policy generally, often follow ideological lines, as is evident in this editorial comment:

> . . . much of the debate about the existing array of federal education programs could be classified easily, if a bit arbitrarily—"liberals" emphasized the value of the programs in making certain that scarce resources were not dribbled away, while "conservatives" attacked the programs for eroding local control over education. The first group accused the second of indifference to the real problems of disadvantaged and minority students; the second group blasted the first for fostering statism under the cloak of civil rights. (Miller, 1981, 49)

Despite these differences, "conservatives" and "liberals" in the United States share a basic belief in equality which has enabled them to achieve consensus at various times by linking educational goals emotionally to equality as an ideal. Equality in the political mainstream of the country, refers to the ideology of equality of opportunity rather than to equality of outcome. The latter ideological emphasis is more common in social democratic, socialist, or communist countries. In addition, there is frequent confusion between *equity* (meaning a proportionate sharing of the pie — fairness) versus *equality* (referring to an equal sharing of the pie).

Thus, conservatives and liberals alike in the United States advocate government action based on the principles of increasing equality of opportunity. Their respective approaches are different — conservatives advocate particularly restrictions on the federal government's right to interfere with opportunities (e.g., deregulation, decentralization, and promotion of the "opportunity society" of the 1980s). Liberals tend to advocate specific government involvements which are intended to increase opportunities for individuals in disadvantaged groups nationally (e.g., programs of the Economic Opportunity Act of 1964). Indeed, the approaches of conservatives and liberals lead to quite different outcomes, neither of which has led to any semblance of equality in life experiences, to the elimination of wide disparities in income and economic opportunities, to fairness in taxation, to elimination of poverty, or to making health care resources equally accessible to all citizens. Radical critics charge that these outcomes prove that both groups, conservatives and liberals, are essentially supporters of *inequality* because they are willing to accept the unfairness and inequality that result from such moderate positions.

The emphasis on the ideal of opportunity is important in understanding the federal role in educational (or social) policy in the United States. Its major purpose has been to increase opportunities for talented individuals to gain a share of the products of their own labor. In the words of Chester E. Finn, Jr., noted educational adviser, the purpose of federal support is, "to weaken the correlation between income and educational opportunity, and to give more people a chance at more education than would have been the case if the federal government had kept out of the field" (quoted in Wilson, 1983, 68).

Balancing federal and state responsibilities has become increasingly complex as the federal role has increased. In the area of elementary and secondary education, this role has been restricted to mandating that all communities provide such education (within certain broad standards) and only providing financial support where localities or states are reluctant or unable to meet these broad federal standards. Higher education has been the primary target of federal financial support, largely in the form of tuition assistance for individuals and reduced taxes for institutions. In keeping with the goals of equal opportunity, such support has attempted to assure that financial hardship does not prevent qualified students from attendance at colleges and universities. In 1981, for instance, $17 billion was spent by the federal government on higher education (Wilson, 1983, 74). For elementary and secondary education, the figure was about one half or one third of that (Rotberg, 1981, 25).

Educational activities are provided through a variety of federal programs—under the Departments of Agriculture, Labor, Health and Human Services, and Defense, among others. Nevertheless, federal support of education represents only a small fraction of the financial costs of education in this country. In 1978, the federal government paid just over 8 percent of the costs of elementary and secondary education while localities and states each paid more than 5 times as much—47.8 and 44.1 percent, respectively. The federal government paid a somewhat higher proportion of the costs of higher education, but the proportion still averaged well under 20 percent. (Jennings, 1981, 6–7). Rotberg (1981, 24) estimates that the federal government pays only 9.5 percent of the total costs of education in the United States, and another estimate places that figure at only 6 percent (Beebe and Evans, 1981, 41).

Unraveling federal involvement in the financing of education in the United States is an elusive task and can hardly be attempted here. Because of the range of programs and variety of funding sources, even simple comparative estimates are difficult to obtain; therefore, we use a variety of sources and a range of estimates in this brief summary. A Carnegie report's conclusion regarding the financing of higher education has been true of federal support of education in general:

> There is probably no single person—perhaps not even any single agency—in or out of government who can define with accuracy all of the ways in which the federal government channels funds to American higher education or the amount of money actually spent or obligated for all of these programs. (Wolk, 1968, ix)

Federal support for the education of older adults represents only a small fraction of overall federal educational expenditures, but unraveling the sources is no less complex. Stanford and Dolar (1978) took on this mammoth task in a chapter in Sherron and Lumsden's *Introduction to Educational Gerontology* (2nd edition, 1985). In a detailed chart covering several pages, they provide information about federal programs, authorizing legislation, specific provisions of the legislation, and agencies responsible for administering the programs. The scope of federal involvement is evident in the variety of legislative provisions cited in 1978:

Adult Basic and Continuing Education Act, Title VII

Adult Basic Education Act

Adult Education Act, Section 222, Title II, III

Appalachian Regional Development Act, 1965

Department of Justice Appropriations Act, 1972

Domestic Volunteer Services Act of 1973

Economic Opportunity Act, 1964

Education Professions Development Act, Section 309

Elementary and Secondary Education Act

General Broadcasting Provisions Act, sections 402 and 412

General Education Provisions Act, Sections 402 and 412

Higher Education Act, amended by Older Americans Act, 1973

Indian Adult Vocational Training Act

Library Service and Construction Act

Migration and Refugee Assistance Act, 1962

Office of Education and Related Agencies Appropriations Act, 1972

Older Americans Act, Title III, IV, VII

Smith-Lever Act

Snyder Act

Social Security Act, Title XX, amended 1974

State and Local Fiscal Assistance Act, 1972

Veterans Educational and Training Amendment Act, 1970

Vocational Education Act, amended 1968

Vocational Rehabilitation Act

[Excerpted from Stanford and Dolar, 1978, 143–150]

Department of Education: A New Era in Educational Policy

Unfortunately, the work of Stanford and Dolar was on the way to becoming outdated even as it went to press, a problem which typically plagues attempts to describe and/or explain federal policies of almost any sort. With his election in 1976, President Carter began to work on reorganizing the Office of Education in order to "enable the Federal government to be a true partner with State, local and private education institutions in sustaining and improving the quality of our education system" (Carter's message to Congress, February, 18, 1978). A product of bitter controversy, the Department of Education emerged in 1979, and various activities related to adult education began to be shifted from the Department of Health, Education and Welfare (now the Department of Health and Human Services) to the new Department of Education. It was the hope of the designers of this structure and their political supporters that Cabinet-level status would strengthen the lines of federal authority, enabling the federal government to assist states and local communities more effectively in addressing the country's educational needs ("Improving the Federal Government's Responsibilities in Education," 1981, 77).

The creation of the Department of Education indicated an acceptance of a stronger, though still limited, federal role in education, although the enabling Act still emphasized the primacy of state and local control and stressed the importance of supplementation rather than substitution by the federal government. Supporters hoped that the Department would ensure a better coordination and administration of national responsibilities (pp. 78, 80), while opponents were unconvinced that this would not mean a relinquishing of local control.

The Lifelong Learning Act: A First

In the midst of this development, an important piece of federal legislation related to the education of older adults was ignored. The "Lifelong Learning Act," passed along with the Education Amendments of 1976, was signed just prior to Carter's election and was hailed as "a landmark of social legislation" (Weinstock, 1978). Setting a goal of educational opportunity to engage in lifelong learning for all citizens "without regard to restrictions of previous education or training, sex, age, handicapping condition, social or ethnic background, or economic circumstance," the Act was the first legislation to specifically mention older adults and retired persons as objects of educational resources. As Ruth Weinstock (1978, 16) proclaimed, "never before has the law recognized as it does now, that the elderly constitute a distinct group . . . for whom 'lifelong learning' is important."

The great promise of the Lifelong Learning Act was never fulfilled, however, because it was never funded. Despite the fact that the bill's original sponsor, Walter Mondale, had been elected Vice President, there was insufficient political support to move Congress to appropriate any of the $40 million which had been authorized for lifelong learning. According to Penelope Richardson (1981), Director of the Lifelong Learning Project from 1976 to 1978, concern that money allocated to lifelong learning would result in reductions in other portions of their budgets led many interest groups to neglect lobbying efforts necessary to convince Congress to act on the appropriation. Richardson notes that those groups which did lobby for an appropriation—community colleges, unions, adult educators, and elder advocates—were simply not powerful enough to counteract the mood of "fiscal conservatism" already apparent during the Carter administration. As a result, the Lifelong Learning Act "served as a consciousness-raising piece of legislation" (Richardson, 1981, 212), but achieved no major breakthroughs. It became lost in the battle over the Department of Education, a struggle which eclipsed any bright hopes of educational reformers.

Conservative opposition to the Department of Education was strong, and elimination of the department became one of the priorities of the Republican party. With the election of President Reagan in 1980, the threat to the department was imminent. A Heritage Foundation report (Docksai, 1981) argued for abolishing the department's Cabinet-level status and refocusing of priorities on information gathering and technical assistance rather than regulation. Distribution of federal money through block grants to the states was seen as a way to limit the Department's size and influence, and thus to return control of programs to states. Efforts to eliminate the Department began with the Reagan administration's first budget, and although Congress acted to preserve the Department and its programs, the administration was successful in making reductions in its influence and its budget.

The basis of Reagan administration's attack against the Department of Education hearkens back to the old constitutional debate:

> The government ought to refrain from doing anything that will encroach on the autonomy of institutions and their governing boards. . . . The Reagan administration is committed to state and local control of education and to institution independence and autonomy in both public and private institutions. (Terrel H. Bell, Secretary of Education, quoted in Wilson, 1983, 81)

In his second term, Reagan appointed William Bennett to succeed Bell as Secretary of Education. Bennet has assumed leadership in advocating educational changes to correspond with the administration's limited view of federal responsibility in education, including advocacy of a voucher system for choice of public or private elementary and high schools, elimination of federal loan programs for higher education (federal grants were already eliminated in the first term).

With the creation of the Department of Education, the bureaucratic structure of educational administration of programs for older adults was changed, but the scope of programming was not. Primary responsibility for administration of educational programs for older adults was subsumed under the Office of Vocational and Adult Education, headed by an assistant secretary reporting directly to the Secretary of Education (see figure 6–1).

A program guide entitled "Education and Training for Older Persons," prepared by the Office of Vocational and Adult Education (1981) details the variety of federal programs serving the needs of older learners. Although subject to change, a summary of that information is provided in Appendix D to indicate the current range of federal activities related to the education of older adults.

In addition to the programs described by the Office of Vocational and

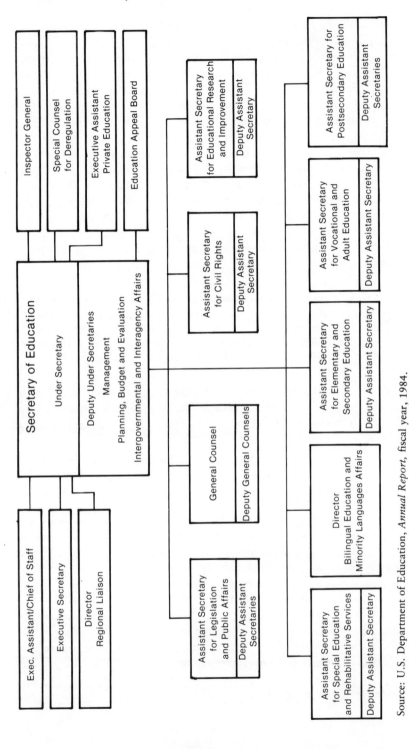

Source: U.S. Department of Education, *Annual Report*, fiscal year, 1984.

Figure 6–1. Organization of the Department of Education

Adult Education, an important role in developing educational programs for older adults is retained by the Administration on Aging under provisions of the Older Americans Act of 1965, reauthorized several times (most recently in 1984). The Older Americans Act provides for shared federal-state-local funding for a variety of services to older adults, including funding for evaluation, training, research, and demonstration efforts to be conducted by state and local governments and other public and private organizations. The term "training" is explicitly used to denote preparation of people for employment in designing, offering, and conducting programs for the aging. Special courses addressing the needs of rural providers are to be funded under the 1978 Amendments.

Title III of the Older Americans Act, the principal source of funding for state and county government planning and service provision, also can be utilized for training of people to provide and coordinate services to older adults. Such plans must be developed in conjunction with Area Agencies on Aging (AAAs), and imagination and creativity by such agency planners and administrators can yield funding for training purposes. Such training can also come under the broad definition of education, although the majority of trainers and trainees are younger, and only a minority are older themselves.

Funds authorized by the Department of Labor under Title V also support education for older adults. This program grants funds for community-service jobs for the unemployed, for persons with low incomes, and for persons over the age of 55 who want to work. Provisions are also made to assist older workers in the transition to part-time employment in community service jobs in social services, home repair, congregate care facilities, hospitals, and so forth. This necessitates "training" of short duration to enable persons to carry out such jobs.

In addition, other federal acts (eg., the Domestic Volunteer Services Act of 1973, as amended) support programs like the Foster Grandparent Program, in which some provisions can be made to provide "training" for older, low-income people to be "foster grandparents." Whether even the federal-state funding of such programs will be continued is, at this time of this writing, an open question.

Determining how to shape the federal role in educational policies for older adults is an onerous task and one which cannot be conceived apart from consideration of the federal role in education in general. Yet, policies are often developed on an ad hoc basis in response to pressures from various interest groups or in reaction to political crises. Some policies, like the Lifelong Learning Act, are merely symbolic responses which have little practical impact on the educational system; others are piecemeal solutions which fail to meet the complex educational needs of the citizenry. In the end we are left with a vast federal bureaucracy which increases in size incrementally each year, and a fragmented, uncoordinated array of individual programs.

Too often those in a bureaucracy who are in the best position to reflect on the broad goals of the organization are so preoccupied with troubleshooting, responding to crises and system maintenance that they do not have or do not take time to examine the fundamental principles which inform and guide their enterprise. However, such reflection is necessary to the development of policy which moves toward a national sense of purpose. It is such a sense of purpose that is generally lacking in our educational system in the United States, and the inability to achieve consensus on the role of the federal government in social welfare and education for all ages confounds us more and more and leaves us with diverse, conflicting, and disconnected social and educational policies, particularly for older adults whose numbers and proportional relation to the rest of the population is increasing, as we noted earlier.

Toward Establishing National Goals

In a rare attempt to step back and consider the fundamental goals of federal policy in education, two officials of the Office of Education in 1975–76 tried to articulate the purpose of a national role in educational policy (Beebe and Evans, 1981). First outlining areas in which there was likely to be general agreement, Beebe and Evans summarized the areas of consensus in five points:

1. The Federal role in American education is small and likely to remain so . . .

2. Although small, the federal role in American education is not concentrated, specialized or focused on any consciously selected mission or area of responsibility. Rather, it has grown up through a process of ad hoc accretion . . .

3. There is also much inconsistency and unclarity about the nature and limits of Federal responsibility . . .

4. Not only does the substance and direction of the Federal role lack clear definition, but the pattern also reflects the ad hoc nature of federal involvement in American education . . .

On this basis, they went on to argue (p. 43) that:

5. Achieving a clarification of the Federal role in education can have important and far-reaching benefits.

(Beebe and Evans, 1981, 41–43)

Clarifying federal responsibilities in education was seen by Beebe and Evans as important in order to control federal expenditures, to concentrate resources on appropriate priority areas, and to maintain a limited role for the federal government in educational policy. While arguing the importance of a national role, they contended that this role should remain limited. Their concern for maintaining the primacy of state and local control of education and restricting federal expenditures echoed "conservative" arguments against federal involvement in education. Beebe and Evans thus articulated a moderate position.

Six criteria were proposed as bases for selecting and evaluating the appropriateness of specific federal policy options in education. The recommendations provide a useful framework for evaluating federal programs and policy options for older adults and thus are included here:

1. In the absence of special and compelling reasons to the contrary, *the provisions of basic educational services is a state and local responsibility.*

2. The Federal government is responsible for *preserving individuals' fundamental rights to equitable participation in the educational system.*

3. The Federal government is responsible for *compensating for Federally-imposed financial burdens), in areas such as Impact Aid and Veterans' Educational Benefits.*

4. The Federal government properly has the responsibility for *"assessing the status and progress of American education."*

5. The Federal government has a primary responsibility, in partnership with the states and with the postsecondary and private sectors, for providing leadership in *improving the quality and relevance of American education,* through research, development, demonstration and evaluation efforts.

6. It is appropriately the Federal government's responsibility to intervene in order to deal with *critical educational problems which have serious national consequences and are beyond the ability (or, sometimes willingness) of state/local governments to solve* [e.g., equalizing educational opportunity.]

(Beebe and Evans, 1981, 44)

It should be noted that these recommendations, while quite useful, do not encompass all of the potentially important responsibilities which the federal government has, in fact, considered appropriate in relation to educational policy. The funding of research and education related to the national defense, a controversial role which has, nevertheless, been a prominent one in recent decades, is not included in this list. Similarly, the federal responsibility in addressing other national problems through educational policy also points to a viable role. For example, the Serviceman's Readjustment Act (G.I. Bill), which revolutionized higher education in this country, was largely designed to reintegrate a large number of servicemen returning from World War II into the society, without displacing existing workers or creating vast unemployment.

Therefore, with the caveat that the criteria established by Beebe and Evans are and must be subject to changing social and economic conditions, two sets of recommendations related to education of older adults will be reviewed against the background of their recommendations: 1) policy statements proposed in the report prepared for the Office of Vocational and Adult Education (1981), and 2) recommendations of the delegates to the 1981 White House Conference on Aging (see appendixes A and B for both sets of recommendations). Representing somewhat opposing views regarding the role of the federal government in the education of older adults, these two proposals are by no means intended to represent the only choices available, but they are representative of the most common positions in this country. In addition to providing details of some of the policy options that have been proposed, they demonstrate the kind of questions worth considering before proposing federal policy options, and might even help reveal future options heretofore not conceived.

1. The report on *Education and Training for Older Persons* contains a list of 21 "exemplary policy statements" covering five aspects of policy development: planning, coordination of service delivery, outreach, supportive services, and instruction. The statements articulate a concern for preserving state and local control of vocational education programs for older persons and encouraging equal access to educational opportunities. Allocation of state and local funds is advised; establishment of local advisory councils is recommended; development of local guidelines for governance is suggested. Several specific recommendations are made about procedures that should be adopted, but these are all proposals for local procedures. No specifically federal responsibilities are indicated. In this regard, the *Education and Training* report conforms to the first criterion in the Beebe and Evans framework—that basic education (specifically, vocational education for older adults) be a state and local responsibility.

In connection with assuring equitable participation, the recommendations do include the statement: "No persons shall be excluded from participation in an appropriate vocational program on the basis of age" and a recommendation that outreach activities (presumably local) be provided in order to attract all those who might benefit from such educational activities. On the surface, this seems to correspond to Beebe and Evans' second criterion. However, there is no indication of how the federal government should act to preserve this desirable condition of equal opportunity, and the expression "appropriate vocational program" opens an escape route for those who would seek to determine some educational activities inappropriate for older adults. The "exemplary policy statements" are thus insufficient on the point of preserving equitable participation.

On the other points, the language of the *Education and Training* report is much less powerful. There are no specific federally imposed costs, and consequently there is no need for federal compensation. A moderate federal role in planning vocational education programs is alluded to in the directives to cooperate with the federally sponsored area agencies on aging, but there are no specific directives for federal responsibility in research, development, demonstration, or evaluation of educational programs involving older adults. A heavy emphasis in the recommendations on coordination of services may, in fact, be seen (in the absence of any more specific recommendations for action) as an unrealistic, perhaps merely symbolic, response.

The most serious limitation in the "exemplary policy statements" is the lack of any statement related to the federal government's role in the event that states or localities are unwilling or unable to provide educational opportunities to older adults. If there is indeed a serious belief in the value of such educational opportunities, then some federal incentives or sanctions must be available to encourage the development and expansion of education for older adults. The lack of any provisions for such encouragement indicates that the recommendations are in fact not recommendations for a federal role at all but rather articulate a position against federal involvement in education of older adults.

This report essentially follows the federal policy models which have been devised throughout the past few years, veering more to the conservative practices regarding the federal role in social, health, and educational policy; it reflects the pendulum swing to the right in the federal-state-local balancing act of tensions which, as noted before, has characterized this country from its early history.

If the federal report on *Education and Training for Older Persons* advocates a minimalist position in regard to federal involvement in education of older adults, the recommendations of the delegates to the 1981 White House Conference on Aging advocate nearly the opposite. A glance at the full text of the recommendations in appendix B reveals that the detailed recommendations are rather comprehensive. For present purposes, we will examine only those recommendations which relate to a federal role in stimulating educational opportunities for older adults, although the other recommendations are no less important.

2. The essence of the 1981 White House Conference recommendations is captured in a statement which was voted on apart from the other resolutions and approved as a "concept" by two thirds of the voting delegates. Addressing the federal role in education of, about, and serving the needs of older adults, the resolution demanded that "exclusion of the aged from education and from training programs legislated for all citizens must cease." The resolution called for expansion of "federal funding of and leadership in" educational programs related to older adults. A strong desire was expressed by the delegates that the federal government should assume a strong role in assuring the rights of older adults to "equitable participation in the educa-

tional system," the second criterion of Beebe and Evans. This is reinforced in earlier recommendations calling for federal education funds to be "targeted in equitable proportion toward older adults." The delegates were in favor of a strong federal role in preserving educational "rights" for all.

The recommendations address the need for divisions of responsibility between federal, state, and local bodies; indeed, many of the recommendations are specifically addressed to state units on aging as well as local community organizations and institutions in both the public and private sector. The recommendations do not follow Beebe and Evans' principle of delegating to states and localities the responsibility for providing all basic educational services; this perhaps represents a failure of the delegates to distinguish those educational responsibilities which should preferably not be assumed by the federal government. Yet, proponents would no doubt argue that maintaining a federal role in all levels of education for older adults is necessitated by Beebe and Evans' sixth criterion — i.e., that there have been and will continue to be serious national consequences due to the failure of states and localities to address the educational needs of older adults and that federal support is therefore needed at all levels of education for the aged. It was the judgment of the delegates that other national priorities for older adults, as expressed in the recommendations about health care, income assistance, employment, nutrition, housing, and so on, could not be assured

> unless older people are entitled to have access to a full range of educational programs in keeping with their needs and interests, to be served by personnel who have been adequately prepared to serve special needs of older persons, and to live in a society which has come to understand more fully the aging process. (White House Conference on Aging, *Final Recommendations,* 1981)

On the federal role in monitoring and improving the quality of educational programs for older adults, the recommendations of the 1981 White House Conference on Aging are strong. A new title under the Older Americans Act is recommended specifically to provide an evaluation of the "educational impact" of the various federal programs affecting older adults. Biennial reports are recommended and are to include information about programs and educational opportunities for older adults, as well as barriers which inhibit elders' participation in such programs. Moreover, the delegates recommended that funding for a variety of research goals be "increased immediately." Specific attention is directed toward research on the normal processes of aging in order to combat ageist stereotypes which inhibit the full participation of older adults in all segments of society. The delegates also urged a strong role for the Commission on Civil Rights (or some other appropriate body) "to fully investigate and document the nature and scope of age prejudice and discrimination in the United States."

The scope of the 1981 White House Conference recommendations indicates that the delegates were not likely to shy away from supporting the federal government's responsibility to compensate states and localities financially for meeting federal priorities. Perhaps one of the most controversial recommendations calls for a "complete range of basic and all other levels of educational programs," with "the highest priority for funding [to be] made available and accessible to all older Americans immediately." As noted above, the delegates argued for the designation of an "equitable proportion" of federal funds for educational and employment programs to be designated for older adults.

What has occurred since these recommendations were made at the White House Conference on Aging in 1981?

The 1984 report of the U.S. Senate Special Committee on Aging makes reference to the expansion of the largely privately financed "Elderhostel" program. In 1984, over 700 private and public colleges and educational institutions in 50 states and Canada served over 80,000 hostelers and over 5000 participated in programs in France, Germany, Scandinavia, the Netherlands, Italy, and Great Britain. The report admits that even with the burgeoning numbers, Elderhostel remains an educational opportunity reserved for mobile, healthy older people with relatively high educational attainment levels.

Intergenerational programs in schools and community centers range from informal and haphazard to those that span several school and neighborhood districts. The federal role in promoting such programs has expanded somewhat through initiatives by the Administration on Aging and the Administration of Children, Youth and Families, both in the Department of Health and Human Services. Three components have been created: 1) an information bank of intergenerational programs across the country, with dissemination of the information to organizations interested in establishing such programs (e.g., "Understanding Aging"); 2) plans to evoke such interest by existing professional organizations; 3) funding of intergenerational demonstration projects on an ad hoc, time-limited basis.

Higher education has not received separate federal subsidies to finance any of their educational initiatives for older learners. Even on the state level, only two or three states provide reimbursement to institutions of higher learning for tuition-waivers which they have granted to older adults (Romaniuk, 1982).

Since 1981, the Reagan administration has proposed consolidating programs into block-grants to states, and this plan was enacted through the Omnibus Reconciliation Act of 1981.

In response to the President's Commission on Excellence in Education

LIBRARY

Report in 1983, the U.S. Department of Education advanced an adult literacy initiative, largely a promotional partnership with the private sector, to reduce adult illiteracy. It was estimated that, of adults aged 60–65, 35 percent lacked competency skills to cope with the minimal demands of today's society. In 1984, the National Institute of Education (NIE) launched a "National Adult Literacy Project," awarding approximately $900,000 to private corporations to develop literacy training and research programs for adults. This again illustrates the private contracting approach to achieve such a formidable task as reducing adult illiteracy in the United States.

Legislative Activities in 1984

Four major education bills were enacted in 1984, partly designed to offer educational assistance to older people: 1) an amendment to the Adult Education Act, 2) the Vocational Education Act, 3) Library Services and Construction Act, and 4) the previously mentioned Labor, Department of Health and Human Services, and Education "package." In October 1984, this legislative package, known as the Educational Amendments of 1984, was signed by the President. It authorizes adult education expenditures of $140 million for fiscal year 1985 (up from $100 million in 1984). However, the increase is primarily designed to assist *states* in providing literacy skills to educational disadvantaged adults.

For comparison, the federal budget in fiscal year 1984 totaled over $840 billion. The Department of Health and Human Services (including the Social Security Trust Fund) represented over $200 billion of that figure; the Department of Labor (including the Unemployment Trust fund) represented approximately $25 billion. By contrast, the entire budget of the Department of Education, including the limited expenditures on adult education noted above, represented just over $8 billion.

The interest of the very small federal library fund is to assist states in upgrading library services as libraries are seen as part of the lifelong learning enterprise. The Library Services Construction Act of 1984 authorizes the training of librarians to work with older people, to conduct special library programs for them, and to purchase special materials, as well as to arrange for an effort to alert older adults about available library services. The Vocational Education Act, even more than previous years, limits the use of federal funds by states to upgrade in some way vocational education programs.

What of the Future?

Despite these activities in 1984, the federal role in older adult education has lessened appreciably since the 1981 White House Conference on Aging, as has the federal involvement in other social welfare programs, and indeed in most domestic programs. This is in tune with the efforts by the Reagan administration to reduce spending in accord with its stance on the appropriate role of the federal government. The present executive office of the federal government takes a limited constitutional view of the federal role, going back to some of the principles of the Founding Fathers of this Republic, notably those held by Alexander Hamilton and Benjamin Franklin, that the national government's major function is to defend the nation militarily, to provide charity to the "needy poor," if it is proved that they *deserve* such help (a throwback to the Elizabethan Poor Laws of 1601 in England and imported to this country by the Pilgrims), and to act as a mediator—if and when called upon—in interstate disputes.

This is a reversal of the political, economic, and social direction from the days of the New Deal when a "reluctant welfare state" was created. The industrial and postindustrial revolutions in modern society made a social insurance state inevitable as has been witnessed in almost all Western democratic countries. In many parts of the developing world, as well as in the socialist nations, "social security" in the fullest sense of the term has become a Number One priority for their populations. And education has been considered part of this schema.

In the United States, since the early 1980s, Congress has not sufficiently demonstrated the leadership or power to do more than put brakes on the dismantling process of the entitlement and other social programs. The social insurance part of the Social Security system has been kept alive to a large extent by convergence of middle-class self-interests among middle-aged and older adults. And the judiciary branch, still composed of many justices appointed by presidents in the pre-Reagan era is likely to support a more narrow interpretation of the Constitution, if a new breed of strict constitutionalist justices (in all federal-level courts) ascends to power and perpetuates the legacy of the Reagan Administration.

The struggle for scarce resources is likely to emerge even stronger in intergenerational terms. For example, a new private organization, "Americans for Generational Equity," was formed in 1986. According to their first public announcement, their central mission is to promote greater public understanding of problems arising among the aging of the U.S. population and to foster increased public support for policies that will serve the economic interests of the next century's elderly. Foundations, institutes, business corporations, and universities are represented on the Board of Directors. The announcement of their first annual conference in 1986, "Tomorrow's Elderly: Planning for the Baby Boom Generation's Retirement," was prefaced with the following statement:

> . . . because of this [Baby Boom] generation's anomalously large size and unprecedented life-expectancy, the United States faces the prospect of a

rapidly aging population during the early decades of the next century. . . . Will the generation's retirement present an unacceptable burden to younger Americans? (Conference flyer, Americans for Generational Equity, 1986)

In light of concerns about generational equity, such issues as educational equity and access are likely to emerge more significantly, and a national policy in social welfare, health and education (including adult and older adult education) appears to be more remote than ever in the present political climate. At the same time, with the "graying of America" it is most urgent now to focus our national attention and invest a share of our fiscal, human, organizational, and temporal resources to enhance the educational opportunities of older persons.

Once such a commitment is made, the issues connected with an equitable allocation of funds for education of the aging within the context of lifelong education can be tackled, and a variety of formulas can be negotiated. Such formulas will have to include demographic facts and trends, an educational philosophy that takes into account expressive orientations, available opportunities and methodologies, to learn and to teach, individual needs, interests, and wants, societal imperatives and benefits, short- and long-range goals, and the influence of individuals, families, constituents. Additional variables must be considered, such as time distribution of learning activities over a total life-span, cultural, social, and technological trends, political and economic conditions and climate (nationally as well as internationally), and the orientation of the federal government vis-à-vis a federal role within the confines of U.S. public policy.

Perhaps the following quotation offers an appropriate exhortation, not only for higher education, but for education at all levels, for people of all ages:

It is necessary for those responsible for the future of higher education to develop an understanding with those responsible for the future of the nation that there is a mutual need for each other, and that the need requires a long-term, systematic commitment if the welfare of the nation is to be enhanced. (Wilson, 1983, 116)

*　*　*

Coda
(Conclusion to Part II)

Older adults are not unique in the thirst for knowledge, understanding and acquisition of skills. They need and want educational opportunities. We have adequate evidence by now to show that given the right circumstances, older adults are able and willing to learn. There is ample evidence to demonstrate that the conditions *necessary* and *contributory* to education of older adults do exist. However, there is still a need to establish why, and in what sense, education of older adults should become a priority. In other words, the question still begs: Is there *sufficient* justification to convince policymakers in the United States to commit a share of this society's resources to the education of older adults? Can we, like Aesop's crow, find the way to quench this thirst? And can we raise the level of educational opportunities for persons of all ages?

Part III
Why Invest in Education in the Later Years?

Eldersong

Dance however you care.
Dare the steps they said
were done. Undo the wraps
of words that cover your
best song. That voice is wrong
that offers you no dancing song
and bids you sit among
the long dull row beside
the hall to watch the young
gavotte and reel. You feel
a rich and deep cadenza, long
as need be for the song
you rung along the years.

—Curt G. Curtin
©1985

7
Lifelong Education as a Right

R esearch from the United States and many other countries provides evidence that older adults need and want education. (In addition to chapter 3, see *Aging International,* 1985–86; Bubolz-Lutz, 1984; *Aging in All Nations,* 1982.) We can confidently begin to present an argument that older people ought to have educational opportunities available to them. But can we make the leap of stating that education is a basic right for persons of any age?

The delegates at the 1971 White House Conference on Aging, armed with McClusky's background paper on the educational abilities and needs of older persons, declared that "Education is a basic right for all persons of all groups" (U.S. White House Conference on Aging, 1971, 1), and they submitted twenty-two recommendations aimed at assuring that this right would become a reality. Recommendations included: increased federal, state, and local funding, expansion of educational and general social welfare programs, greater responsiveness to the needs and desires of older learners, including the need for bilingual education and development and/or strengthening of existing programs which were sensitive to ethnic and cultural differences of participants, increased outreach, especially to those who had been ethnically, racially, socially, and economically deprived, and several specific suggestions about curriculum designs and contents, consciousness-raising, leadership training, and preretirement planning. With a nod toward justifying the increased expenditures called for in such a major program expansion, the report noted that education was "one of the ways of enabling older people to have a full and meaningful life" and "a means of helping them develop their potential as a resource for the betterment of society" (p. 1).

The delegates to this second White House Conference on Aging had no illusions that older adults actually had enjoyed any entitlement claim to these educational rights. Their reports documented the vast array of educational needs which were largely unmet in the private and public sectors and remained to be addressed through public policy. Even by the time of the 1981 White House Conference, only 3.1 percent of those over the age of 65 indicated that they had participated in any form of organized education, a much lower proportion than those in younger age groups (see chapter 3). Lumsden and Sherron (1978, 95) reported in their article that "education in this country is the right of young people but is a luxury for older adults." And though widespread activity following the 1971 White House Conference on Aging had expanded educational opportunities for older adults, this remained a future goal at the next White House Conference (U.S. White House Conference on Aging, 1981, 20). The use of the term *rights* was a rhetorical device, used to add emphasis and ammunition for the political battles ahead. In fact, the language of *rights* was used at the 1971 conference in relation to everything from health care, safety, and housing to the right to be informed and to be heard (U.S. White House Conference on Education, 1971).

The zeitgeist of the late 1960s and early 1970s certainly influenced the language as well as the mood of the delegates. Indeed this was an international mood, evident even in 1982, when the delegates to the U.N.-sponsored World Assembly on Aging in Vienna adopted in their "International Plan of Action" (which was endorsed by the U.N. General Assembly in 1983) twelve recommendations specifically devoted to education out of a total of sixty-two. They recommended that "as a basic human right, education must be made available without discrimination against the elderly. Educational policies should reflect the principle of the right to education of the aging, through the appropriate allocation of resources and in suitable educational programmes" (*Aging in All Nations,* 1982, p. 81; see appendix C for complete recommendations related to education).

There is danger in an indiscriminate use of the concept of rights, as A.I. Melden (1982) has suggested in another context. The risk is that there is a tendency to depend on the emotional reactions associated with a perceived violation of rights in order to avoid the more difficult problem of developing cogent arguments to support one's cause. Indeed, although the rhetoric of the 1971 and 1981 White House Conference reports is bolstered by some evidence and logical argument, there continues to be a need for justification for a major societal commitment to provide and assure lifelong education for everyone as called for at the White House Conferences on Aging.

There is no attempt here to suggest that older adults (or anyone else, for that matter) should not have available educational opportunities and be engaged in lifelong learning. Rather, the point is made here that there is need to make explicit the basis on which such opportunities for continuing education, particularly for people in their later years, should exist, and to develop defensible arguments for it.

Moral Right to Education?

In calling education a basic right, the delegates to the U.S. White House Conferences on Aging and the delegates to the U.N. World Assembly on Aging seemed to imply that this was a moral entitlement, an inalienable human right, like life or liberty. It is the protection of moral rights that most concerns A.I. Melden in arguing against a broadly inclusive use of the term *rights*. He warns that not only does such an extension of the concept of moral rights enable one to evade the responsibility for defending important public policies, but that more importantly and more dangerously, it may actually confound the aims of those who use such terminology by making those who do not believe in basic inalienable human rights suspicious "that those of us who do talk about human rights are employing an inflated rhetoric that serves only to buttress our strong moral convictions" (Melden, 1982, 276).

Melden argues that human rights are fundamental, held in common with all human beings, and morally basic. In addition they are "unalienable" and "cannot be waived or relinquished." In analyzing this concept of rights, Melden uses the example of income support programs (or income maintenance); Melden argues against considering income support a basic human right; it is not fundamental because other moral rights can exist in the absence of a right to income support; it is not held in common with all human beings, because only those in need of income support would have the "right;" it is not morally basic, in Melden's terms, because its absence as a right does not inhibit the establishment of special moral relations among human beings. Melden suggests that income security be considered part of the "requisite setting" for enjoyment of the basic rights of life and the pursuit of a life worth living (he does not specify what type of life is worth living) but that it not be considered a moral right.

Melden's distinction between moral right and requisite setting for enjoying that right is more than a semantic distinction. It provides a framework for distinguishing those elements which are most fundamental to the existence of social relationships from those which enhance social interactions. In making such a distinction, Melden draws from and reinforces the work of John Rawls, whose theory of social justice has had profound influence on subsequent discussions of social rights and social welfare.

In *A Theory of Justice,* Rawls (1971) proposes that differences in life prospects are just if the greater expectations of the more advantaged improve the expectations of the least advantaged — and the basic structure of society is just throughout, provided that the advantages of the more fortunate further the well-being of the least fortunate. Society's structure is perfectly just, provided that the prospects of the least fortunate are as great as they can be. He further states that:

> All social values — liberty and opportunity, income and wealth, and the bases of self-respect — are to be distributed equally unless an unequal distribution of any, or all, of these values is to everyone's advantage. (Rawls, 1971, 219)

Although the importance of equality or fair inequality in the distribution of social values is stressed, it is not accurate to conclude that individuals have rights to these social values. Rawls draws from this general view two *principles of justice,* only one of which is based on rights:

> *Principle 1.* Each person is to have an equal right to the most extensive basic liberty compatible with a similar liberty for others.

> *Principle 2.* Social and economic inequalities are to be arranged so that they are both (a) reasonably expected to be to everyone's advantage, and (b) attached to positions and offices open to all. (Rawls, 1971)

The rights noted in the first principle are defined narrowly by Rawls to include political liberties, freedom of speech and thought, freedom from unwarranted arrest, and the right to property. Such are the fundamental rights of individuals which cannot be traded or taken away, and which exist for all citizens in a *just* society. Other social values (income, wealth, opportunity) are not fundamental for the individual and are allowed to be distributed unequally—as long as such distribution is in keeping with the guiding assumption, that such distribution is to everyone's advantage. And if such distribution is not to everyone's advantage, the greatest benefit must go to those least advantaged; otherwise the situation is unjust, but not necessarily a deprivation of rights.

The case against considering income support or maintenance a right is a complex one, and others (e.g., E.M. Burns, N. Itzin, S.M. Miller, R. Riessman, M. Rein, R.M. Titmuss) have argued in favor of considering income support or income security as a basic human right. Itzin (1958), for example, chooses to emphasize the necessary interdependencies of all humans as the fundamental basis of rights. She argues that the justification for this social responsibility "may be found in individual awareness of imperfection and incompleteness in a world where each one is susceptible to the need for assistance because he is imperfect and incomplete in himself." Thus we must guarantee one another mutual support, and a right to subsistence income is part of that guarantee.

A right to income support can be derived from the moral right to life, since in most post-agrarian societies income is the main instrument through which the biological foundations of life can be secured; e.g., food, shelter, clothing; the basic survival needs are accessible to most people via a mechanism of income, in the marketplace or through governmental (tax) sources, be it in kind, in money, or via transfer payments.

For our purposes here, it is not necessary to resolve the debate regarding a moral right to income maintenance. However, applying Rawls's principles and Melden's interpretation of these human rights principles to education reveals that education may be seen as an important ingredient to a meaningful human existence without necessarily being considered a *moral right.*

Rather than loosely and rhetorically defending a moral right to education, it is more fruitful to recognize the problem which such argument may produce and of which Melden warned—that an appeal to moral rights should not be used to avoid the process of justifying specific public policy options based upon defined principles.

Emphasizing the importance of developing a solid rationale for any purported moral right, Paul Vernier (1982) suggests four conditions which should be satisfied by advocates claiming to argue for a particular moral right:

1. to develop convincing arguments to justify the right
2. to indicate which persons or organizations are responsible for assuring that the right is enforced
3. to address the problems of allocating resources
4. to explain the responsibilities of those enjoying the rights.

Vernier's conditions are sound principles for advocacy of any public policy. Following these four conditions, advocates of the right to education for older adults must be prepared to explain why such education should be provided, who is responsible to provide it, how priorities should be established among other competing resource needs, and what, if any, are the responsibilities of older learners.

It is worthy of note here that public grammar school education for children and younger adults was first established as a privilege, later as a right and a requirement; such a concept of right was essential if attendance for the young was to be made compulsory, on the assumption that individuals had certain functional responsibilities of citizenship in a democracy, responsibilities which required that certain things had to be learned. Public education was thus established as "universal, free, and compulsory," with required school attendance beginning as early as 1852 (Dye, 1984, 159). "This was an inevitable development in any society demanding literacy and skills for labor force and political reasons" (Kahn, 1979, 82). These political reasons also included the self-interest of local, state and national politicians to develop a loyal electorate of assimilated Americans who would know how to pull the political lever to express their choice, thus assuring aspiring or established politicians a dependable constituency.

Legal Right to Education?

Even if Vernier's and Melden's conditions are accepted and it is assumed that education is not sufficiently justified as a basic moral right, some may want to consider it a *legal right*. A true legal right is a justiciary right; if the provisions (benefits or services, for example) are not given as specified under the law, the claimant may call upon the courts to enforce the right. Such a right is the reciprocal side of concomitantly specified obligations (e.g., benefits under Title II, Old Age Insurance and Disability provisions, of the Social Security Act) are related to a formula of regular payments which employers and employees must pay under the law.

What kind of specific educational obligations might be established for older learners? How would courts enforce this right to learning? Kahn essentially makes the point that "a true rights concept has reached social services only gradually and in a modest sense." He notes that elementary and secondary education (for youth) are among the few social service rights available in this country. By contrast, health care can only be considered a right in a limited sense, according to Kahn, given that it is provided and financed unevenly, depending on individual ability to pay. Kahn suggests that education at the college level (through community colleges and four-year colleges) is a right in a few places in the United States but more often a privilege. He would no doubt agree that education of older persons is at best only a partial right in this country. "For the present, then, we face the reality that many personal services in the voluntary and public sectors are privileges or partial rights, not full rights" (Kahn, 1979, p. 84).

Kahn then poses the question: "Do social services lend themselves to sufficient specification for such purposes?" He answers that . . . elementary and secondary education offer an encouraging precedent, but many social services are far less easily specified. . . . It will require considerable deployment of doctrine, the spelling out of clear provisions to ensure user access to service before full service rights may be said to exist" (Kahn, 1979, p. 85). An analogy to continuing education in the later years using Kahn's statement regarding personal social services can be drawn. Perhaps lifelong education should be available as a political right of citizenship. In order to explore the appropriateness of this option in the United States, it is necessary to reflect on the nature of political rights in this country.

The emphasis in the U.S. Constitution is on liberties rather than rights; on those properties and freedoms that the government cannot take away rather than properties and freedoms that the government provides to its citizens. Although stated as rights to life, liberty, and the pursuit of happiness, these are really liberties which the government is forbidden to restrict without serious and just cause. The right to vote and to receive equal protection under the law may have received official public recognition very late for several minority groups, but this official recognition was still based on the assumption that these *rights* were inalienable, that they had always existed even though they were not enforced. Although belatedly, the Voting Rights and Civil Rights acts upheld the principle that the government cannot prevent any of its citizens from participating in the political process and that the government must protect the liberties of all citizens regardless of race, religion, or national origin.

The assumption of those who drafted the constitution was that the people were the constituent power, and therefore that they, ipso facto, possessed these rights which were articulated in the Constitution. As an expression of citizens' rights, the Constitution is thus a statement of basic liberties, based on the premise of inalienability because of the basic humanity of the citizen.

Regardless of whether one supports this rather limited view of rights, it is important to recognize its widespread influence on all public policymaking and implementation in the United States. Until the early part of this century, a libertarian emphasis dominated political decision-making, and even at the height of the progressive era the deemphasis on rights granted to individuals severely restricted the range of options for developing social welfare programs. Whereas many countries, e.g., Germany, as early as the 1880s, developed public pension programs based on a right of citizenship, the designers of the Social Security program in the United States did not use the term *right* but referred to it as an *entitlement* based primarily on prior work experience (Axinn and Levin, 1980).

While Austria, Canada, Germany, Great Britain, Sweden, and Switzerland, among many other industrialized and even nonindustrialized countries, developed national health services, the United States delayed until the 1960s to provide partial medical insurance coverage. To the aged, "Medicare" (Title XVIII of the Social Security Act) has been provided and administered on a national scale, based on past work history of the individual worker, as an earned right; to the indigent citizen, "Medicaid" (Title XIX of the Social Security Act) has been based on a means-test (the burden of proven need is placed on the needy applicant, more appropriately labeled "supplicant"), and benefits are financed through a federal-state public assistance program, administered by states and local municipalities. Twenty years after their inception, these programs have not only *not* reduced the proportion of income that older adults must spend on health care but, in fact, they have sharply increased the amounts older people have to spend on health care today.

Despite many government programs—income maintenance, food stamps, housing subsidies, fuel assistance, health-care financing—citizens of the United States do not enjoy any rights to food, clothing, shelter, or health care. Many individuals go without these requisite for the maintenance and enjoyment of the right to life. Since the 1970s, largely because of increased social insurance benefits, older people have fared better as a group in this regard than younger people. However, many still live on marginal incomes and in poverty; each year many still die of malnutrition, hypothermia, and lack of health care for curable illnesses. Therefore, while a charter of educational rights is being defended in other Western countries, e.g., Great Britain

(Laslett, 1984; Groombridge and Rogers, 1976), such a defense is more problematic in the United States in light of the conditions mentioned and the ideological positions which have found support in this country.

An example of the political objections to establishing broad welfare rights in the United States can be found in James Fallows's article, "Entitlements" (1982). Capturing the mood of the country under President Reagan, Fallows highlights windfalls available to some individuals under a system which establishes benefits on the basis of rights rather than on individual need. He argues that the broad application of entitlements, coupled with automatic cost-of-living increases, has made programs like Social Security unsustainable and has forced us to look again at who needs help rather than assuming that everyone has a right to assistance. He warns that "all causes are in jeopardy as long as more and more of us are 'entitled' to support from everyone else" (Fallows, 1982, 59).

Much attention in the 1980s has focused on potential intergenerational conflicts arising from the increasing numbers of older adults and special privileges accorded to them. These concerns center on justice between generations rather than justice within a particular generation. Recent articles in the *Washington Post* (Taylor, "The Coming Conflict As We Soak the Young To Enrich the Old," 1/5/86), *The Atlantic Monthly* (Longman, "Justice Between Generations, June 1985), and *Scientific American* (Preston, "Children and the Elderly in the U.S.," December 1984) warn that the increasing proportion of older adults in the population and the continuation of generous age-based benefits for the old will eventually lead younger individuals, in Longman's words, to "say 'enough' and rise up in revolt against their elders."

Most gerontologists in the United States believe that the appearance of intergenerational conflict is a fabrication of the Reagan administration and their powerful supporters as well as such conservative "think tanks" as the Hoover, Manhattan, and Enterprise Institutes and the Heritage Foundation, which have framed issues in such a way that attention is focused on choices between generations, when choices are really between rich and poor or between domestic and military spending. This point was made vividly at the Thirteenth International Congress of Gerontology, held in New York City in July, 1985. Independent presentations by five prominent U.S. gerontologists, Robert Binstock, Marjorie Cantor, Robert Morris, Bernice Neugarten, and James Schulz, all arrived at the same conclusion; intergenerational conflict is a myth, not a reality.

The increasing tendency in our society to view older persons as "burdens" can be related to our heavy emphasis on individualism and the assumption that individuals should strive for independence. We seem to forget at times the social nature of human existence, Aristotle's dictum of a *Zoon politikon,* that humans need to support one another in order to assure their very survival as a species. A more appropriate emphasis is on interdependence, on respecting and valuing the individual contributions of all persons to the human group and to society's needs and imperatives for survival. Such a view of human potential recognizes individual autonomy without assuming that individuals who are dependent in some aspects of their lives are any more burdensome or any less human, than anyone else. In the course of a lifetime, we are all mutually dependent.

In a major exploration into the historical roots of our social welfare policies, (*Rethinking Social Welfare: Why Care for the Stranger?* 1986a) Morris has struggled with the various bases for "caring for the stranger" from biblical times up to the present day. He finds evidence to support a guarantee of "a healthy survival . . . freedom from arbitrary interference, avoidable ill health and deep ignorance" (p. 196), based on the influence of these factors on the autonomy of individuals. Indeed, by this rationale, a right to education, at least that type of education which is designed to dispel "deep ignorance," might seem an equal partner in assuring the well-being of society. However, in developing the elements for a political consensus around a "minimum but significant core for national social responsibility" (p. 216) in the United States, even Morris limits his core recommendations to income, work, and a national health system. The effort to achieve consensus on national priorities is not enhanced, it seems, by demands for educational entitlements for older adults.

The appearance of intergenerational conflict has been fueled by attacks on the Social Security program, attacks which have undermined public confidence that the program will serve future as well as present generations of older people. At a time when presidential rhetoric has expressed concern for only the "truly needy," a narrowly defined group which is not assumed to include all those who eat at soup kitchens, the apparent exemption of older adults from a share of federal spending cuts has doubtless caused some ill-feeling among several segments (not only younger ones) of our population. There has not yet been a major public outcry about age-entitlements, but it would be optimistic to assume that the potential for such confrontations has passed.

The problem in overusing the concept of rights is evident in Fallows' argument. He makes no distinction between entitlements to military, civil service, or Social Security pensions. In fact, in his definition of entitlements— "benefits for which people qualify automatically, by virtue of their age or income or occupation"—he includes unemployment compensation, farm supports and housing subsidies, quite a broadening of the usual definition of entitlement. There is thus no distinction between the special benefits of individual programs and the more debatable "right" to an adequate standard of living as envisioned in a program like Social Security. Also, the specific features of existing programs, e.g., the cost-of-living adjustments, are included in Fallows' broad conception of entitlement—that to which one is presumed to have a right. Thus when some aspect of a program needs to be modified, as was presumed necessary in the 1983 fiscal crisis of the Social Security Trust Fund, opponents like Fallows argue for the elimination of the right to benefits rather than arguing for changes which modify the program to provide the greatest advantage to the least advantaged in consonance with Rawls's conception.

Itzin (1958) notes that establishing rights on the basis of political or economic reasons is problematic because it places greater emphasis on the political or economic system than upon the individual. The individual's right is then simply a matter of utility for the system. Discussions of political or economic considerations may be relevant to other issues of public policy, but rights need to be more fundamental; they must not be susceptible to changing ideological, political, economic, or social conditions.

Income in old age has been more nearly a *right* of citizenship in this country than any other social welfare benefit. Yet even this has been under considerable attack in the 1980s.

In what sense, then, is it useful to argue for a right to education in such a social context? If the most basic aspects of physical survival cannot call upon sufficient political endorsement to endure shifts of political winds, if all citizens are not assured those rights or requisite settings for survival, then a right to education seems even less defensible on such grounds.

Education may be essential for the pursuit of lives worth living for older as well as younger adults. Should not the emotional, moral, legal, or political appeal of educational rights rather be forsaken in favor of arguments about why, how, by whom, and at what cost the society should invest in education for its older citizens? Without the issue of basic rights to cloud the discussion, there appears to be more merit to developing and marshaling political, economic, sociological, and philosophical arguments for establishing a national policy of lifelong learning.

Social Necessity of Lifelong Learning

The members of the Technical Committee on Education at the 1981 White House Conference on Aging did not abandon the language of educational rights, but added an important dimension to make a case for education of older adults. They declared that education was not merely a right of all citizens but also a "necessity for a society struggling to achieve a fuller measure of social justice for all Americans" (U.S. White House Conference on Aging, 1981, 43). Much of the Technical Committee's report is an argument for the need and value of education for older adults, rather than for a basic right.

The 1981 Committee report is less technical than McClusky's prior report for the 1971 Conference. There are no updates on the learning abilities of older adults; theories of educational needs and types of education are not expanded upon; what little information there is about the demographic profile of older learners is relegated to the Appendix. Instead, the authors of the report, under the leadership of Bernice Neugarten—who also served as the Committee's Chair—make a bold attempt to argue the case for expanding and improving education for older learners, education for personnel serving older adults, and education about aging.

The case for education of older adults is made on the basis of three arguments: benefits for older learners, benefits for the educational system, and benefits for society.

1. Benefits for Older Learners

Any society is organized to meet the collective needs of its population. Unfortunately, the collective solutions developed for a given social system are never completely complementary to the individual needs of all members of the society. Thus the individual and society are often in conflict over priorities and needs. It is essential, therefore, that the policies of a society be developed with an eye toward balancing the individual's needs and the society's imperatives (Lowy, 1985b, 49).

Education can be a tool for meeting the individual needs of older adults while also complementing the needs of the society. As noted in chapter 4, the educational needs of older adults are as extensive and various as those of younger individuals. The 1981 White House Conference Committee report on education suggests a variety of individual benefits to be gained from continuing education.

The report notes that older adults can increase their coping or survival skills through educational programs. For example, they can improve their economic status by learning how better to manage money, by discovering how to make better consumer decisions, and by finding out about financial assistance programs such as Social Security, Supplemental Security Income (SSI), housing subsidies, and food stamps which may increase their purchasing capacity and improve their economic standard. They may learn to cope with chronic health problems, especially through mutual aid/self-help groups which have become popular educational experiences for many older persons (Cutler; Silverman, 1980).

As stated before, older adults like younger adults can gain by keeping abreast of technological changes, especially if they want to remain working or attempt to embark on a second career. Education can increase their knowledge and skills, thus broadening the range of work or employment opportunities that may be available to them. New challenges may be found in paid or unpaid employment which may satisfy the need to maintain an active, constructive role in society, provided, of course, that jobs do exist. Such participation in the mainstream can go a long way to assure that older adults are not socially isolated and may provide life enrichment to them and their families.

2. Benefits for the Educational System

The 1981 White House Conference on Aging report alludes to benefits for the educational system through the participation of older adults. Citing John Dewey's abhorrence of the terminal view of education as preparation for adulthood, the authors suggest the possibility that the focus on lifelong learning can help to transform the educational institutions to better deal with the demands of rapid technological change. They emphasize that the need to provide education outside of traditional settings is a challenge which may help to make education more responsive and effective.

The three types of barriers to educational activity for older adults which had been described by Cross (1979) are reviewed in the White House Conference report: 1) situational barriers (e.g., costs, transportation, physical handicaps); 2) dispositional barriers (e.g., attitudes of potential students or educators which limit participation); and 3) institutional barriers (discriminatory policies, inaccessibility, lack of counseling, inconvenient scheduling and registration). Overcoming such barriers, particularly in traditional educational institutions is viewed as a constructive challenge which will eventually prove beneficial for the young and the old. (This was discussed in somewhat more detail in chapter 4.)

The report emphasizes the benefits to educational institutions in using older adults as resources as well as beneficiaries or clients. The authors cite estimates of the number of older adults involved as educators, concluding that "it is possible that more older Americans are engaged in education, broadly considered, as educators than as learners" (p. 17). They emphasize the vast resources to be tapped by forward-looking educational institutions which utilize the resources of older adults as teachers as well as learners.

3. Benefits for Society

Despite the potential tensions between the goals of society and the goals of individuals, Neugarten and the other members who developed the report on education for the 1981 White House Conference on Aging find mainly benefits to the society in expanding educational opportunities for older adults. Social benefits are seen to be in three main areas: adapting to an aging society, enhancing political participation, and increasing productivity.

First, the society gains a better understanding of the aging process and how to adjust to an aging population. The authors suggest that the involvement of older adults in social problem-solving can open up new avenues for addressing poverty and discrimination, improving the quality of life not only for older adults but for all members of the society.

The authors emphasize the potential for society to benefit through the participation of older adults in the political process. Given the high percentage of older adults who vote, compared to persons of younger ages, it is particularly important that elders be knowledgeable about the political issues at stake. In this way, they can contribute to constructive changes in society, helping to improve their own lives and those of their fellow citizens.

Anticipating complaints about costs of such expanded educational services for older adults, the authors stress that the potential resources available from older adults more than justify any expenditures on educational activities. Older adults can return much to the society through increased productivity and self-sufficiency. The authors cite a report (Tibbits, 1980) estimating that as many as 3 million adults over the age of 65 are interested in training for new job skills. Such untapped resources can only limit the society's potential for growth.

In addition to justifying the commitment to education on the basis of benefits to the individual, the educational system, and the society, the 1981 report also begins to address other conditions necessary for the defense of public policy. (The complete recommendations of the Technical Committee, adopted by the full assembly of delegates to the 1981 White House Conference on Aging, are provided in appendix B. A discussion of their feasibility and appropriateness is included in chapter 6.)

The members who prepared the recommendations for the Technical Committee on Education contend that "the benefits derived from a more literate and just society—and more enlightened and self-fulfilled older persons—will far outweigh the cost of the educational initiatives proposed in this report" (U.S. White House Conference on Aging, 1981, preface). That, of course, depends on the level and ratio of future expenditures and the corresponding contributions of older adults. However, the evidence cited so far suggests that benefits of an expanded commitment to lifelong education are worth the investment.

Given the history, tradition, and philosophy of this country regarding the shaping of public policy, particularly in the economic and social sectors, it is most unlikely that lifelong education will be considered a political or legal right for people or be viewed as an entitlement, even under more liberal political administrations than the present one. That is why lifelong education has to base its argumentation on the conception of the interrelationship between the individual and the society and to consider their mutual obligations.

The decision to expend resources on one area of education, such as educational gerontology, must be justified on political, sociological, economic, and philosophical grounds. The report of the 1981 White House Conference on Aging began the process of justification. Later chapters of this book attempt to expand and develop these arguments.

8
Merging the Instrumental and Expressive: Toward a Humanistic Philosophy of Education

If education is to be seen as an individual and social obligation, the definition of education becomes particularly critical, because it specifies the level of this obligation. We have earlier adopted Peterson's definition of education: "planned learning that occurs from maturation and that is seriously undertaken . . . education is distinct [from learning] in that the change [in knowledge, attitudes, or behavior] is identified beforehand by the teacher, or the student, or both."

Such a definition of education is broad in that it extends beyond traditional schooling and includes formal and informal learning situations in which there is some educational goal established at the outset. The definition, however, does not include learning that is incidental or a concomitant part of maturation because, important as all such learning is, there seems hardly any way to examine individual responsibility or social obligation to do that which is either unconscious or uncontrollable from the inside of the person or from the external environment. Obviously, the distinction is not completely clear-cut; there are situations in which persons may choose to become involved in activities in which they are aware that learning does take place (e.g., volunteering to deliver meals to home-bound individuals) but in which the learning is not the primary goal of the activity. Depending on the extent to which learning *is* a primary, intended goal of the activity, this may or may not fit our definition of education. Although the definition allows some room for wider interpretation, it is still useful since it encompasses what we plan to examine in relation to educational responsibility and obligation.

There is some advantage in dividing the concept of education into primary components in order to analyze the individual and social value of assuming such educational responsibilities. A division which has been found relevant and useful by many educators and gerontologists is the dichotomy between *expressive* and *instrumental* education. Susceptible to the usual criticisms of dichotomous thinking (because it too narrowly restricts the range of choice), such a classification may be better conceived as two ends of a continuum in which there are various levels of overlap in between. Nonetheless, the distinction of education that is primarily expressive (learning activities for their own sake) from those which are primarily instrumental (learning activities directed toward and therefore secondary to some future goal) provides useful insights.

Motivations for Learning: Instrumental versus Expressive

Londoner (1978), one of the original architects of the distinction between expressive and instrumental education, attributes the earliest uses of the terms to the sociologist Talcott Parsons. The terms were first used in developing his theory of how social systems operated, though there is, in Parsons' discussion, no specific reference to the educational system. In *The Social System,* Parsons (1964) develops a theory of society that assumes that different types of people can function and work together to maintain an ongoing society with some semblance of order and stability, because these individuals have been socialized to accept the basic value system they share. The social order is organized on the basis of this value system, so that individuals who choose to behave in accordance with it can receive desirable social rewards such as status, prestige, money, love. In this way, the society works toward consensus and stability and is assured long-term survival.

Parsons distinguishes two major orientations guiding individuals as they pursue goals within the social system: *expressive orientations,* those characteristics of activities which provide immediate gratification or satisfaction in and of themselves; *instrumental orientations,* those which are subsidiary and require postponement of immediate gratification for some future goal.

Parsons' "adaptation, goal-achievement, integration, pattern-maintenance" model, most frequently cited and critiqued as a "conservative approach to analyzing society" (Siporin, 1975, 33), is not complete without two additional models: 1) his "theory of deviance," in which deviance is seen as a product of failure on the part of *society* (not individuals) to provide conditionally rewarding roles; and 2) his "theory of social change," which explains social change through changes in the allocation of rewards that produce strain, new innovative ways of coping, new structures, and eventually new values (Parsons and Shils, 1962, 77–88). In contrast to the *general system* model (Bertalanffy, 1967), Parsons' *social system* model, which focuses on human adaptations within a society or organization, is particularly useful for conceptualizing difficult human conditions as social problems such as poverty, discrimination, ageism, lack of acceptance of lifelong learning, and so on. Parsons' model emphasizes the role of societal institutions to change in allocation of its rewards, e.g., rewarding those institutions which offer educational opportunities to older people to learn and study, and thereby give evidence that people in their later years can indeed learn. (De Hoyos and Jensen, 1985).

Londoner (1978) credits Havighurst (1964, 1969) with first using the sociological terms instrumental and expressive in the field of education. Distinguishing between two major types of educational activity, Havighurst applied the same labels and motivations used by Parsons to propose two broad categories of educational goals: instrumental and expressive. Shortly thereafter, Londoner (1971) himself adopted the categories, stressing the importance of instrumental education, which appeared at the time to have been neglected for older adults.

Instrumental education, as described by Havighurst and Londoner, is pragmatic, directed outside of oneself and oriented toward future utility; it thus seeks to improve a person's life situation. Havighurst suggests several activities which are assisted by instrumental education:

1. Preparing for an occupation
2. Becoming a competent responsible worker
3. Rearing children
4. Setting adolescent children free
5. Making a comfortable home
6. Becoming an informed and responsible citizen
7. Adjusting to bodily changes

(Havighurst, 1976, 44)

Although Havighurst does not link his framework to the categories of learning needs, several of the categories described by McClusky (1974), including coping needs, contributory needs, and influence needs, can be related to instrumental education at first sight. Education which provides skills for survival or future security helps fulfill the coping needs: that which is vocationally oriented, which focuses on development of skills and training for jobs, volunteer work or nurturing human service roles prepares individuals to fulfill contributory needs; and education for citizenship or political activity equips individuals to satisfy needs to influence those around them. Such educational activities are directed at future goals, enhancing the learner's potential to contribute to the production of society's resources and thus fulfills this instrumental function.

Expressive education, by contrast, is education for its own sake, where the goal of learning is learning itself (Havighurst, 1976; Londoner, 1978). Havighurst suggests that there are many activities which are not assisted by instrumental education but which can be enhanced by learning whose base is expressive. Strengthened interpersonal relationships among friends and family and enhanced commitments to organized groups may follow from the personal growth which is stimulated by education that is expressive. While the focus of such education is on learning for its own sake, such learning may enhance the learner's ability to adjust to losses and crises in life. Expressive, contemplative, and transcendental needs are best met through expressive educational activities.

Londoner stresses the importance of distinguising between expressive and instrumental educational activities in identifying and assessing the needs of older adult learners. His own preference is that priority be given to instrumental education because most older adults, in his words,

> are committed to surviving and will be more likely to respond to activities designed to meet these survival needs/goals than to recreational and/or liberal educational pursuits. Their basic goals are instrumental . . . and consequently, their needs are instrumental because they are committed to instrumental, survival goals. (Londoner, 1978)

Much work in the 1970s was devoted to attempts to determine empirically whether the needs of older adults are primarily instrumental or expressive. A review of such studies appears in Londoner's chapter (1978). In the earliest such study, Hiemstra (1972) surveyed a group of senior center participants to determine their preference among a variety of educational activities which had been classified as instrumental or expressive. A distinct preference for instrumental activities was discovered. Follow-up studies by Hiemstra (1975, 1976) produced similar results favoring instrumental education as the choice of older adults. Reports in studies by many Senior Centers today tend to emphasize even more the preference for instrumental education (Lowy, 1985a).

Not all empirical studies support instrumental education as the preference of older adults. Londoner (1978) reviews a variety of studies (many unpublished) which indicate the variety of opinion about the relative merits of instrumental and expressive education: Whatley (1974) and Goodrow (1975) found no significant differences between preferences for instrumental or expressive education; Bauer (1975) found expressive activities to be preferred. Several studies concluded that the differences in preferences for instrumental as opposed to expressive activities were related less to age and more to educational background. Those with less education preferred instrumental education (Burkey, 1975); white-collar workers preferred expressive education (Hiemstra, 1973, 1976); married people participated in more instrumental projects than did the unmarried (Hiemstra, 1975, 1976); and women preferred expressive educational activities (Marcus, 1976). Figure 8–1 provides yet another view. Reasons for taking adult education courses are either job-related (suggesting instrumental inclinations) or non–job-related (more likely to include expressive inclinations). A clear preference was noted among males

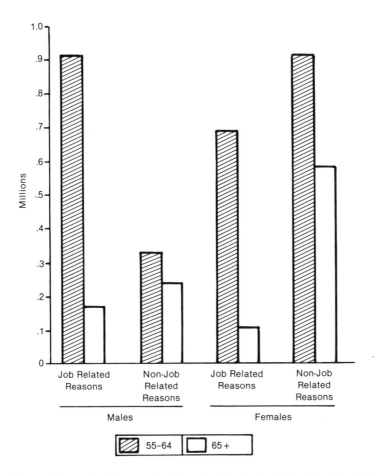

Source: National Center for Education Statistics, Participation in Adult Education: 1981.
Note: Job related reasons includes: to get a new job in current or former occupation or in new occupational field: to improve or advance in current job. Non-job related reasons includes: for American citizenship, for general education, to train for volunteer work and for personal or social reasons.

Figure 8–1. Older Persons' Primary Reasons for Taking Adult Education Courses, 1981

aged 55–64 for job-related activities, while females 55–64 and 65 and over emphasized non–job-related reasons for taking courses. Job-related reasons were least important for the older participants (male and female) in the study.

Aside from the obvious problems of restricting preferences to a dichotomous scale, Londoner suggests that a major reason for the discrepancy in survey results is the fallacy in classifying educational activities as inherently instrumental or expressive. On the contrary, Londoner argues, such a classification of educational activities depends on the goals of the individual student. "The same educational opportunity can be simultaneously instrumental and expressive; how it is perceived and used by the actors is the crucial point" (Londoner, 1978, 87–88). He argues that both major types of educational activity are important to older adults and that the categories are useful not for determining which type of education should be offered, but for assessing how best to meet the learning needs of older adults.

Educational Philosophies Underlying Instrumental/Expressive

The debate over the relative merits of instrumental versus expressive education recalls the much older debate over liberal versus progressive or vocational education, at its height in the late nineteenth and early twentieth centuries in this country. It is striking to note the similarities in definitions. Vocational education, like instrumental, is focused on the future and the world outside the student. R.W. K Paterson says of vocational education that it "treats its students, no doubt justifiably and with their willing consent, as means to the ultimate production of valuable goods and services" (Paterson, 1979, 42). It is training for jobs, helping the student to develop skills in order to work and earn a living.

The best of liberal education fits the expressive category, where the individual is the center of learning, engaged in an interaction with the history of human thought, doings, and feelings. In keeping with the assumptions of expressive education, Paterson says of liberal education that it "regards its students exclusively in the light of their status as conscious selves whose personal development or increased fullness of being is rightly held to be an end in itself" (1979, 42).

The purpose of both liberal and expressive education is to expand self-awareness, to examine serious questions of value, and to develop an ability to reason and to make ethical judgments. In studying fundamental questions of being, the student of liberal education develops an ability to reason which, Paterson argues, can diminish if not regularly attended to. Continuing liberal education for adults is thus essential for the advancement of human understanding, for movement toward social justice (although it is arguable whether this is necessarily so).

Not all of what goes by the name of liberal education is truly expressive or liberal in its nature. And certainly liberal education is not synonymous with higher (i.e., college or university) education. Much of the technical information imparted in college courses in management, gerontology, medicine, and policy programs is really instrumental; many non-credit, non-academic programs—Elderhostel, the NCOA Senior Center Humanities Program, the Great Books program, for instance—provide a more liberal, or expressive, educational experience than that which is provided in much of higher education. Educational programs in senior and multiservice centers frequently offer a range of activities which include instrumental and expressive elements. As Londoner says, it is the goals of the student rather than the programmatic elements which determine whether an educational experience is predominantly instrumental or expressive.

Whereas Londoner champions instrumental education as most essential for older adults because of their goals of survival, Moody suggests that it is liberal, or expressive, education which is most worthy of attention in the later years. The accumulation of life experience, combined with a changed and changing perspective of time as "what's left," offers a special opportunity for older adults to examine the ultimate questions of meaning, to accept as "the major developmental task of old age" the life review process (Moody, 1978, 36). Through the liberal arts, through the review of life experience, Moody argues, older learners can transcend their past roles, can escape the past limitations on their view of themselves. Such transcendence of the past is essential to the human quest for growth and expanded consciousness, and thus he suggests that this is the only type of education deserving of attention in old age.

There is a problem with an educational philosophy for older adults which forces a choice between the instrumental and expressive aspects of the learning experience, and therefore neither the liberal nor the progressive educational philosophy will quite satisfy our needs. Too great an emphasis on the expressive focus of liberal educational philosophy runs the risk of elitism by attracting only those who, through previous education or life experience, have developed an appreciation of the search for meaning. Too often this search becomes the prerogative of the well-to-do who are not overwhelmed with survival tasks resulting from low incomes, poor education, sex, race, and ethnic discrimination, if not oppression and hazardous working conditions. Elderhostel, a vastly successful program by any account, gives evidence of the danger of an exclusive emphasis on liberal education: for despite the lack of restrictive entrance requirements, the number and proportion of college graduates in the program has remained high, about 60 percent. Over 80 percent of the participants have some experience with higher education. By comparison, 15–17 percent of the older population has such a background (Berkeley, 1985). Not only does the emphasis on expressive education run the risk of ignoring the educational needs and interests of large numbers of older adults, it also raises doubts about a collective search for meaning which may ignore the experiences of large segments of the population.

An instrumentally based, progressive philosophy of education might appear at first glance to be less biased. However, a focus on instrumental educational activities or goals can be elitist in another way. Such goals reinforce the view that productivity is the measure of humanity, that educational activities are to be measured in terms of their development of human productive potential alone. Thus job re-training or second-career programs are measured by the numbers of students placed in paid employment, craft programs by success of graduates in producing (preferable saleable) objects, citizenship classes by participating in political processes (within the system); even basic reading and health education programs are, at least hypothetically, measured by the increased self-sufficiency of students, which would decrease the number of social and health services needed that are paid for by the taxes, i.e., which come out of the public purse.

This purely instrumental view of education can lead to a further reduction of public services and demean the value of learning for the sake of learning. The emphasis on progressive education as the only national responsibility can (and to a certain extent does today) encourage the development of a two-tiered system of education in which the poor, those in minority groups and the handicapped, are segregated into educational programs which expand and exploit their productive capacities while the well-to-do are able to reserve for themselves the insight of expressive education.

In a paper entitled "The Elderly as Surplus People: Is There a Role for Higher Education?" Morris and Bass (1986) examine the role of the able elderly in an aging society and discuss the capacity of older persons as economic and social resources. They propose a "secondary labor market" which employs older people in more flexible work situations, primarily in the human service delivery system. They further argue that higher education would have a significant role to play by training the elderly for such work roles, in fact emphasizing a primary, if not exclusive, instrumental focus and orientation for educational programs and initiatives with regard to older adults. They are not oblivious to expressive needs or orientations, but rather build their argument around the assumption that such a proposal offers the possibility of a meaningful life for the fifteen or twenty years after the age of sixty. In this view, such a work orientation is beneficial to the older person (otherwise wasted and roleless) and to the market-economy.

Although they suggest that the establishment of such a secondary labor market should aim to increase the range of available services rather than replacing existing services, Morris and Bass do little to address what the labor-market implications might be for those sectors in which a secondary market economy may be developed. What impact this would have on wages, salaries, labor unions, and the emerging confrontations of the young with the older generation, are important concerns which should be alleviated before embarking on such a policy. It is also important that such new work roles for older adults not be seen as the only avenues for meaningful existence in the later years.

As an educational philosophy for older persons, the progressive philosophical position has the potential to entrap us into accepting the human worth of older adults as measured in economically productive terms. Referring to elders as "resources" increasingly suggests this tendency, especially when used in arguments against mandatory retirement or advocacy for the hiring of older workers. Realistically, however, many older adults are incapable of contributing to productivity in the market sense; moreover, many older adults may find their abilities to *produce* quite diminished when compared to their previous capacities and energy-levels. Without some other measure of their own worth, they must judge themselves worth *less* to society as society signals to them that they are nonproductive and of limited worth. It is indeed a serious problem if we as a society continue to value human worth primarily through a productive role in a market-oriented society. The problem becomes even more serious when we review the demographic data (see chapter 3). The concept of a "role-less role" (Burgess, 1960) for the aged is likely to affect larger and larger numbers of people and their families. It was Peck (1956) who originally specified that one of the major developmental tasks in the later years was to "move from work-pre-occupation to ego-differentiation, to redefine one's worth on other ways than work," to arrive at a sense of "who-ness" rather than "what-ness" to redefine oneself in terms of being rather than doing (Lowy, 1985b).

Robert Hudson, in a presentation for the Ollie Randall Symposium at the November 1985 meeting of the Gerontological Society of America in New Orleans, responds to this productive view of the worth of older adults by emphasizing the danger of a political trend to identify the "able-elderly" as a political interest group separate from older adults who are more frail and less able to assume productive roles. Hudson warns that this division has the potential to undercut hard-won gains in social benefits which have improved the living standards of older adults as a group. Instead, Hudson argues, increasing attention to the able members of the older population may lead to policies which not only allow and encourage older adults to work and assume other productive roles, but also, in the long run, may lead to policies which "force participation among the not-so-able-elderly through further disability policy restrictions, pension modifications, etc." (Hudson, 1985, 7). Hudson warns that

> the ascendence of able-elders as a self-identified and socially identified population will also contribute to an erosion of social citizenship and the citizen's wage based upon it. There is a real danger that, in celebrating the rise of the able elderly, we allow institutional commitments to the old as citizens to be transformed into residual programs for the very old as social outliers. (Hudson, 1985, 13)

How can we avoid this danger if society does not validate non-work roles, does not offer older persons alternative roles to affirm their identity? Simone de Beauvoir emphasized the need for alternative roles for older adults:

> Leisure does not open up new possibilities for the retired man; just when he is at last set free from compulsion and restraint, the means of making use of his liberty are taken from him. He is condemned to stagnate in boredom and loneliness, a mere throw-out. (de Beauvoir, 1972, 542)

We must find ways to encourage a variety of new and existing roles for older adults. For those who are unable or choose not to assume their past work roles, we as a society must help them to find new opportunities, whether economically productive or not, to find meaning and fulfillment in the later years.

The progressive philosophical position cannot suffice because it misses the important potential of older adults that has been described already. For there is indeed (or should be) a special opportunity that older adults can have to reflect on their life-experiences from a unique vantage point. While the temporal vantage may be shared by all individuals in a certain generation, other social and economic vantages may differ widely. The individual and collective reflections of older adults may thus contribute important insights into future social conditions. A philosophy of education for older adults cannot have the potential to devalue human worth; thus, the progressive philosophy of education, in avoiding the search for meaning beyond human productivity, must—like the liberal philosophy—be found insufficient as a philosophy of education for older adults.

Toward a Humanistic Philosophy of Education

Victor Frankl (1963) speaks of the "search for meaning" as an all-encompassing need of human beings at any stage in life. Robert Butler (1982, 238) also points out that "at no other time in life is there as potent a force toward self-awareness operating as in old age."

The epistemological theory of aging, which suggests that people are capable of increasing degrees or levels of knowledge as they grow older was voiced first by Plato as the basis of his view that we should undertake the study of philosophy in old age "to commence the long struggle to overcome the illusions of life," and later by Schopenhauer who said "At that time of life [old age] what a man has to himself is of greater advantage to him than it was ever before." This view has found empirical support (e.g., by K.W. Schaie, Lowenthal, Denny, among others).

This is all the more reason why a philosophy of education in the later years needs to encompass both the instrumental and expressive goals of older adults. The liberal and progressive schools of educational philosophy cannot meet this goal separately:

> To merely extend the scale of present efforts would have little impact on the educational needs of older people whose level of educational attainment is low, who are members of minority groups, who are physically handicapped, and who are poor. (U.S. White House Conference on Aging, 1981, 36)

If the liberal and progressive educational philosophies cannot encompass and provide a raison d'être for meeting the learning needs of older adults, then what of the other philosophical schools identified by Elias and Merriam (1980)?

Behaviorism cannot serve as a major educational philosophy for older adults because it ignores, even denies, any search for meaning which holds such importance for persons in their later years. Moreover, the behavioral philosophical position relies primarily on an external view of what is to be learned—the educator's view—and does not dwell on the internality of the learner. It is mechanistic, and operant conditioning is one of its basic tenets in its approach to learning. Rewards and punishments as external "agents" do not allow for sufficient self-exploration and search for creativity. Instrumentality, "roleless role," is the outcome of learning endeavors. This does not mean that progressive or behavioral positions could not or should not be part of an educational philosophy for lifelong learning. They simply are not sufficiently encompassing to include a *l'art pour l'art* approach as one of the major goals of such learning.

Some would say that the *radical* philosophy, as we have previously described it, is most relevant for older adults, since it does integrate the instrumental with the expressive aspects of education. The radical approach incorporates the teaching of basic survival skills—reading, computation, health care, nutrition—with an analysis of the historical and social context. It simultaneously combines a search for survival with growth to higher levels of consciousness.

There is the danger in the radical philosophy of education, however, that its conclusions are often preordained and do not generally accept a serious reevaluation and reexamination of material by students. The experiences of older adults may thus be examined to identify and address sources of oppression, but not necessarily to refute other theories of human and social behavior. A tendency toward absolutism in radical philosophy quite frequently refuses to admit of the possibility of faulty judgment, errors in basic assumptions about the nature of people in their social environment, and about different value-systems in a variety of cultural contexts.

It may be helpful, as a heuristic device, to think in terms of a matrix, which attempts to emphasize a primary orientation of educational activity (expressive or instrumental) and to interrelate McClusky's need categories (see figure 8–2). Such a paradigm allows for a greater or lesser focus of direction on an educational continuum. For example, a person with coping needs may be instrumentally oriented (e.g., wanting to learn how to repair his/her house). This person's expressive orientation may lead him/her also to learn how to acquire speed-reading skills to quench his/her thirst for absorbing literature. And since all needs may at one time or another demand to be met, this matrix provides us with a holistic overview rather than a segmented one to assess, examine, and plan educational activities accordingly.

While this heuristic device offers an inclusive rather than a merely dichotomous view of educational needs and orientations, it does not substitute for a philosophy of education that better responds to these three questions: Why should older adults invest in educational activities? For what purpose should a society invest in education for those who are at the end of the life cycle? How will people in their later years find a validation of their social roles? Presently our implicit assumptions about productivity and elders as a resource respond in the following manner: older adults validate themselves through evidencing their productive capacities in a market-oriented society. Yet we do know that such a society does not facilitate "ego-differentiation;" it does not provide the opportunity to review self and to find meaning in one's own existence in the social world, if not in the universe. Can a philosophy of education include all of these expressive and instrumental orientations?

Let us take a look at the *humanistic* philosophy of education. As discussed earlier, humanistic philosophy operates on the assumption that human beings are free and creative, with unique, innate possibilities for growth and self-actualization. People are viewed from the point of view of their potentialities rather than from a deficit model or a utilitarian position. There is an implicit faith that people in their later years are capable of solving their own problems in a reasonably satisfactory manner and, if needed, can, yes even should, make use of external help and assistance to manage their own problems. Persons in their later years continue to grow and continue to experience the "here and now," linking the past with the present and future. (This belief in continuing growth has been a hallmark of the life-cycle developmental school of psychology as well and increasingly empirical evidence is being marshaled to support this belief [e.g., Neugarten, 1977, 1979; Lowenthal, Kastenbaum, 1971, 1979; Havighurst, 1972].)

Humanists hold that human nature is fundamentally good, but they also recognize the necessity of dealing with problems of evil although they by no means agree on what the solutions are to such problems. Humanists believe that the highest fulfillment of human nature is evidenced in growth, self-actualization, and collective social responsibility.

Instrumental Orientations

Educational Needs	Coping	Contributive	Influencing	Expressive	Transcendental
Coping					
Contributive					
Influencing					
Expressive					
Transcendental					

Expressive Orientations

Figure 8–2. Instrumental and Expressive Orientations Matrix

Humanistic principles have been adopted by groups considered politically conservative (e.g., the "New Humanist" movement which emphasizes the study of the classics), as well as by those considered politically radical—groups which argue for unfettering people from oppressive chains by emphasizing the "human qualities" that need to be liberated. Humanistic educational philosophy can encompass aspects of progressive, liberal, behaviorist, and radical positions. The development of acute personal and collective consciousness can lead to major social and economic changes, and, in this sense, education can be what Gross (1977, 164) calls "a lever for life change." It can be a tool that empowers people to grow and change and to make significant changes in the society around them. Yet it need not assume that existing social structures (e.g., democratic capitalism) must be fully destroyed in order to create societal conditions which are more responsive to individual growth and social justice.

Humanism has gone out of fashion in the 1980s owing, in large part, to the attacks of right-wing and fundamentalist religious groups against secular humanism. However, secular humanism is not a "subversive religion" as some have called it. In fact, by no means are all humanists secular. There are many who consider themselves religious or theistic humanists; they believe in a supernatural supreme being, yet they affirm that human behavior is ultimately the responsibility of human beings to control and to be held accountable for. In describing connections between humanism and fundamental values of American society, Nicholas Gier summarizes the common beliefs of religious and non-religious humanists:

> Humanists believe that human beings have intrinsic value and dignity. They believe that human beings are autonomous centers of value with free will and moral rights, including those of free expression and inquiry. They also use reason, not divine revelation, as the guide for moral action and education. (Gier, 1982, 28)

Gier argues that the "principles of humanism turn out to be the principles of our state [U.S. government], not of any particular church," and that these principles are compatible with religious and non-religious views.

Although the roots of humanism are closely linked with the philosophy and methods of liberal education, it is important to make a distinction between *humanistic studies* and a *humanistic philosophy of education*. The former refers to the study of humanities, i.e., the arts, literature, philosophy, theology, and several of the social sciences, such as anthropology and history. This is essentially the curriculum of the liberal arts, encompassed in the liberal philosophy of education. Out of such study of the best of human thought and the search for meaning in human existence, humanism as a philosophy has itself arisen.

However, as a philosophy of education, humanism is here conceived more broadly than the liberal philosophy, and thus can encourage the fulfillment of both the expressive and instrumental orientations of the continuum and goals of learning for older adults. Such a broad use of the concept is not meant to expand the definition of humanistic education to the point that it loses all meaning. Rather, this use seeks to identify the essence of the humanistic — belief in the value and dignity of all human beings — and to suggest that all education directed toward and in the service of older adults should, indeed must, uphold such a philosophy.

As a practical matter, emphasis on the worth and dignity of every individual directs the humanistic educator to meet the learner at his or her own level of need (whether in Maslow's terms the need is for survival, security, community, affection or self-actualization) and to engage the learner in a study of philosophical ideas, practical techniques, aesthetics or crafts — whatever the subject matter — in a spirit of free inquiry. It need not matter whether the learning task is undertaken for its own sake or for the sake of a future goal.

To summarize concisely what has been said so far:

1. Learning in the later years is neither primarily instrumental nor primarily expressive; it encompasses both orientations and goals and allows for meeting survival, utilitarian, contemplative, expressive, influencing, contributory and transcendental needs.

2. Learning in the later years must be directed toward meeting a series of bio-psycho-social-emotional developmental tasks as people grow older, such as: maintaining coping capacities, restoration, rehabilitation, and functional health; trading off losses with gains, helping in the search for the meaning of life past, present, and future — integrating identity, performing roles as a citizen, and so on. Such tasks demand as full an engagement of all dimensions of the human person he/she is potentially capable of — physiological, biological, somatic, psychic, cognitive, social, cultural, ideological, and spiritual.

3. Realization of one's growth potential in the view of reducing resources of self and others is a difficult task, at best.

4. In our judgment, the philosophical rationale for lifelong learning is best examplified by the humanistic philosophy of education. A humanistic philosophy encourages, indeed demands, an atmosphere between teacher and student, between facilitator and learner in which mutual learning is achieved. This means that people learn from one another through fostering and nurturing interdependent relationships. There is a lateral relationship which offers opportunities for equitable gains through cooperative teaching and learning. Hierarchical patterns are decreased, as it is recognized that each partner has something to contribute to the other, cognitively, affectively, and behaviorally. Conflict and confrontational situations are acknowledged as normal, as are harmonious conditions; the question here is how to manage conflict

rather than to deny or avoid it. In fact, conflict and harmony, dissent and consensus, are expected to permeate the learning environment and to stimulate as well as invigorate the learning process.

5. Why educate older adults? Given their perspective of time, older adults are likely to be capable of special reflection on the meaning of their lives. This capability should be developed, fostered, and enhanced. Such reflection may become an important resource in a rapidly changing, fast-moving society; it can serve as a reflective stance and pace which assists in the resolution of complex human and societal problems through contemplation, thereby creating intervals and intermissions. (We know that in music, the pauses, intervals, and intermissions are integral parts which bring forth the essence, the rhythm of the work.) However, as a society, we must provide educational opportunities to older adults not because they will necessarily provide material or non-material resources, not because older adults may continue to be productive contributors to society—although it is good when this happens. We should educate older adults, first and foremost, because they are human beings who have value and dignity in their own right and whose "late freedom" makes it more than ever possible to find nourishment in learning. An educational philosophy which respects this ultimate worth of older persons must give recognition to the variety of needs, capacities, and potentialities of older learners and must move our society to devote a share of its social and material resources to helping its citizens to reach their greatest individual and collective self-realization and emancipation. From an ecological perspective, this in turn will enrich the society and pour out from its enriched reservoir its increased wealth, thus reinvigorating itself and its members in a never-ending stream.

Such a philosophy, going back to Socrates, Plato, and Aristotle, finds its present psychological counterparts in Rogers, Maslow, Perls, Frankl, Neugarten, and many others. Its sociological and educational counterparts include Parsons, Merton, Havighurst, Bruner, Whitehead, and Knowles. And in the social welfare field, such names as Titmuss, Marshall, Brian-Able, Rein, Miller, Kahn, Morris, and Cohen, to name a handful, add the appropriate luster.

9
Linking Social Welfare, Social Work, and Education

A central question of this book, "Why education in the later years?" involves a basic concern about allocation of societal resources — resources which even in the most affluent of societies are scarce in relation to the many types of purposes and uses to which they can be allocated and for which many interest groups compete. Indeed, if there were not the problem of scarcity in the social system, education of older adults would hardly need justification any more than any other societal program or benefit. However, the choice to devote more resources to education of older people in order to meet the various needs of a growing elder population invariably involves some trade-offs. The availability of another program, service, or benefit must be reduced or eliminated altogether if a new opportunity — the large-scale education of older adults — is to demand a larger share of a society's resources.

Economists call this the *opportunity cost,* the trade-off made by using resources for a certain purpose measured in terms of the opportunities given up by not using the resources in their best alternative use. Regardless of whether such a trade-off is between resources devoted to education of older people and those devoted to the education of children and younger adults, between education of older people and other societal benefits or services for the old, between public education of older people and private expenditures, or between social welfare programs in general and programs for national defense, some trade-off is called for in any move that seeks to increase the education of older adults on a nationwide scale.

Allocation of its resources is one of the major functions that every society has to perform. It is also a function which people must perform in their own lives, whether as individuals, as members of families, or as members of peer or other groups. People must continually make choices between competing demands on their time, energy, finances, emotional stamina, activities, and so on. We have sought to address two major questions in this book: 1) Why should older adults allocate their own resources to educational activities? 2) Why should a society allocate a share of its resources to the education of older adults?

The answers to these two questions are not necessarily the same or even complementary. Although the relationship between the individual and the society is a symbiotic, interdependent one, conflict between the goals of individuals and those of the society is an ever present fact of social relations. The built-in conflict between *human needs* and *societal needs* is a normal, ongoing phenomenon. This has been a historical condition since social organization was created to make life manageable. Society must solve certain problems to continue to exist and make adaptations to all types of changes, especially when these are accelerated, as in the postindustrial world. People must solve their problems to insure their continued existence within the social matrix, to fulfill their varying needs and aspirations, which are frequently at odds with societal imperatives. These natural tensions produce a disequilibrium between societal demands and a person's capacity to cope with them externally and internally. To achieve this capacity is a major purpose of the socialization process of the young.

It was Merton (1957) who first dealt with the "adult socialization" experience, in contrast to the majority of sociologists and educators who confined socialization to the years of childhood and youth. The recognition of lifelong adaptation to ever-changing life-developmental tasks and societal changes came relatively recently and has had a significant impact upon adult education and education in the later years, as well as upon social welfare and social work. The result has been a publicly mandated social mechanism to negotiate the imbalance between individual and societal needs through the creation of a series of health, social, economic, and educational policies.

In turn, these have brought about the emergence of specialized occupational groupings to implement such policies. Occupations such as those of physicians, nurses, lawyers, social workers, educators, became professionalized and reached their height of elite professionalization during the industrial revolution, notably in the Western world. An emphasis on rationality and empiricism emerged from this period with an emphasis on the scientific method as the avenue for discovering the truth. The hallmark of the period was specialization and expertise.

After the ascendance of a new liberal political and social philosophy in the late 1950s and 1960s in the United States and several other Western countries (evidenced in the student revolts of the 1960s in France and Germany, for instance), a new development of social consciousness began to emerge in the United States through the Civil Rights and women's movements, the "War on Poverty," and the protests against the war in Vietnam. Whereas the belief in science, rationality, and empiricism had encouraged political developments in the early part of the century which fostered the emergence of a professional class to implement such policies, by the late 1960s professionalism was questioned as the sole arbiter of knowledge, skill, or expertise.

Three powerful concepts were debated, correlated, and utilized to examine the role of professionals as well as that of the interdependence of people and their social structure: 1) economic and social justice (Rawls); 2) inequality (Roby, Miller, Titmuss); and 3) new property rights (Reich), which eventually led to the awareness of *entitlements* as part of new property rights. Charles Reich (1964) and Harry Jones (1958) had elaborated a legal doctrine that argued in effect that "the new income" (i.e., transfer payments) or "the social wage" meant that in this modern world, income depended not only on money in accumulated wealth, cash, or credit but also on guaranteed assets, services, and social resources. Particularly relevant were pensions, social insurance programs, housing and social services, including education, health, neighborhood amenities for recreation, leisure, and participation (Kahn, 1979, 81).

Although a "reluctant welfare state" (Wilensky and Lebeaux, 1965) was erected incrementally, it is questionable whether the doctrine of "new property rights" was ever part of the ideological basis for what was a pragmatic, cumulative venture. The zeitgeist of the 1960s, and even the early 1970s, made advocacy of new property rights relatively attractive to various groups of people, notably the activists of the time, including the Gray Panthers. However, the appeal has been short-lived. Despite the relatively rapid technological and socioeconomic changes in the United States since the Kennedy and Johnson administrations, a major turnaround toward reducing federal responsibility for social problems was introduced in the 1970s and accelerated by the Reagan administration in the 1980s. This trend toward limiting federal responsibility for social welfare has been described and encouraged in Charles Murray's (1984) popular polemic, *Losing Ground: American Social Policy, 1950–1980*. Its economic counterpart is reflected in the theory that has been dubbed "supply-side" economics.

This free market approach to the economy has emphasized decentralization and reduction in the functioning of the federal government in domestic, regulatory, and social welfare matters (in contrast to strengthening it in the foreign and defense sectors). This is a move toward greater and greater residualism, and away from institutional social welfare (Wilensky and Lebeaux, 1965), as well as an avowed disaffirmation of Rawls' philosophy of economic and social justice in favor of Nozick's (1981) and Gilder's (1981) affirmation of the "trickle-down" theory. According to Gilder, social policies should provide incentives (tax cuts) to the economically well-off and venturesome risk-takers in the corporate and non-corporate world; Neo-conservatives question the concept of basic entitlement to anything (Greider, 1981) except entitlement to compete for whatever opportunities exist in an essentially middle- and upper-middle-class "free society."

The idea of freedom *to* venture forth and acquire material wealth has superseded the idea of freedom *from* social insecurity, want, and economic need. Galbraith's (1958) notion that private wants will be given precedence over public needs has been significantly confirmed in the 1980s, as pointed out by Lester Thurow and other economists, not to mention social welfare theorists (e.g., Rein, Kahn). This is most evident in the health and educational sectors, where privatization (e.g., proposals of a voucher system for private schools and private health care) threatens quality and quantity of care for the young and the old, as Francis Moore (1985) of Harvard has pointed out. "Elite professionalism" with its built-in super-subordinate stance, its distinction between the all-knowing professional versus the naive, non-knowing patient, or client, had been attacked widely and with reasonable success in the liberal era of the 1960s and 1970s by designing and administering health, social welfare, and educational services—e.g., Health Maintenance Organizations (HMOs), health and social service centers, neighborhood centers, use of volunteers, rise of para- and nonprofessionals to positions of status, unionization of professionals, advisory and decision-making bodies drawn from members in the community, growth of community schools and colleges, learning centers for adults and older adults.

In the present political climate, the power of "elite" professionals is reasserted in a new way, via privatization, non-accountability to the larger public good, private-fee and contracting arrangements with corporations, social institutions, and third-part payors. Even social work, which has been one of the most organizationally based, nonprofit professions, is presently deemphasizing to some extent agency-based operations and is increasingly looking to the private marketplace for clients, replicating the ancient structure of the private patient and professional fee model, though still on a sliding scale, according to the client's ability to pay.

What will these political, economic, social, and cultural trends in the United States (and in several other Western countries, though to a significantly lesser extent) portend for education in the later years? Let us first look at the possible benefits of education for the individual person, then move to the possible benefits for our society.

Value to the Individual

Every human being has certain needs which she or he strives to fulfill in a lifetime. The hierarchy of human needs developed by Maslow (1968) provides a useful framework for evaluating the benefits of education in relation to these needs. The individual benefits derived from pursuit of educational activities can be understood in relation to the individual's place in the hierarchy of needs. The choice of educational activity and the benefits derived from it will be determined largely by the extent to which the individual has satisfied basic needs (food, clothing, shelter, security) and can begin to address other levels of need (love and belonging, esteem, achievement, self-actualization). This is also related to McClusky's (1974) categories of need (discussed in chapter 4) which are not necessarily hierarchical.

An older adult who is confronted with daily threats to basic survival because of low income, illness, or lack of adequate shelter may find some assistance in meeting these basic needs through education which enhances basic survival skills. Many older adults (and not merely older people) have found that a low income can be stretched a bit further with improved budgeting skills; still others have found that knowledge of income assistance or benefit programs has enabled them to increase their economic and social resources and/or decrease their financial expenses or social debits. Information about Supplemental Security Income (SSI) benefits, acquired through reading a brochure in the library or grocery store, talking with case managers or social workers, or attending a community forum, can be quite helpful to older adults not only in enhancing their own survival but in freeing them to pursue different, if not higher goals. Similarly, education which provides job skills can equip some older adults to increase their income through part- or full-time employment, even on a temporary basis.

So it is with the other needs in Maslow's hierarchy. Educational activities can contribute to increased personal and social security by enabling older adults to learn more about crime prevention, legal rights, housing regulations, and advocacy to protect long-term social benefits. The need for a sense of love and belonging can be addressed through programs in acquiring skills to improve interpersonal relationships and to become engaged in community activities. Older adults can improve their chances for achieving recognition and esteem by improving skills to enhance leadership qualities or job opportunities. And self-actualization can be better realized by increasing self-knowledge, achieving a sense of fulfillment, and pursuing more successfully the search for meaning in life. That is why learning activities are intimately connected with social welfare functions and social work activities, as noted by Siporin (1975) in his treatise on social work practice.

A key to obtaining individual benefits via educational activities is the strengthening of an individual's sense of personal control and mastery over her or his own life situation. Empowerment, as discussed earlier, had become one of the central themes in discussions of various movements for social change in the 1960s and 70s, and is still on the political and community development agenda today. Empowerment seeks to help individuals to discover how their own personal resources can be channeled effectively to create desired changes in private or social relationships (see, for example, Lee Staples, *Roots to Power,* 1984).

Gallant (1985) notes that an important step in the process of empowerment is to change the nature of the relationship between individuals and the programs and institutions that serve them. In relation to a social services program for elders, he suggests that we must stop viewing people as *clients;*

instead, Gallant proposes that all elders in the service areas be considered members of the service program rather than clients, a distinction which not only avoids labeling, but which acknowledges the prerogative of members to exert control and influence on the decisions of the service agency, achieving greater equalization between the two parties.

The goals of empowerment call into question standard approaches to policy development which treat individuals as recipients of services rather than as constituents or active participants in the conditions and interventions that affect their own lives. Rappaport (1981) describes the responsibility of policymakers who are truly committed to enhancing individual autonomy:

> Our aim should be to enhance the possibilities for people to control their own lives. If this is our role, then we will necessarily find ourselves questioning both our public policy and our role relationship to dependent people. We will not be able to settle for a public policy which limits us to programs we design, operate or package for social agencies to use on people. (Rappaport, 1981, 55)

If education is also to serve as a tool of empowerment, greater equalization and more equitable social justice, then social policymakers, administrators, and educators must develop procedures (even if they involve greater effort) which provide for maximum participation of older adults in the planning, development, execution, and evaluation of educational programs in which they participate. Following Gallant's advice, we may want to adopt a new label to describe adults' and older adults' education, to replace the label of the disempowered "student." Indeed, older adults may need to assume control themselves to design their learning experiences, rather than wait for benevolent administrators and educators to offer them opportunities for greater participation in their own educational activities.

Such an approach by older adults would challenge existing assumptions about the individual benefits of lifelong learning, as it would suggest that one of the basic questions now should read: "Why should we, as older adults, choose to devote time in the later years to educational activities?" The change in focus would undoubtedly reveal new insights into the value of education throughout the life-span from the perspective of the individual, new "margins of power" which would strengthen the potential for growth and fulfillment in later life.

Value to the Society

Society also benefits from educating older adults. One of the major benefits frequently cited is that older adults are a largely untapped source of human potential which can make significant contributions to the productivity of the nation. Many older adults are able to work and want to do so. A survey by Harris (1981) revealed that 75 percent of those retired would prefer to be working either part- or full-time. Drewes (1981, 15) argues that the extent to which older adults will contribute to the productive labor force depends on the social incentives provided. "If older Americans are viewed as a valued resource worthy of the investment for its development, they stand ready to contribute."

Moody (1976) has contended that a rationale for education for older adults based on its role as an investment in the future "makes little sense on economic grounds." However, along with many others, he has found the benefits accruing to the economy worthy of a second look (Moody, 1986). Studies comparing older and younger workers have revealed that older adults are often more dependable, have lower absentee rates and fewer accidents on the job than younger workers. (See Schulz, 1985, 47–69, for an excellent discussion of this point.) Age is simply not a good predictor of productive capacity. A 65-year-old person in good health may be able to work for twenty more years, while a 30-year-old person in poor health may no longer be able to work at all. Educational programs which help older adults update their skills or train for second (or third or fourth) careers can help to maximize the valuable resources which these individuals have to offer. "The productive involvement of older citizens, wise with experience in all aspects of local life, is a priceless community asset for preserving community vitality" (Academy for Educational Development, 1974, 68).

As already observed, learning to assume caretaking functions for family members becomes a modern imperative and—what is more—such functions can be taught and learned (see, for example, Brody [1981], Horowitz [1985], Lowy [1985b], and Seltzer [1978]). Older persons can transfer these acquired skills to non-family members as well, such as friends, neighborhoods, community service centers, and civic organizations. Here the instrumental and expressive motivations are often linked, and the output can become advantageous to social institutions in the private and public sectors, directly benefiting society.

Development of a new pool of older workers (paid or unpaid) will only be a social benefit, however, if the society's unemployment rate is not too high and if older workers do not simply replace younger workers. The secondary labor market proposed by Morris and Bass (1986), discussed earlier, or other mechanisms devised for including greater numbers of older workers in the labor force, should not simply displace other workers, and it should not lower salaries and wages for existing workers. We must find ways to include all members of the society who want and are able to do "productive" work. We must find new avenues to enable individuals to contribute to the good of society, as well as new mechanisms for distributing the fruits of such contributions, without creating greater inequities of rewards based on surplus labor by an aging population.

This is easier said than done in a society that is just beginning to become aware of the existence of a significant sector of citizens who are capable of contributing to the Gross National Product and until now had largely been written off as a surplus population to be kept in a dependent state. Creative macroeconomic ideas that encompass this new phenomenon of an older population in the United States need to be generated and tested out in the context of a rapidly changing sociopolitical world.

Another important societal benefit of education in the later years is the strengthening of the democratic process. A democracy cannot function well if its citizens are ill-informed or apathetic. Active participation of the citizenry fortifies the democratic process, especially when such participation is based on an understanding of the issues involved and intelligent discussion of problems. Older adults are active participants in the political system as voters. They have consistently held the highest voting record of any age group, constituting about 16 percent of voters (Binstock, 1972), a much higher representation than their proportion in the population. A *Los Angeles Times* exit poll in 1984 reinforced and slightly increased this earlier finding: Seventeen percent of all voters were aged 60 and over. While only about 52 percent of persons aged 35–44 and 60 percent of those 45–54 voted in 1982, 64 percent of persons 55–64 voted in the same election, as did 65 percent of people 65–74 (*Aging America,* 1985–86). The proportion of older voters, like the proportion of voters in other age categories, are even higher in election years which coincide with the presidential election, and thus the percentages were even higher for older adults in 1980, for instance, when 71 percent of elders voted. However, elders do not vote as a group any more than do younger or middle-aged voters; older adults are a heterogeneous political constituency, and there is no reason to assume that availing themselves of increasing educational opportunities will change that fact (Binstock, 1972, 1981).

Since older adults are active participants in the political process as voters, as campaign workers, as lobbyists, and as candidates, the society has much to gain if such participation is based on knowledge of issues and understanding of the political process. This is true of younger as well as older adults, of course; the special contribution of older adults is the reinforcement that such education must be a lifelong experience if, as Fisher predicted, "the quality of any national thinking can be improved."

Given the demographic trends noted, it is clear that education of older adults has another important societal function: preparation for an aging society. Older adults are our most valuable teachers about what it is like to be old. With a growing population of older adults, the society must learn how to adapt its institutions and policies to best serve the needs of future generations of older adults.

Older adults can serve as important role models for children, for youth and for young and middle-aged adults. Seeing older adults engaged in learning and growing—even in view of "normal" crises and problems of aging—can provide inspiration and challenge to the next generation. Older role models may move the society toward a more flexible view of roles, encouraging more people to grow and adapt to changing social conditions and needs. Older persons can be psychological resources, performing what Butler (1975) calls the "elder functions": transmitting values and traditions—particularly during periods of rapid change—as well as symbolically teaching younger persons to integrate the concepts of death and dying as part of life (Kastenbaum). A society could emerge in which persons of any age could be easily able to take on new roles in work or study, and to move in and out of these roles as their interests and circumstances direct. As the World Assembly on Aging (1982) recommendation number 44 states: "Educational programmes [should be developed] featuring the elderly as the teachers and transmitters of knowledge, culture and spiritual values." Such a society would, in all likelihood, be better equipped to meet the demands, pitfalls, crises, and joys of the technological, social, and philosophical challenges of the twenty-first century.

Some have argued that the societal benefits of education for older adults can be measured against other social expenditures, such as social welfare outlays, which may be reduced. The Academy for Educational Development (1974) suggested that encouraging older adults to participate in educational activities could lead to an increased independence and a diminished need for social services among the elderly. Weinstock (1978, 135) argued in a similar vein that "education prevents health problems and is therefore less costly than maintaining the elderly in hospitals and nursing homes." And the Technical Committee on Education for the 1981 White House Conference on Aging suggested that educational programs could provide a key to problems of poverty, poor health, and discrimination, bringing benefits which would "far outweigh the cost" of the report's recommendations.

Such arguments, while attractive, are difficult to depend on in a practical world. Prevention of social problems is difficult to prove empirically; the arguments are elusive because it is rarely possible to demonstrate convincingly what might have occurred in the absence of a social intervention. Similar arguments made confidently about the potential of home care services to reduce unnecessary institutionalization of older adults (clearly a more direct link than the relationship between educational programs and institutionalization), have been frustratingly difficult to prove. As Brody (1979a) has pointed out in that context, rather than arguing cost-effectiveness, it is probably better to stress the potential of such programs to enable older adults "to live at better levels of health and well-being" (p. 1829). It is important to emphasize what can and cannot be measured in economic and other quantitative terms. Conceptions of social justice and social welfare cannot readily, if ever, be measured merely in dollars and cents. Social justice, social well-being, functional competence, and a "good old age" are qualitative by nature and need qualitative indicators as well as quantitative measures.

To be sure, a series of scales and assessment instruments exist that have been designed to measure mental health, morale, life-satisfaction, and physical well-being. Such instruments are useful in assisting clinicians, researchers, policymakers, and administrators to arrive at judgments and decisions regarding treatment procedures or policy actions on behalf of the aged (Kane and Kane, 1983). Case studies, qualitative measures, and ethnomethodological methods are increasingly employed in order to find additional validation of data, and also to arrive at greater insight into those factors of human existence which are subjective and qualitative by nature and defy quantification (Pieper, 1985). This is essential because, as the eminent biologist R.C. Lewontis (1981, 13) points out, "the 'objective facts' of science turn out over and over again to be the cooked, massaged, finagled creations of ideologues determined to substantiate their prejudices with numbers."

Beyond Survival

Individual and societal benefits of education for older adults point to important and valuable resources which contribute to the survival of individuals and society. These goals are not always complementary, however. The socialization of individuals in order to strengthen social institutions may conflict with the desire of individuals to pursue their own interests and/or to question the social norms. Tensions will always arise between the needs of the social system and those of the individuals in the society, as we have noted earlier. While it is frequently presumed that the social institutions in our society are established for the benefit of human beings, and designed to change to benefit individuals, and not vice versa, there is a necessity not only for mediation between the conflicting goals of person and society but, more importantly, for the identification of a sense of purpose which goes beyond the mere survival of individuals or the society.

Shared Goals of Education and Social Work

It is here that links between the goals of social welfare, social work, education, and humanism become evident. The social worker and the educator serve as mediators between the competing interests of individuals and the society; they enable individuals to grow and adapt to the society's expectations; they attempt to influence the society to change in order to better meet the needs and interests, of its members. "Social work is a social practice mechanism that intervenes in order to mediate tensions between society's imperatives and people's needs, desires, expectations and aspirations" (Lowy,

1974, 26). Indeed, social work is an educational enterprise, albeit a specialized one, whose purpose is "to guide and reinforce people's efforts to find and use their own powers" (Frankel, 1969). Likewise, education can be seen as a social service which is provided to meet various needs of individuals of all ages and to facilitate their role performances in a changing society.

Ultimately, both social welfare and education as fields and social work and education as occupations are philosophically oriented toward enhancement, growth, development, and change of people within a social environment, in continuing transaction of persons-situations-milieu. By utilizing purposive change strategies with persons, groups, organizations, and communities, conditions can be maximized to enhance people's lives as members of their social network in their communities and can give them a meaningful place and role in society.

Education and Social Work as Planned Change

What are some of the purposive change strategies and processes?

We return to Kurt Lewin's (1947, 1951) field-theoretical approach. His approach relies on planned change through modification of interpersonal relations, facilitating a democratic problem-solving process. Edgar H. Schein (1969) describes these interactional change processes as going through three states that were originally defined by Lewin as: 1) unfreezing, 2) changing, 3) re-freezing.

1. If change is to occur, it must be preceded by an alteration of the present condition, behavior, and attitudes, "making something solid into a fluid state."

2. Once the existing equilibrium has been upset—the solid state has become fluid—energies will be directed to make changes which will establish a new equilibrium.

3. After change has taken place, the "new state" needs to be firmed up, to become solidified again in order to function. However, if another planned change is to occur, this new solidified state needs to be "unfrozen" to be ready for modification. Essentially this process is a dialectical one (Schein, 1969, 31–33).

Building upon these theoretical concepts, Roland Warren (1965) and Bennis, Benne, and Chin (1969) designed three prototypical planned-change strategies, which are interchangeable and this can be turned into a mix of strategy-arrangements. These depend on the nature of the conditions to be changed, the context of the situation, the goals informed by values to be sought, the background of the participants involved, the time and place when and where it occurs, and the skill of the facilitators. Since learning is fundamentally a changing process, these interventive stances have relevance to education as they have to social work or, for that matter, to any field that engages in purposive planned change.

Three Prototype Change Strategies

1. The empirical-rational: consensus (collaborative) strategy
2. The normative-reeducative: negotiation (campaign) strategy
3. The power-coercive: (confrontational) strategy

The collaborative strategy is based on an assumption that people are essentially rational and want to change (e.g., to learn), but they need relevant data, information, and expertise in order to arrive at a consensus on issues, on how to solve a problem, or how to advance their knowledge and skills; they want to collaborate with others to do so.

The negotiation or campaign strategy assumes that people act more in accord with their beliefs and emotions, which are supported by socio-cultural norms. A change in actions or positions involves learning new attitudes (toward young and old, for instance). Appropriate learning and teaching techniques include group programs which involve people, primarily as group members, and make them sensitive and susceptible to the consequences of group processes such as group pressures, feelings, and normative expectations.

The power-coercive strategy uses power as a major tool for change, since there are major issue differences. Techniques include making petitions (e.g., in the social or educational policy arena) making persistent demands, staging protests and/or demonstrations, and promoting legislative action. The emphasis is on confrontation rather than on collaboration.

While social work, notably its community organization and social action arm, has been engaged in the development of several of these strategies in pure or modified form, they have just as much utility and value in education for adults, including older persons (Lowy, 1985b; Rothman, 1979; Staples, 1984).

Through an attempt to understand the past, the present, and the future, social work and education seek to develop conditions in which people can find personal and social fulfillment and growth. Out of a belief and a commitment that societies, communities, and people as individuals, family and group members can deliberately change, both fields emphasize education in the sense of *Bildung* at any time or stage of life.

There is no dichotomy between education and social welfare; a choice to support education is a choice to support social welfare services, and vice versa, because education is also a vital service. Lawson (1975) argues against drawing a connection between social work and education on the grounds that free inquiry is essential for education in a democracy. He suggests that the tension between the individual and the society must be carefully balanced in the education of adults in a democratic society because of the danger that one individual (the educator or facilitator) should seek to lead, guide, or change other individuals who are presumed to be free and equal. Lawson (1975) warns against using the educator as an agent of social change because such a view might lead to limitations on the freedom of educational inquiry, because only some specific social changes are considered justifiable by those who determine the direction of the change. We would make the counter-argument that competent social work practice enables people to determine their own destinies by releasing their capacities to change themselves and/or their surroundings in a society that moves toward greater social justice and generational equity.

In the 1985 Annual Report of the Solothurn (Switzerland) School of Social Work, the rektor (dean) points out that plans are in the making to link more and more social work and educational curriculi, because many tasks of educators and social workers require common knowledge and skill foundations. Common and separate content areas have to be further analyzed, but a general tendency to coordinate and link whenever possible is unmistakably noted in the Report.

The idea of connecting social work and education has found fruition in a dual-degree program at Boston University. Beginning in the fall of 1986, students wishing advanced degrees in both education (M.Ed. or Ed.D.) and social work (MSW) may enroll in a course of studies which enables them to work simultaneously toward both degrees and to receive certification in either or both fields.

> Students who have been accepted into both schools will submit an educational plan to a Joint Education and Social Work Liaison Committee. This will include proposals for course work, field work and research. . . . The plan will be consistent with the respective requirements of both schools and it will indicate the significance of the programmatic connection between education and social work for the student. (Proposal accepted by Boston University Schools of Education and Social Work, March, 1986)

It will be interesting to find out how many other academic institutions in the country plan similar types of programs. Subsequently, it will be important to determine who avails themselves of this opportunity, whether adult and older adult education will figure significantly as areas of concentration. Most important, it will be necessary to evaluate how this "marriage" fares over time. This move gives a signal that social work and education shall travel together and express their commonality rather than their separateness.

Why Survive?

Ultimately social work and education must be justified not only in terms of their contributions to survival of people and of society, or even the survival of our civilization. The question must be, as Butler (1975) raised it, why survive? What are all of us surviving *for?* What is the ultimate meaning of human existence throughout the generations?

Paterson emphasizes the importance of looking beyond the individual, social and societal benefits of education, beyond survival as a justification for any educational endeavor. He proposes that an equally important responsibility of societies is to assist people to develop into better human being who are more "intensely alive" and "intensely aware of the world." He suggests that it is the responsibility of society to urge its members toward a growing consciousness of their inner selves and of their relationships to other individuals:

> A just society cannot remain indifferent as to whether its members are lifeless machines, docile languorous animals, or living, active, wakeful and intelligent human persons. (Paterson, 1979, 232)

Each society has a responsibility to educate both its children and its adults because the growth of human potential which is unleashed through educational activities is the most effective means of achieving conditions of social justice.

> ... to its adult members, too [the just society] had educational duties of the utmost seriousness, based ultimately on the general moral principle that we have an obligation to help our fellow men to make the most of themselves and to reach the highest level of humanity and of personal worth that they are capable of attaining. (Paterson, 1979, 232)

It is this ability of educational activities to enable individuals and societies to reach the highest fulfillment of human potential which justifies education for persons of any age. It is only out of the belief in the importance of such a search for continued growth and meaning that a national sense of purpose for lifelong learning can find its true justification. The following statement by an older student provides a most dramatic expression of the point that we can offer:

> Well, it's really wretched to be ignorant—I mean it. We're only on this planet for so long. We don't have a lot of power over what happens to it. Some lunatic can push the button right now or next week or whatever, and all this beauty is going to go pfft! I have no control over that. I have no control over how long anybody in my life lasts. I have no control over the economy. I

have no control over aging. The list of what I don't have control over is very long and very depressing; but, by God, I do have control over my mind and what I can learn while I'm here. It's like a gathering-in. When I go, I want to go with something. If we go off into nothingness then we go off into nothingness; but if we go off into another life, or if we go to heaven or whatever, I want to be able to say: I did this; I learned this; I saw it; I heard it; I cared; I was awake; I did my job—which, I think, is to learn as much as you can about the world you live in. My God, it's the only one we've got! And it may be the only life we've got. Bit if it's pfft! afterwards, then I don't want to spend all the time until I get to nothingness preparing for it by being and doing nothing. There'll be long enough to be nothing. (Roazen, 1985)

To enable us to be all that we can be: that is the justification for social work; it is also the justification for education. Ultimately, the aim of all social policy is to facilitate this process of becoming.

10
Conclusion

In the preceeding discourse, we have attempted to respond to the need and prerequisites for an educational philosophy for older adults. In so doing, we have explored a variety of educational philosophies: the liberal, the progressive, the behaviorist, the radical, and the humanistic. We have argued that an educational philosophy suitable for older learners must be founded in a belief in the older learner's potential for creativity, enhancement, and growth, that it must support the learner's need to learn in an atmosphere of mutual respect and freedom of inquiry, and that it must respond to the variety of learning needs shared in different degrees by persons of all ages, but particularly those needs which we have in our years, in accord with the bio-psycho-socio-emotional developmental tasks of older adults. We have suggested that the humanistic philosophy of education is best suited to this challenge.

Calling for an educational philosophy which values older adults as individuals does not imply that older learners are unique; indeed, we have noted that Dewey's general educational philosophy — aimed particularly at the education of young children — and Knowles's educational approach for adults are equally rooted in humanistic principles. We have emphasized that the education of older adults does not call for special philosophies, theories, or methods only suitable for this population, but that such education calls for the best that we have learned about how to encourage and enable persons of all ages to learn, to grow, and to change. Hence, we have based our educational philosophy on a long tradition of humanistic thought, reaching back to the beginnings of Western civilization in ancient Israel, Greece, and Rome.

By focusing attention on the education of older learners, we have attempted to avoid segregating them, but rather to highlight the contributions that older learners can make to our thinking about education in general. In this respect we have agreed with others who suggest that the greater likelihood of approaching death places a special emphasis on the transcendental needs and on the educational and other health and social service choices that older adults may have to make. Therefore, older learners may be less patient with oppressive educational and service methods which limit their chances for autonomy and growth; they may feel freer to challenge educational procedures, methods, and content. Teachers with a "pedagogical" bent, who enjoy and favor passive, compliant students may have reason to worry about a greater influx of learners whose motivations for learning are less likely to be enhanced by existing educational carrots (credentials) and sticks (grades). But those who truly wish to see education flourish, who see personal, intellectual, and emotional growth as among the highest aims of human strivings, can find cause for celebration in the increased presence of lifelong learners.

In articulating a humanistic philosophy of education for older learners, we have attempted to respond to the three core questions which form the base of any educational philosophy.

1. To the question, *What is to be learned by older adults?* we have answered that no knowledge, attitude, or skill is to be assumed unimportant for older learners, that our humanistic philosophy of education calls for beginning with learners where they are and enabling them to grow and change. We have considered the full range of instrumental and expressive learning activities relevant for older adults and have suggested that educational activities be directed to meeting the variety of learning needs as they emerge and meet, singularly or in bundles. Coping, expressive, contributory, influencing, and transcendental needs are vital for all older adults, though to different degrees and at different times.

2. To the question, *What is the purpose of education in the later years?* we have responded that the individual and societal benefits of education for older adults are diverse and significant. We have also noted the important implications for educational reform which can arise from a greater inclusion of older adults in a full range of learning designs, processes, and activities. Nevertheless, we have concluded that the essential purpose and justification for education in the later years must come from values which extend beyond the support of social, economic, political and educational systems; this sense of purpose must be based on more than the survival of individuals or societies. It must be and is fundamentally related to the purpose of human survival, to the development of a human cosmic consciousness toward a greater understanding and role in the future of the universe.

For this reason, we have found it important throughout the book to link the goals and policies of social welfare, social work, and education. We have argued that the goals and objectives of these policy arenas are inextricably connected in the human search for an individual and societal sense of purpose. Our beliefs about why we as a people should struggle to survive and why we should assume responsibility for ensuring the survival of others, are at the root of our social policies; to the extent that we as individuals or as a society affirm that such policies should encourage and foster growth and development of persons and groups, to that extent we support the humanistic aims of social welfare policy, of which education and social work as fields and disciplines are important components.

3. Finally, we have begun to examine *What is the role of society in educating older adults?* This is a question which each society must answer, taking into account its history, traditions, heritage, values, political and economic situations, and avowed or hidden goals. We have analyzed specific precedents in the United States which suggest the extent to which lifelong learning has a place in national policy. We have argued that educating persons of all ages is an important national goal, but we have also noted the long-standing, consciously set limits on the federal government's role in providing such education. It is therefore most important for each state, each local community, indeed each educational institution, to examine its policies and to consider the importance of lifelong learning among its various aims, given the fact that no coherent or comprehensive national policy has ever existed, nor is likely to exist in the foreseeable future. The lessons of our social welfare policies, are instructive, because even in periods of dire social and economic stress, in contrast to most Western societies, this country has barely accepted a minimum national income maintenance program, preferring "residual" solutions over "institutional" arrangements.

Many questions remain as the United States and countries throughout the world struggle to determine the appropriate role of public policy in encouraging education at all stages of the life cycle. Among the challenges for the future, the following issues and questions should be on the agenda:

1. *How have older adults transformed formal education?* We have alluded to the hopes and expectations of educators in various countries regarding the potential of older learners to transform their educational institutions. As more and more older learners engage in activities in formal educational institutions, it will be important to determine whether, how, and to what extent these expectations are being realized.

2. *What future educational models should be created?* Rosenmayr (1983) suggests that the old educational models are simply not adequate for the period of the "late freedom." Perhaps the existing models can be transformed or new models can be created. Will the most responsive and viable programs be age-integrated or age-segregated? Will tuition waivers, currently popular in U.S. higher education, provide any useful role in the future, or will they be found to exacerbate prejudices against the old, automatically making them into second-class citizens? Will greater flexibility between the roles of teacher and student find its way into traditional institutions, as it has in many experimental programs?

3. *What mix of public/private, federal, state, and local resources should be employed to encourage and provide education of persons of all ages?* How and where can an equitable allocation of federal resources be made for education of adults and older adults? As a proportion of the U.S. Department of

Education's budget? As a proportion of the total social welfare costs for older adults? By some other criteria? What combination of federal, state, local and private, nongovernmental resources is most appropriate in support of education of older adults, and in support of educational policy in general? Given even major shifts in the dominant national ideology, is there some baseline policy that can be justified on ethical or pragmatic grounds?

As Robert Morris (1986b) notes in his review of Charles Murray's *Losing Ground,* "despite the defects in Murray's reasoning, it is not possible to ignore the fact that programs designed to date have not dealt with the problems noted. He advocates further probing and convincing explanations about these dilemmas and creative policy and program initiatives that require well-reasoned explanations" (Morris, 1986b, 74). Morris further warns that if such well-reasoned explanations are not forthcoming by social workers or others, our major democratic resources (i.e., state and national government resources) for coping with common human needs may be undermined.

4. *What responsibilities do all citizens bear for their own growth and development?* Assuming that such responsibilities exist, how can they be encouraged and facilitated? What mechanisms are available already and which ones need to be created?

Questions 1 and 2 can be addressed largely through empirical research, some of which has already begun and is described earlier in the book. The latter two questions are intimately involved in the assessment of the value of human life and the determination of how (and whether) to strive for conditions of social justice as Rawls had defined it. These latter questions can be *informed* by empirical research, but their ultimate justification must come from ethical argument and moral suasion. These are fundamental value questions which must be approached through systematic study of philosophy, ethics, epistemology, history, art, literature, sociology, and politics. Answers cannot be obtained by *scientific* means or through empirical evidence alone; rather, they must, as Keats said, be "proved on our pulses."

We face a great challenge in the coming century, particularly when we review the demographic data. We must learn to balance individual interests with national interests, to weigh national priorities against the balance of international concerns in a world economy. We must find peaceful resolutions to conflicts. To do this, we must acknowledge our human and national interdependencies, and we must find ways to stretch the limits of our mental capacities in order to reach our highest potentials as individuals, as members of societies, as world citizens. Les Brown's (1986) *Annual State of the World Report* contends that the meaning of "national security" has changed in the past few years. "Global geo-politics," he says, "is being reshaped in a way that defines security more in economic than in traditional military terms." Being printed in nine languages, this report will find its way into 122 nations, east and west (*Time,* February 24, 1986). Lifelong education will become a powerful tool in this reshaping process; individuals, families, institutions, organizations will, *nolens volens,* be transmitters of this message, and older persons of this and future generations may become pioneers of a new educational system, the parameters of which are still unknown to us.

The issues and questions posed here will shape these parameters and may move us toward an intergenerational, intercultural, humanistic world. Learning and teaching, the mutual interactional process called *education,* offers people and societies the instruments to shape and reshape their lives and the lives of those who follow them. As part of that reshaping process, we must learn how to articulate the worth and dignity of individuals without trumpeting independence and productivity as the hallmarks of human dignity. For it is *interdependence* which truly binds us to other persons. Focusing our attention on interdependence, we might then begin to develop policies which promote economic, social, and personal growth for all individuals, so that we as humans in a social setting, helping and supporting one another, may develop to our fullest potentials.

Aristotle has said that "education is the best provision in old age." What he could not have surmised or known in his era, was that for our complex, technological and technocratic world, education is an essential provision at any age, since the very existence of humankind and its habitat, the earth, are at stake.

Appendix A
Recommendations for Federal Role in Educational Policy for Older Adults

Exemplary Policy Statements

Planning

The needs of older persons should be given explicit consideration in the planning of vocational education programs, services and activities.

A written action plan for the provision of vocational education to older persons should be prepared.

Plans for the provision of vocational education to older persons should be developed in cooperation with area agencies on aging and other community organizations concerned with the needs of older persons.

Local advisory council membership should provide for the representation of older Americans.

State and local funds should be allocated to meet the basic costs of vocational education programs for older persons.

Coordination of Service Delivery

Vocational education programs, services and activities should be coordinated with other public and private organizations providing services to older persons.

Working cooperative relationships should be established with area agencies on aging and other community services agencies using statewide cooperative agreements as the vehicle.

Vocational education should work cooperatively with employers and other community groups to ensure that the resources of older persons are productively employed.

Source: *Education and Training for Older Persons: A Program Guide*. Washington, D.C.: U.S. Department of Education, Office of Vocational and Adult Education, March 1981.

Cooperative relationships should be established with sheltered employment facilities to provide support for those older persons needing such services.

Vocational education should coordinate with such agencies and services as are necessary to insure that a full range of supportive services is available to older persons so that they can profit from vocational education and training.

Outreach

Vocational education should actively seek to serve all older persons who might profit from vocational programs, services and activities.

Procedures should be established for identifying, locating and advising older persons of all vocational education program options available to them.

Procedures should be adopted for processing referrals of older persons for vocational education from any public or private source.

Vocational education should seek to work with employers to serve older employees who may desire a second career.

Supportive Services

Appropriate supportive services should be provided to assist older persons in benefiting from vocational education.

Opportunities for comprehensive vocational assessments should be provided each older person enrolled in vocational programs.

Career and retirement counseling should be provided older persons in conjunction with vocational assessment.

Local guidelines should be established governing use and interpretation of vocational assessment instruments and work evaluation measures as applied to older workers.

An assessment report should be prepared and used to assist older persons in the selection of appropriate vocational programs/services.

Sufficient qualified staff should be provided to conduct and/or assist in vocational assessment of older persons.

Instruction

No persons shall be excluded from participation in an appropriate vocational program on the basis of age.

Appendix B
Summary and Detailed
Recommendations of 1981
White House Conference on Aging

The following is a summary of the Recommendations; the complete text follows this summary.

Summary Reports of the Conference Committees

Committee 10:
Education and Training Opportunities

Chairman: Bernice L. Neugarten
Vice Chairman: Gerald Felando
Staff Director: John K. Wu

I wish to begin by thanking these persons, the other members of the staff who worked so diligently and effectively, the resourse persons, the observers, and especially the two volunteers who gave us special assistance, Ms. Julia Hambelt and Mr. Henry Drennan. There are 157 members of this Committee.

After two very excellent keynote addresses by Mr. Harold Johnson and Ms. Margaret Arnold, the Committee began its deliberations by reviewing the rules of the Conference, and by establishing a quorum.

The group was an excellent and hard-working one. After agreeing on a tentative agenda, a preliminary preamble, and after adopting three resolutions, the Committee recognized that to continue in this time-consuming manner was counter productive. Therefore, the Committee managed to work out a procedure whereby each member had the opportunity of making input and a procedure by which more than 109 separate proposals were combined into a relatively small number of major recommendations.

Reprinted from *Final Report, The 1981 White House Conference on Aging* Nov. 30, 1981–Dec. 3, 1981; Vol. 2, Process Proceedings; Summary Reports of the Conference Committees; Committee 10: Education and Training Opportunities, pp. 92–93.

Because of time limitations, I shall summarize and paraphrase.

Our report will open with a preamble: "It is the considered opinion of the Committee on Education that education is not only an inherent right of all age groups, it is a necessity for a society struggling to achieve a fuller measure of social justice for all Americans irrespective of age, race, sex, economic status, color, handicap, territorial residence, or national origin. Specifically, it is our collective judgment that the recommendations of other White House Conference committees cannot be implemented effectively unless older people have access to a full range of educational programs in keeping with their needs and interests, unless they are served by personnel who have been adequately prepared to serve their needs, and unless older people live in a society which has been enlightened about the processes of aging."

Our major recommendations are grouped according to that sector of the society which we believe bears the major responsibility for implementing each one.

First, under the heading,"The Role and Responsibilities of the Federal Government": ". . . A complete range of basic and all other levels of educational programs to improve the economic status, health, social functioning, and life satisfaction of older people should be given the highest priority for funding and made available and accessible to all older Americans immediately. These must be offered under a wide variety of auspices including both public and private organizations. High on the list should be job training and retraining programs, work-related preretirement training, skills and knowledge training, leadership and volunteerism training, survival, and cultural opportunities. Included here are programs for displaced homemakers and work/training for those women and men who need to work and who lack readily marketable job skills. Attention should be given to both formal and informal learning opportunities by both paid and volunteer teachers who are older persons."

A number of specific recommendations are then addressed to specific government agencies and programs, including but not limited to the Older Americans Act, the Adult Education Act, and National Endowment for the Humanities programs.

All personnel involved in the delivery of educational services should be required to have gerontological and/or geriatric training. The Federal government needs to work with institutions of higher education as well as with professional, scientific, and community organizations to develop an educational strategy to prepare personnel, including adults themselves.

Because many of the problems of older persons are due to lack of scientific knowledge, funding through many Federal agencies must be increased immediately for gerontological, geriatric and policy research, and research training; the new and old information should be made available for incorporation into appropriate curricula at all levels of education, beginning with early childhood education.

To combat ageism, it is recommended that the U.S. Commission on Civil Rights or some other appropriate body fully investigate and document the nature and scope of age prejudice in the United States, and prepare a series of recommendations detailing intervention strategies, including those addressed to the public education systems, the informal educational agencies, the mass media, and business and industry.

Under "The Role and Responsibilities of State Government":

State governments should continue to share responsibility with the Federal government and the private sector. Each State should designate a unit of its government to define and rank priorities regarding the educational needs of its older residents from all socioeconomic and geographical areas. These units should be granted resources for a leadership role in the development of needed programs to monitor financial aid programs in the field of education and to ensure that discriminatory practices based on age are corrected.

Special attention should go toward educating personnel administrators in both the public and private sector.

Because medical schools, nursing schools, pharmaceutical schools, and other training programs for health care providers should include emphasis on the problems and treatment of persons of advanced age, training in these areas, wherever appropriate, should be considered as a condition for graduation certification, and licensure.

Under "Role and Responsibility of Educational Institutions and Professional and Scientific Organizations":

We urge educational institutions at all levels and educational organizations, both formal and informal (for example, libraries and museums) to give high priority to developing programs to educate and train senior adults, personnel serving the elderly, and the general public.

In a similar vein, scientific societies and associations of professionals serving older people must devote more attention to the implications of an aging society for their respective membership. Educational programs in geriatrics and gerontology must be developed for both preservice and in-service practice.

Under "Role and Responsibility of Organizations in the Private Sector":

It is essential that private profit and nonprofit organizations, including business, industry, trade unions, and voluntary health, civic, social welfare and religious organizations, take steps to guarantee appropriate accessibility to older adults in all their educational programs. Private sector organizations should become advocates for both educational opportunities for the elderly and for public education about aging. It is important that the private sector be encouraged to provide education for retirement.

Under the heading, "Older persons":

Older Americans must themselves assume responsibility to advocate for their own interests with those who control and direct the provision of educational services and programs and should, independently and through their organizations, engage in programs designed to preserve and facilitate the teaching of the wisdom and knowledge gained through their years of experience. Older Americans should seek opportunities whereby they will be actively involved with students in all levels of education as teachers and in a wide variety of supporting roles.

This preamble and these major recommendations—spelled out in greater detail than reported here—were adopted in a single action of the Committee on Wednesday morning by vote of 105 to 7. The Committee then voted the adoption of four brief additions and then voted—in line with the Rules of the Conference—to make use of supplemental statements and additional views, as deemed appropriate by individual members.

All these actions were completed by 11 AM on Wednesday, and with no further business before the body, the Committee was adjourned.

Supplemental Statements

The Committee delegates entered 19 supplemental statements. Three made additions and corrections to the main Committee report. Six addressed the needs of special interest groups—rural, Native Americans, transportation, and peer counseling. Eight statements suggest specific training and educational programs, including development of low-cost training packages, citizenship education, study circles, minority and bilingual professionals to serve the elderly, and new work options for older persons. Two additional resolutions concern fostering volunteerism through reciprocal learning and teaching programs in the private sector and improving the status of ACTION.

Additional Views

The delegates entered 14 additional views for the record. Three addressed the Federal role in terms of tuition tax credits, support of education for self-sufficiency, and lack of need for a new Federal aging agency. Four others concerned advocacy training, leadership roles, peer teaching, and use of elderly expertise. Four additional views focused on special group needs of Native Americans, residents of territories and trusts, minorities, and the visually impaired. Three others were miscellaneous.

Madam Chairman, I respectfully submit this report in the name of our Committee on Education, and in doing so, I should like to commend all those who worked so diligently and so harmoniously in its preparation.

Detailed 1981 White House Conference Recommendations

Committee 10: Education

Recommendation: *Number 423*

It is the considered opinion of the Committee on Education that education is not only an inherent right of all age groups, it is a necessity for a society struggling to achieve a fuller measure of social justice for all Americans irrespective of age, race, sex, economic status, color, territorial residence, handicap, or national origin. Specifically, it is our collective judgment that the recommendations of other White House Conference on Aging Committees cannot be implemented effectively unless older people are entitled to have access to a full range of educational programs in keeping with their needs and interests, to be served by personnel who have been adequately prepared to serve special needs of older persons, and to live in a society which has come to understand more fully the aging process.

Recommendation: *Number 424*

Complete range of basic and all other levels of educational programs including multi-career and re-education, to improve the economic, health, social functioning and life satisfaction of the elderly should be given the *highest priority for funding* and made available and accessible to all older Americans immediately. Federal education and employment funds shall be targeted in equitable proportion toward older adults, including displaced homemakers, to assure career counseling, work training, and job placement in a variety of occupations for those women and men who need to work and who lack readily marketable job skills.

These must be offered under a wide variety of auspices including both public and private organizations, agencies and institutions including but not limited to: aging organizations, colleges, and universities, senior centers, public schools, news media, religious organizations, libraries and labor unions.

High on the list should be job training and retraining programs, vocational rehabilitation programs, work related preretirement training programs, skills and knowledge training, leadership and volunteerism training, survival and cultural and recreational opportunities. Attention should be given to both formal and informal learning opportunities and conducted by both paid and volunteer teachers.

The above programs will represent a major step in the march towards entitlement to education for the aging only if the following steps are taken in implementation:

1. In the reauthorization of the Older Americans Act a title be included for encouragement and facilitation of *networking* resources and services for older Americans through diverse outlets;

2. Action's Older American programs such as RSVP, Senior Companions Program and Foster Grandparents should be continued and their funding expanded;

3. In the reauthorization of an Adult Education Act a special title be added to provide services and programs to the elderly, and all titles now authorized for their use should be funded;

4. A title equivalent to the Library Services Act Title IV for services to older Americans (authorized under LSCA following the 1971 White House Conference on Aging but never funded) should be included in whatever national library legislation replaces LSCA after 1981.

5. AoA Title IV-A (short and long term training) should be continued and fully funded.

6. The National Endowment for Humanities' Senior Humanities Program should be continued and expanded, as well as other NEA/NEH programs geared to seniors.

7. Tax credit should be established for older persons who donate 50 hours or more per year to non-profit agencies.

Recommendation: *Number 425*

Older Americans must themselves assume responsibility to advocate for their own interests with those who control and direct the provision of educational services and programs.

Recommendation: *Number 426*

Older Americans should, independently and through their organizations, engage in programs designed to preserve and facilitate the teaching of the wisdom and knowledge gained through their years of experience with life.

Recommendation: *Number 427*

Older Americans should seek opportunities and create programs whereby they will be actively involved with students in all levels of educational institutions as teachers and in a wide variety of supporting roles.

Recommendation: *Number 428*

A new title under the Older Americans Act should be created to provide for review of the educational impact of all programs designed to improve the economic status, health and social functioning of the elderly and should be given the necessary resources to evaluate the programs conducted by relevant Federal agencies (e.g., Education, Health and Human Services and particularly the Administration on Aging, Labor, Agriculture, Housing and Urban Development, Community Services Administration, and Action) in carrying out their respective endeavors.

The designated unit should collect data about programs, identify barriers to their utilization by older persons, and prepare an evaluative report on educational opportunities for the elderly on a biennial basis. The report should be sent for appropriate review and action to the Secretary of Health and Human Services, to the Select Committee on Aging, and the appropriate Oversight Committees.

Recommendation: *Number 429*

The quality of educational services, and all other services available to older people depends directly upon the quality of the personnel who provide them. All personnel involved in the delivery of such services should be required to have gerontological and/or geriatric training. The Federal government needs to work with institutions of higher education as well as with professional, scientific, and community organizations and with the health professions to develop an educational strategy to prepare personnel, including older adults themselves. Education in this area should emphasize the importance of dialogue between the professional leadership and those being served. One part of the educational strategy to meet personnel needs over the next decade should be to consider how the roles and responsibilities of professionals and para-professionals in fields such as health and education, recreation and service, may be shaped and reshaped so that older persons are better served and their potential realized. It must be recognized that changes in traditional professions and disciplines and the development of new career lines are necessary to be sensitive to the unique social, emotional, recreational and cultural circumstances of older adults. Therefore, the Federal Government is urged to give increased financial and policy support over sustained periods of time to education programs designed to prepare personnel to serve the elderly, including training of older adults themselves. It is further recommended that the skills, knowledge, and background of older adults be used as resources in the planning and implementation of educational programs. Finally, it is recommended that such educational programs be viewed as an integral part of a broad strategy intended to improve health and human services, housing services, and other programs planned to assist the elderly.

Recommendation: *Number 430*

Many of the problems encumbering the aged are due to the lack of scientific knowledge about the processes of normal aging, the aging society, and the circumstances of older people. To improve education and service programs it is recommended that funding through many Federal agencies be increased immediately for gerontological, geriatric and policy research and research training. Such a strategy must allow for the expansion of investigator initiated research as well as government directed research. Research and research training must be concentrated in the nation's colleges and universities to ensure the preparation of personnel able to maintain and improve the gerontological and geriatric research enterprise in this nation. It must be emphasized that increased research funding and activities must be undertaken by many Federal agencies (e.g., Education, Health and Human Services, Social Security Administration, Labor, Agriculture, Veterans Administration, Energy), because the range of problems affecting the aged and the aging society cut across departmental domains. To guarantee a greater degree of cooperation among the relevant agencies, one unit should be selected by the President, or designated by Congress, to inventory all aging related research and to publish periodic reports. An access and retrieval system should be implemented to facilitate the retrieval and use of the most up-to-date information.

To ensure a better understanding of the aging process, it is recommended that Federal efforts assure that such information be made available for incorporation into appropriate curricula for all levels of education, beginning with early childhood education.

Recommendation: *Number 431*

State governments will continue to share responsibility for educational programs with the Federal government and the private sector. Therefore, the

Committee recommends that each state designate a unit of its government, working in the fields of education and/or aging, to define and rank priorities regarding the educational needs of its older residents of all socio-economic levels and geographical areas. These units should be granted adequate resources for a leadership role in the development of needed programs by appropriate agencies of government, educational institutions, and other public and private organizations in their respective states. Each state should collect qualitative and quantitative information about the programs and levels of participation. A public report should be prepared and distributed biennially by the state.

Recommendation: *Number 432*

The above mentioned units of state government are requested to continually monitor financial aid programs in the field of education, including those funded by the Federal government but administered by the states, to make certain that discriminatory policies and practices based on age are identified and corrected.

Recommendation: *Number 433*

The deleterious effects of ageism have not permitted the elderly to participate fully in the shaping and management of our society. As a means of expanding opportunities for older Americans to increase their contributions to this nation, it is recommended that the U.S. Commission on Civil Rights, or some other appropriate body, be directed to fully investigate and document the nature and scope of age prejudice and discrimination in the United States. Further, it is recommended that the designated agency prepare a series of recommendations detailing intervention strategies—including the use of educational programs and the media—to better inform the American public about the processes of normal aging and the responsibilities, contributions and potential of the aged. Such recommendations are the following:

1. To develop and implement a national policy in mass-media programming and presentation for the purpose of producing positive images of the elderly.
2. To assess the role of public education systems in order to assist them in promoting knowledge about the aging process, the concept of life long learning, and the interaction of youth with older persons.
3. To minimize negative media images by encouraging the older person to participate in public and private programs and by responding to stereotypes found in the media.
4. To enlist business and industry to educate persons about aging, and to modify employment and retirement policies.

Recommendation: *Number 434*

Medical schools, state medical societies, nursing schools, pharmaceutical education, medical education programs, and training programs for health care providers should increase specific emphasis on physical, mental and emotional problems and the treatment of persons of advanced age. Training in the areas, where appropriate, should be considered as a condition for graduation certification, and licensure.

Recommendation: *Number 435*

To achieve the objectives of pre and post retirement planning, it is recommended that state governments:

1. Encourage the development of programs to meet the pre and post retirement needs of the elderly which include educating personnel adminstrators and employees in flexible work schedules, including part-time jobs, shared jobs, and phased retirement to encourage greater and longer labor force participation by older workers and to allow for more individualized work and leisure opportunities.

2. Establish state agencies where needed to provide such services.

3. Institute feasibility studies to determine precisely what are the needs of the elderly with respect to pre and post retirement planning and job development.

4. States should enact legislation with funding to develop work options and pre and post retirement programs.

5. The state should take the lead in encouraging the private sector to participate in like programs.

Recommendation: *Number 436*

Strengthen educational and counseling services to assist persons, regardless of age, who have special needs in dealing with death and dying, inflation, consumer problems, applications for governing benefits, fraud, crime and abuse, advocacy, spiritual growth and other issues of concern.

Recommendation: *Number 437*

The state governments should provide the leadership and the funding necessary for the development of curriculum materials on the aged and the aging process, and provide adequate monitoring to assure and facilitate the implementation of these materials at all school levels.

Recommendation: *Number 438*

Scientific societies and associations of professionals serving the elderly must devote more attention to the implications of an aging society for their respective memberships. Educational programs in geriatrics and gerontology must be developed both for service professionals in training as well as those professionals who are currently in practice. It is their responsibility to delineate the ways in which their members can and should better serve the aged and increase public understanding about the effects of an aging society on all age groups and social institutions.

Recommendation: *Number 439*

As our society is aging, it is also experiencing other profound changes affecting all ages as a result of the technology explosion and urbanization. These and other societal changes have extraordinary implications for educational institutions at all levels, professional associations and scientific societies. It seems likely that multiple programs will be much more commonplace—indeed essential—in the immediate future. Therefore, we urge educational institutions at every level and educational organization (such as, but not limited to, the American Council on Education, Association of American Universities, American Association of Community and Junior Colleges, National Association of State Universities and Land Grant Colleges, and the American Library Association) to give high priority to the development and implementation of programs to educate and train on an on-going basis senior adults, personnel serving the elderly, and the general public. There shall be equal access to all educational programs by older persons in such areas as admissions, financial aid, course content and location, teaching methods and training opportunities that presently serve to exclude or minimize the participation of older adults. In order to adjust for current age discrimination, a significant percentage of scholarship aid should be allocated to older adults preparing for second careers on the basis of need and potentials. We urge colleges, universities and other appropriate institutions to pay attention to the special educational needs of specific groups, such as, but not limited to, the rural elderly, older women, ethnic and racial groups, and the handicapped elderly. Knowledge about aging should be included in teacher preparation programs, in curricula for students at all age levels, and in training for any personnel who will be delivering services to older persons. Inasmuch as the education and training of senior adults is currently an adjunct, irregular and unstable function, the Committee urges that education and training for later life be established in the 1980s as a regular, fully-funded and priority function of educational institutions.

Recommendation: *Number 440*

The Committee urges that education of the elderly acknowledge the physical, mental, spiritual, social, recreational, cultural and psychological needs of the elderly.

Recommendation: *Number 441*

Expansion of pre-retirement programs is imperative if future generations of older Americans are to enjoy their later years.

Recommendation: *Number 442*

It is essential that private profit and non-profit organizations, including business, industry trade unions, and voluntary health, civic, social welfare and religious organizations, take whatever steps are necessary to guarantee appropriate accessibility to older adults in all educational programs. Particular efforts should be undertaken to guarantee the inclusion of those elderly who may be handicapped by poverty, illness, disability, social isolation, gender or minority status. It is important that private sector organizations become advocates in regard both to educational opportunities for the elderly and to public education about aging. It is also important that the private sector be encouraged to provide education for retirement. In the case of nationally organized units of private and voluntary organizations, we believe it is incumbent upon their leadership to put in motion steps to guarantee that educational programs under their auspices provide the broadest possible opportunities for the elderly to participate as planners, teachers and learners.

Recommendation: *Number 443*

Be it resolved, that Federal funding of and leadership in (1) education and training of the aged, (2) education of all ages about aging and the aged, and (3) training of experts to serve the needs of the aged must be expanded. A comprehensive Federal program of dissemination of exemplary programs must be put into operation at once. Exclusion of the aged from education and from training programs legislated for all citizens must cease.

Implementation:

Passage by Congress of laws and then passage of Congressional appropriations.

Note: This statement was approved as a "concept" by an approximately two-thirds vote, considered separately from the other resolutions.

Appendix C
U.N. International Plan of Action on Aging

Reprinted from *U.S. Perspectives: International Action on Aging. A Background Paper prepared by the American Association for International Aging for the Select Committee on Aging, House of Representatives, 98th Congress, Second Session, January 1985* (Comm. Pub. No. 98–478, Washington, D.C.: GPO); Appendix 2: Text—International Plan of Action on Aging.

APPENDIX TWO

TEXT: INTERNATIONAL PLAN OF ACTION ON AGING*

PREAMBLE

The countries gathered in the World Assembly on aging,
Aware that an increasing number of their populations is aging,
Having discussed together their concern for the aging, and in the light of this the achievement of longevity and the challenge and potential it entails,
Having determined that individually and collectively they will (i) develop and apply at the international, regional and national levels policies designed to enhance the lives of the aging as individuals and to allow them to enjoy in mind and in body, fully and freely, their advancing years in peace, health and security; and (ii) study the impact of aging populations on development and that of development on the aging, with a view to enabling the potential of the aging to be fully realized and to mitigating, by appropriate measures, any negative effects resulting from this impact,
1. *Do solemnly reaffirm* their belief that the fundamental and inalienable rights enshrined in the Universal Declaration of Human Rights apply fully and undiminishedly to the aging; and
2. *Do solemnly recognize* that quality of life is no less important than longevity, and that the aging should therefore, as far as possible, be enabled to enjoy in their own families and communities a life of fulfillment, health, security and contentment, appreciated as an integral part of society.

FOREWORD

1. Recognizing the need to call world-wide attention to the serious problems besetting a growing portion of the populations of the world, the General Assembly of the United Nations decided, in resolution 33/52 of 14 December 1978, to conven a World Assembly on Aging in 1982. The purpose of the World Assembly would be to provide a forum "to launch an international action programme aimed at guaranteeing economic and social security to older persons, as well as opportunities to contribute to national development". In its resolution 35/129 of 11 December 1980, the General Assembly further indicated its desire that the World Assembly "should result in societies responding more fully to the socio-economic implications of the aging of populations and to the specific needs of older persons". It was with these mandates in view that the present International Plan of Action on Aging was conceived.
2. The Plan of Action should therefore be considered an integral component of the major international, regional and national strategies and programmes formulated in response to important world problems and needs. Its primary aims are to strengthen the capacities of countries to deal effectively with the aging of their popula-

---

*Adopted August 6, 1983, U.N. World Assembly on Aging; and endorsed U.N. General Assembly, December 3, 1983.

tions and with the special concerns and needs of their elderly, and to promote an appropriate international response to the issues of aging through action for the establishment of the new international economic order and increased international technical co-operation, particularly among the developing countries themselves.

3. In pursuance of these aims, specific objectives are set:

(a) To further national and international understanding of the economic, social and cultural implications for the processes of development of the aging of the population;

(b) To promote national and international understanding of the humanitarian and developmental issues related to aging;

(c) To propose and stimulate action-oriented policies and programmes aimed at guaranteeing social and economic security for the elderly, as well as providing opportunities for them to contribute to, and share in the benefits of, development;

(d) To present policy alternatives and options consistent with national values and goals and with internationally recognized principles with regard to the aging of the population and the needs of the elderly; and

(e) To encourage the development of appropriate education, training and research to respond to the aging of the world's population and to foster an international exchange of skills and knowledge in this area.

4. The Plan of Action should be considered within the framework of other international strategies and plans. In particular, it reaffirms the principles and objectives of the Charter of the United Nations, the Universal Declaration of Human Rights (General Assembly resolution 217 A (III)), the International Covenants on Human Rights (General Assembly resolution 2200 A (XXI)) and the Declaration on Social Progress and Development (General Assembly resolution 2542 (XXIV)), the Declaration and the Programme of Action on the Establishment of a New International Economic Order (General Assembly resolutions 3201 (S-VI) and 3202 (S-VI)) and the International Development Strategy for the Third United Nations Development Decade (General Assembly resolution 35/56) and also General Assembly resolutions 34/75 and 35/46, declaring the 1980s as the Second Disarmament Decade.

5. In addition, the importance of the following, adopted by the international community, must be stressed, for the question of aging and the aging of populations is directly related to the attainment of their objectives:

(a) The World Population Plan of Action; [1]

(b) The World Plan of Action for the Implementation of the Objectives of the International Women's Year; [2]

(c) The Programme of Action for the Second Half of the United Nations Decade for Women; [3]

(d) The Declaration of Alma Ata (on primary health care); [4]

(e) Declaration of Principles of the United Nations Conference on Human Settlements (HABITAT); [5]

(f) The Action Plan for the Human Environment; [6]

(g) The Vienna Programme of Action on Science and Technology for Development; [7]

(h) The Programme of Action to Combat Racism and Racial Discrimination [8] and the Programme of Action for the second half of the same Decade; [9]

(i) The Buenos Aires Plan of Action for Promoting and Implementing Technical Co-operation among Developing Countries; [10]

(j) The International Labour Organization (ILO) Convention No. 102 concerning minimum standards of social security;

(k) ILO convention No. 128 and Recommendation 131 on invalidity, old-age and survivors' benefits;

(l) ILO Recommendation No. 162 concerning older workers;

(m) The Programme of Action of the World Conference on Agrarian Reform and Rural Development; [11]

(n) The World Programme resulting from International Year of Disabled Persons; [12]

(o) The Caracas Declaration adopted by the Sixth United Nations Congress on the Prevention of Crime and the Treatment of Offenders; [13]

(p) The Recommendation on the development of adult education, adopted by the General Conference of UNESCO at its nineteenth session (Nairobi, 1976);

(q) ILO Convention No. 157 concerning maintenance of social security rights, 1982.

I. Introduction

A. DEMOGRAPHIC BACKGROUND

6. Only in the past few decades has the attention of national societies and the world community been drawn to the social, economic, political and scientific questions raised by the phenomenon of aging on a massive scale. Previously, while individuals may have lived into advanced stages of life, their numbers and proportion in the total population were not high. The twentieth century, however, has witnessed in many regions of the world the control of perinatal and infant mortality, a decline in birth rates, improvements in nutrition, basic health care and the control of many infectious diseases. This combination of factors has resulted in an increasing number and proportion of persons surviving into the advanced stages of life.

7. In 1950, according to United Nations estimates, there were approximately 200 million persons 60 years of age and over throughout the world. By 1975, their number had increased to 350 million. United Nations projections to the year 2000 indicate that the number will increase to 590 million, and by the year 2025 to over 1,100 million; that is, an increase of 224 per cent since 1975. During this same period, the world's population as a whole is expected to increase from 4.1 billion to 8.2 billion, an increase of 102 per cent. Thus, 45 years from now the aging will constitute 13.7 per cent of the world's population.

8. It should be noted, furthermore, that in 1975 slightly over half (52 per cent) of all persons aged 60 and over lived in the developing countries. By the year 2000—owing to the differential rates of increase—over 60 per cent of all older persons are expected to live in

those countries, and it is anticipated that the proportion will reach nearly three quarters (72 per cent) by 2025.

9. The increase in the numbers and proportions of the aging is accompanied by a change in the population's age structure. A declining proportion of children in a population increases the proportion of older persons. Thus, according to the United Nations projections, the population aged less that 15 years in the developing regions is expected to decline from an average of about 41 per cent of the total population in 1975 to 33 per cent in 2000 and 26 per cent in 2025. In the same regions, the population of 60 years and over is expected to increase from 6 per cent in 1975 to 7 per cent in 2000 and to 12 per cent in 2025, thus reaching the level observed in the developed regions in the 1950s. In those latter regions, the population below the age of 15 is expected to decline from 25 per cent in 1975 to 21 per cent in 2000 and to 20 per cent in 2025; however, the group aged 60 and over is expected to increase as a proportion of the total population, from 15 per cent in 1975 to 18 per cent in 2000 and 23 per cent in 2025. It should be noted that these are averages from vast regions and that considerable variations exist between countries and at the subnational level.

10. According to model life tables, increasing life expectancy at birth could imply an increase in life expectancies at age 60 in the developed regions of approximately one year between 1975 and 2025. In the developing regions, the projected increase would be roughly 2.5 years. Men of the age of 60 could thus expect an average of over 17 years of further life in the developed regions by 2025 and of over 16 years in the developing regions. Women could expect about an additional 21 and 18 years, respectively.

11. It should be noted that, if present trends prevail, the sex ratio (that is, the number of men per 100 women) will continue to be unbalanced in the developed regions with, however, a slight improvement. For instance, this rate, which in 1975 was 74 for the 60–69 age group will be 78 in 2025, with a rise from 48 to 53 for the over-80 age group. In the developing regions, this rate will be 94 in 2025 against 96 for the 60–69 age group, and 73 against 78 for the over-80 age group, signifying a slight decline. Thus, women, in most cases will increasingly constitute a majority of the older population. Gender-based differences in longevity may have some impact of living arrangements, income, health care and other support systems.

12. Another important consideration is the trend in urban-rural distribution. In the developed regions, two-thirds of the aged were in urban areas in 1975, and this proportion is expected to reach three quarters by the year 2000. In the developing regions, three quarters of the aged were to be found in rural areas. Nevertheless, the increase in the proportion of the aging in urban areas in these countries could be considerable and exceed 40 per cent by the year 2000. These changes can be influenced by migration.

B. HUMANITARIAN AND DEVELOPMENTAL ASPECTS OF AGING

13. The demographic trends outlined above will have significant effects on society. The achievement of sustained development requires that a proper balance be preserved between social, economic

and environmental factors and changes in population growth distribution and structure. Countries should recognize and take into account their demographic trends and changes in the structure of their populations in order to optimize their development.

14. For this purpose a substantial financial effort will be needed on the part of Governments and the international institutions concerned. Actually however, the economic situation of most of the developing countries is such that they are unable to release the means and resources needed for carrying out their development policy successfully.

15. In order to enable these countries to deal with the basic needs of their populations, including the elderly, it is necessary to establish a new economic order based on new international economic relations that are mutually beneficial and that will make possible a just and equitable utilization of the available wealth, resources and technology.

16. The present International Plan of Action on Aging deals both with issues affecting the aging as individuals and those relating to the aging of the population.

17. The humanitarian issues relate to the specific needs of the elderly. Although the elderly share many problems and needs with the rest of the population, certain issues reflect the specific characteristics and requirements of this group. The sub-topics examined are health and nutrition, housing and environment, the family, social welfare, income security and employment, and education.

18. The developmental issues relate to the socio-economic implications of the aging of the population, defined as an increase in the proportion of the aging in the total population. Under this heading are considered, *inter alia,* the effects of the aging of the population on production, consumption, savings, investment and—in turn—general social and economic conditions and policies, especially at times when the dependency rate of the aging is on the increase.

19. These humanitarian and developmental issues are examined with a view to the formulation of action programmes at the national, regional and international levels.

20. In some developing countries, the trend towards a gradual aging of the society has not yet become prominent and may not, therefore, attract the full attention of planners and policy makers who take account of the problems of the aged in their over-all economic and social development planning and action to satisfy the basic needs of the population as a whole. As outlined in the preceding section, however, United Nations projections show that:

(a) A marked increase in the population over the age of 60 years is expected in the future, particularly in the segment of those aged 80 years and over;

(b) In many countries, the increase in the proportion of the over-60 population is expected to become apparent over the next few decades, and especially during the first quarter of the twenty-first century; and

(c) Increasingly women will constitute the majority of these elderly populations.

21. The issue of the aging of populations, with its vast implications both for over-all development at the national level and for the welfare and safety of older individuals, is therefore one which

will concern *all* countries in the relatively near future; it already affects some of the more developed regions of the world.

22. The measures for the optimum utilization of the wisdom and expertise of elderly individuals will be considered.

23. The human race is characterized by a long childhood and by a long old age. Throughout history this has enabled older persons to educate the younger and pass on values to them; this role has ensured man's survival and progress. The presence of the elderly in the family home, the neighbourhood and in all forms of social life still teaches an irreplaceable lesson of humanity. Not only by his life, but indeed by his death, the older person teaches us all a lesson. Through grief the survivors come to understand that the dead do continue to participate in the human community, by the results of their labour, the works and institutions they leave behind them, and the memory of their words and deeds. This may encourage us to regard our own death with greater serenity and to grow more fully aware of the responsibilities toward future generations.

24. A longer life provides humans with an opportunity to examine their lives in retrospect, to correct some of their mistakes, to get closer to the truth and to achieve a different understanding of the sense and value of their actions. This may well be the more important contribution of older people to the human community. Especially at this time, after the unprecedented changes that have affected human kind in their life-time, the reinterpretation of life-stories by the aged should help us all to achieve the urgently needed reorientation of history.

II. Principles

25. The formulation and implementation of policies on aging are the sovereign right and responsibility of each State, to be carried out on the basis of its specific national needs and objectives. However, the promotion of the activities, safety and well-being of the elderly should be an essential part of an integrated and concerted development effort within the framework of the new international economic order in both the developed and the developing parts of the world. International and regional co-operation should, however, play an important role. The International Plan of Action on Aging is based on the principles set out below:

(a) The aim of development is to improve the well-being of the entire population on the basis of its full participation in the process of development and an equitable distribution of the benefits therefrom. The development process must enhance human dignity and ensure equity among age groups in the sharing of society's resources, rights and responsibilities. Individuals, regardless of age, sex or creed, should contribute according to their abilities and be served according to their needs. In this context, economic growth, productive employment, social justice and human solidarity are fundamental and indivisible elements of development, and so are the preservation and recognition of cultural identity;

(b) Various problems of older people can find their real solution under conditions of peace, security, a halt to the arms race and a rechannelling of resources spent for military purposes to the needs of economic and social development;

(c) The developmental and humanitarian problems of the aging can best find their solution under conditions where tyranny and oppression, colonialism, racism, discrimination based on race, sex or religion, *apartheid,* genocide, foreign aggression and occupation and other forms of foreign domination do not prevail, and where there is respect for human rights;

(d) In the context of its own traditions, structures and cultural values, each country should respond to demographic trends and the resulting changes. People of all ages should engage in creating a balance between traditional and innovative elements in the pursuit of harmonious development;

(e) The spiritual, cultural and socio-economic contributions of the aging are valuable to society and should be so recognized and promoted further. Expenditure on the aging should be considered as a lasting investment;

(f) The family, in its diverse forms and structures, is a fundamental unit of society linking the generations and should be maintained, strengthened and protected, in accordance with the traditions and customs of each country;

(g) Governments and, in particular, local authorities, non-governmental organizations, individual volunteers and voluntary organizations, including associations of the elderly, can make a particularly significant contribution to the provision of support and care for elderly people in the family and community. Governments should sustain and encourage voluntary activity of this kind;

(h) An important objective of socio-economic development is an age-integrated society, in which age discrimination and involuntary segregation are eliminated and in which solidarity and mutual support among generations are encouraged;

(i) Aging is a life-long process and should be recognized as such. Preparation of the entire population for the later stages of life should be an integral part of social policies and encompass physical, psychological, cultural, religious, spiritual, economic, health and other factors;

(j) The Plan of Action should be considered within the broader context of the world's social, economic, cultural and spiritual trends, in order to achieve a just and prosperous life for the aging, materially as well as spiritually;

(k) Aging, in addition to being a symbol of experience and wisdom, can also bring human beings closer to personal fulfillment, according to their beliefs and aspirations;

(l) The aging should be active participants in the formulation and implementation of policies, including those especially affecting them;

(m) Governments, non-governmental organizations and all concerned have a special responsibility to the most vulnerable among the elderly, particularly the poor, of whom many are women and from rural areas;

(n) Further study on all aspects of aging is necessary.

III. Recommendations for Action

A. Goals and Policy Recommendations

26. The Plan of Action can only include proposals for broad guidelines and general principles as to the ways in which the international community, Governments, other institutions and society at large can meet the challenge of the progressive aging of societies and the needs of the elderly all over the world. More specific approaches and policies must, by their nature, be conceived of and phrased in terms of the traditions, cultural values and practices of each country or ethnic community, and programmes of action must be adapted to the priorities and material capacities of each country or community.

27. There are, nevertheless, a number of basic considerations which reflect general and fundamental human values, independent of culture, religion, race or social status: values induced by the biological fact that aging is a common and ineluctable process. The respect and care for the elderly, which has been one of the few constants in human culture everywhere, reflects a basic interplay between self-preserving and society-preserving impulses which has conditioned the survival and progress of the human race.

28. The pattern by which people are judged to have reached old age at a point set only in terms of the number of years they have completed, and where the loss of employment status may entail their being placed on the sidelines of their own society, is one of the sad paradoxes of the process of socio-economic development in some countries. The aim of that development was originally to improve the general living standards, health and well-being of the population at large, including the elderly.

29. The close historical interaction between the socio-economic and technological development of the industrialized countries from the last century onwards, and the old-age security systems they adopted as a part of the same process, should be analysed and kept in mind; however, other options corresponding more closely to the circumstances and needs of the developing countries ought also to be considered.

30. Aging is simultaneously a sign of and a result of socio-economic development, in the quantitative as well as the qualitative sense. One major example of the effects of the imbalance between the sectoral approaches taken to national and international development during the past decades is the fact that advances in medicine and public health have by far out-paced progress over the same period in production, income distribution, training, education, housing, institutional modernization and social development in general terms. The developing countries are in this sense about to "age" without all the sectors necessary to ensure balanced and integrated development being able to follow at the same pace and guarantee a decent living standard for the dramatically increasing numbers of elderly people foreseen for the next few generations.

1. General policy recommendations

31. The following summarized considerations, based on the above remarks, may provide guidelines for the consideration of policies and specific actions:

(a) The progressive aging of societies, the continuing increase of the elderly population both in absolute and in proportional terms, is neither an unexpected, unforeseeable event nor a random result of national and international development efforts. It is the first and most visible outcome of a sectorally based approach to socio-economic development all over the world and should be accompanied by equally efficient interventions in other areas in order to ensure balanced growth and integrated development;

(b) With a long-term view to slowing down the over-all aging of the community, Governments may be able to take the measures necessary to adjust or avoid imbalances between age groups, while preserving the right to life of the elderly;

(c) To this end, policies and actions should be inspired by the determination to give further qualitative content and meaning to a quantitative process in order to make sure that the generally expanding life-span of individuals the world over will be accompanied by efforts to fill these extra years with a sense of purpose and accomplishment, and that people will not be relegated to a marginal and passive role after a certain age level;

(d) As the transition into old age is a gradual and individual process, notwithstanding the statutory retirement age limits adopted in some countries and cultures, all policies and programmes should be based on the fact that aging is a natural phase of an individual's life cycle, career and experience, and that the same needs, capacities and potentialities usually prevail over the entire life-span;

(e) As most people can expect to survive their own retirement age by a substantial number of years, the concept of "preparation for retirement" should not continue to be conceived as a last-minute adaptation, but be proposed as a life-long consideration from adulthood onwards—as much to the individual for his or her future benefit, as to policy-makers, universities, schools, industrial work centres, the media and society at large. It should serve as a reminder that policies on aging and for the elderly are an important society-wide concern, and not solely a question of caring for a vulnerable minority. For this reason, this calls for a general policy of prevention;

(f) Policies to meet the challenge of a growing, healthier and more active elderly population—based on the view of the aging of society as an opportunity to be utilized—automatically benefit the individual aging person, materially and otherwise. Similarly, any effort to ameliorate the quality of life for the elderly, and to meet their diverse social and cultural needs, enhances capacity to continue interacting with society. In this sense, the developmental and the humanitarian aspects of the question of aging are closely intertwined;

(g) It is imperative that, when considering the question of aging, the situation of the elderly should not be considered separate from the over-all socio-economic conditions prevailing in society. The elderly should be viewed as an integral part of the population. They should also be considered within the framework of population groups such as women, youth, the disabled, and migrant workers. The elderly must be considered an important and necessary element in the development process at all levels within a given society;

(h) Aging is apparent in the working-age population long before the number of persons over 60 increases. It is essential to adapt the labour policy as a whole and technology and economic organizations to this situtation;

(i) This consideration should be accompanied by recognition of the fact that for the elderly in general—and particularly for those beyond a certain higher age (the "old old")—policies have to be considered and programmes implemented in response to their specific needs and constraints. Sectoral interventions in such fields as health and nutrition, housing, income security, and social, cultural and leisure activities are as necessary for the elderly as for other population groups, and should be provided for by each country or community according to the means available to it. It is recognized that the extent of the provision that can be made, and its timing, will be affected by prevailing economic circumstances;

(j) Policies and action aimed at benefiting the aging must afford opportunities for older persons to satisfy the need for personal fulfillment, which can be defined in its broader sense as satisfaction realized through the achievement of personal goals and aspirations, and the realization of potentialities. It is important that policies and programmes directed at the aging promote opportunities for self-expression in a variety of roles challenging to themselves and contributory to family and community. The principal ways in which older people find personal satisfaction are through: continued participation in the family and kinship system, voluntary services to the community, continuing growth through formal and informal learning, self-expression in arts and crafts, participation in community organizations and organizations of older people, religious activities, recreation and travel, part-time work, and participation in the political process as informed citizens.

32. A priority consideration for all countries is how to ensure that their vast humanitarian efforts in favour of the elderly do not result in the maintenance of a growing, relatively passive and disenchanged sector of the population. Policy makers and researchers, as well as the mass media and the general public, may need a radical change of perspective in order to appreciate that the problem of aging today is not just one of providing protection and care, but of the involvement and participation of the elderly and the aging. Eventually, the transition to a positive, active and developmentally oriented view of aging may well result from action by elderly people themselves, through the sheer force of their growing numbers and influence. The collective consciousness of being elderly, as a socially unifying concept, can in that way become a positive

factor. Since spiritual well-being is as important as material well-being, all policies, programmes and activities should be developed to support and strengthen the spiritual well-being of the aging. Governments should guarantee the freedom of religious practices and expression.

2. The impact of aging on development

33. The trend towards the successive aging of population structures is bound to be one of the main challenges to international and national planning efforts during the last decades of this century and well into the twenty-first. In addition to the general considerations outlined above on the status and predicaments of the elderly sections of societies, and the review of the needs and potentialities of the elderly, attention should be given to the vast and multifaceted impact which the aging of populations will have on the structure, functioning and further development of all societies of the world. The role of the public and private sectors in assuming responsibility for some of the functions now provided by the family in developing countries will probably have to increase under such circumstances.

34. In the first instance, it is evident that aging, both in terms of absolute numbers and in terms of the relative proportion of the elderly in any society, will necessarily change the structure and composition of the economically active population. The most basic manifestation of this phenomenon will be the gradually deteriorating ratios between the economically active and employed sectors of society and those dependent for their sustenance on the material resources provided by these sectors. Countries with established social security systems will depend on the strength of the economy to sustain the accumulated charges of income-basis and deferred retirement benefits for a growing elderly population and the costs of maintaining dependent children and of ensuring training and education for young people.

35. Changing dependency ratios—in terms of the number of old people depending for their material safety on younger, economically active and wage-earning people—are bound to influence the development of any country in the world, irrespective of its social structure, traditions of formal social security arrangements. Problems of a social nature are likely to emerge in countries and regions where the aging have traditionally benefited from the care and protection of their next of kin or the local community. Those relationships may become increasingly difficult to maintain when the number of dependent elderly increases while at the same time traditional care-providing structures, such as the extended family, are undergoing radical change in many regions of the world.

36. As mentioned above, the total dependency ratio in many countries may eventually be maintained at close to present levels, owing to the progressively decreasing number of non-employed and dependent children and youths resulting from shrinking birth rates. There remains, however, a political and psychological problem related to the perceptions of the relative urgency of covering the material and other needs of population groups not directly participating in production and public life. The costs of programmes in favour of the younger generations may be more easily acceptable in

view of their value as a form of investment in the future; conversely, such costs in favour of the elderly—especially when not directly related to individual savings or wage-related benefits—are less easily accepted, particularly when they weigh heavily on already overstrained national budgets.

37. The problem of deteriorating dependency ratios, and hence of guaranteeing even minimal material security for older people with reduced capacities for earning, will be most acute in the rural areas, particularly in the less productive, subsistence farming areas of the developing countries, which already suffer from an escalating flight of the younger and more active sectors of the population towards the urban areas in search of wage-earning employment. This trend naturally leads to an even more insecure future for the older persons left behind and—in a vicious circle of further deprivation—reduces the chances of further stimulating public investment in agriculture and services which would benefit the remaining farmers.

38. To some extent this phenomenon could be considered as partially offset or at least mitigated by the transfer of sustenance funds back from the younger people who have found salaried employment in the urban and industrialized areas. In many cases, the size of the remittances indicates an effort not only to help sustain the family, but to save for future investments, productive or not. For the immediate future, this phenomenon may help to soften the effects of the rural exodus and provide a certain level of material safety for the older and inactive left behind. Nevertheless, it can hardly be seen as a long-term reliable compensation for the migration of the young, active people from the rural areas or from their own countries. Concentrated efforts aimed at improving the socio-economic conditions prevailing in rural areas are indispensable, particularly considering the migrants' return to their country of origin.

39. Rural development should be seen as a key to the over-all problem of the aging in large parts of the world, as much as it is a key to balanced and integrated national progress in countries with an essentially agricultural economy. To some extent, policies to improve production and productivity in rural areas, to stimulate investment, create the necessary infrastructures, introduce appropriate technologies and provide basic services, could strengthen the generalized social security systems in force in other and more industrialized countries.

40. The slowly expanding life-span of the population even in developing areas constitutes a hidden resource for national economies which, if properly stimulated and utilized, might help to compensate for the exodus of younger people, decrease the real dependency ratios, and ensure the status of the rural elderly as active participants in national life and production, rather that as passive and vulnerable victims of development.

41. A desirable compensation for the emigration of young people to other countries would be an improvement in the continuity of social benefits in terms of contributive rights to a pension, including favourable provisions for financial transfers in whatever form the benefits are granted to migrant workers. This would be not only equitable, but also consistent with the stimulation of the de-

velopment of the economy of the home country. Bilateral and multilateral social security agreements must be developed to this effect. Other measures should accompany these efforts, notably in terms of providing housing for repatriates. While aging migrants have the same needs as other elderly people, their migrant status gives rise to additional economic, social, cultural and spiritual needs. In addition, it is important to recognize the role the older migrants could play in the support of their younger counterparts.

42. In countries with fully developed social security systems linked to compulsory retirement age levels over-all aging is, and will continue to be, one of the most important structural factors affecting the composition of the labour force. This phenomenon should not be considered solely in terms of its repercussions on the elderly. Because of their sheer dimension and close interaction with other sectors and processes affecting the active labour force, retirement policies cannot be treated in an isolated manner as a separate phenomenon. For various countries the most visible relationship is that between arrangements for retirement and problems of unemployment, especially among young peope about to enter the labour force.

43. Much has already been said about that relationship, and various governmental actions have been considered or taken to respond to it. Whatever the apparent wisdom of lowering retirement age levels in order to open up employment opportunities for the young, such action can hardly be seen as anything but a short-term and partial solution of one social problem through the creation of another, probably longer-lasting one. More innovative actions should be considered at both extremes of the labour force structure.

44. On the other hand, the wide varieties in personal interests and preferences among people approaching retirement age could, without too many administrative or organizational changes, be taken into account in a system of elastic retirement plans catering to the individual. Where retirement is preferred, different age levels for voluntary early retirement can be established with reduced benefits and counterbalanced by extended employment periods for those older persons whose job constitutes their main commitment, and occasionally their main reason for living. Other arrangements, such as part-time or occasional work or consultancies are already in use, especially at the higher technological and administrative levels, and could be extended to a greater part of the labour force. In order to implement this measure, provision should be made for training and retraining and the development of new skills.

45. The interrelationship between the employment and income needs of the young and the elderly raises particularly acute problems for women, whose longer life expectancy may mean an old age aggravated by economic need, isolation and with little or no prospects for paid employment.

46. Where social security systems based on accrued retirement benefits exist, the growth in the number and longevity of retired persons is now emerging as a major aspect of the husbandry of national economic resources, and is sometimes presented in terms of a gradual freezing of a large share of national wealth for so-called non-productive purposes. On the other hand, it will probably

be recognized that the accumulation of retirement funds could constitute a stabilizing factor in the national economy, in the sense of providing for long-term and conservatively utilized sources of funding on a substantial scale, whose impact on otherwise fluctuating economic systems can be beneficial. In such systems, the purchasing power of the pensions paid should as far as possible be maintained.

47. Similarly, most pension payments from retirement funds represent deferred earnings by the individual retiree. The natural use of pension payments for immediate material needs rather than for long-term and insecure investments may also be a stimulating factor in societies heavily dependent on individual spending and consumption for their economic health.

48. Where formal retirement benefit systems do not yet exist, the economic implications of the aging of societies are for the time being largely negative, and will probably continue to be so, unless serious and far-reaching efforts are made to turn this liability into a potential benefit for the whole of society. Governmental initiatives to promote material development and social well-being, and international action to sustain such initiatives, could be taken jointly in an effort to prepare for the future of those approaching old age in areas where traditional structures of protection are about to dissolve.

3. Areas of concern to aging individuals

49. The recognition that all aspects of aging are interrelated implies the need for a co-ordinated approach to policies and research on the subject. Considering the aging process in its totality, as well as its interaction with the social and economic situation, requires an integrated approach within the framework of overall economic and social planning. Undue emphasis on specific sectoral problems would constitute a serious obstacle to the integration of aging policies and programmes into the broader development framework. Although the recommendations in the following narrative have been divided under broad headings, it should be recognized that there is a high degree of interdependence among them.

50. Within the framework of recognizing this interdependence, particular attention could be given to co-ordinating preventive efforts in order to combat the detrimental effects of premature aging. From birth onwards, the detrimental effects of premature aging on the individual could be avoided by:

—An educational effort designed specifically to make young people aware of the changes which will occur as they grow older;

—A healthy general life-style;

—Appropriate adjustments to working hours and conditions;

—Splitting up each individual's time and responsibilities among various types of activities so that he can have several different jobs as he grows older, and achieve the best possible balance between time spent in leisure, training and work;

—Constant adaptation of the man to his work and, more important, the work to the man, and changing the type of work in accordance with the changes in each person, in family circumstances, and in technological and economic development. In this sphere, occupational medicine and permanent education should play an essential role.

51. In resolution 1981/62, the Economic and Social Council called upon the Secretary-General to elaborate a set of general guidelines for consumer protection. Furthermore, the Food and Agriculture Organization of the United Nations has adopted a Code of Ethics on International Trade in Food and the World Health Organization an International Code of Marketing of Breast Milk Substitutes to protect children's health. Elderly consumers should be protected, since the good health, safety and well-being of the elderly are the objective of the World Assembly on Aging.

(a) Health and nutrition

52. While the rapidly increasing number of old people throughout the world represents a biological success for humanity, the living conditions of the elderly in most countries have by and large lagged behind those enjoyed by the economically active population. But health, that state of total physical, mental and social well-being, is the result of interaction between all the sectors which contribute to development.

53. Epidemiological studies suggest that successive cohorts of the elderly arriving at the same age have better levels of health, and it is expected that, as men and women live to increasingly greater ages, major disabilities will largely be compressed into a narrow age range just prior to death.

Recommendation 1.—Care designed to alleviate the handicaps, re-educate functions, relieve pain, maintain the lucidity, comfort and dignity of the affected and help them to re-orient their hopes and plans, particularly in the case of the elderly, are just as important as curative treatment.

Recommendation 2.—The care of elderly persons should go beyond disease orientation and should involve their total well-being, taking into account the inter-dependence of the physical, mental, social, spiritual and environmental factors. Health care should therefore involve the health and social sectors and the family in improving the quality of life of older persons. Health efforts, in particular primary health care as a strategy, should be directed at enabling the elderly to lead independent lives in their own family and community for as long as possible instead of being excluded and cut off from all activities of society.

54. There is no doubt that, with advancing age, pathological conditions increase in frequency. Furthermore, the living conditions of the elderly make them more prone to risk factors that might have adverse effects on their health (e.g., social isolation and accidents)—factors that can be modified to a great extent. Research and practical experience have demonstrated that health maintenance in the elderly is possible and that diseases do not need to be essential components of aging.

Recommendation 3.—Early diagnosis and appropriate treatment is required, as well as preventive measures, to reduce disabilities and diseases of the aging.

Recommendation 4.—Particular attention should be given to providing health care to the very old, and to those who are incapacitated in their daily lives. This is particularly true when they are suffering from mental disorders or from failure to adapt to the environment; mental disorders could often be prevented or modified by means that do not require placement of the affected in institutions, such as training and supporting the family and volunteers by professional workers, promoting ambulant mental health care, welfare work, day-care measures aimed at the prevention of social isolation.

55. Some sectors of the aging, and especially the very old, will nevertheless continue to be vulnerable. Because they may be among the least mobile, this group is particularly in need of primary care from facilities located close to their residences and/or communities. The concept of primary health care incorporates the use of existing health and social services personnel, with the assistance of community health officers trained in simple techniques of caring for the elderly.

56. Early diagnosis and treatment are of prime importance in the prevention of mental illness in older people. Special efforts need to be taken to assist older persons who have mental health problems or who are at high risk in this respect.

57. Where hospital care is needed, application of the skills of geriatric medicine enables a patient's total condition to be assessed and, through the work of a multidisciplinary team, a programme of treatment and rehabilitation to be devised, which is geared to an early return to the community and the provision there of any necessary continuing care. All patients should receive in proper time any form of intensive treatment which they require, with a view to preventing complications and functional failure leading to permanent invalidity and premature death.

Recommendation 5.—Attentive care for the terminally ill, dialogue with them and support for their close relatives at the time of loss and later require special efforts which go beyond normal medical practice. Health practitioners should aspire to provide such care. The need for these special efforts must be known and understood by those providing medical care and by the families of the terminally ill and by the terminally ill themselves. Bearing these needs in mind, exchange of information about relevant experiences and practices found in a number of cultures should be encouraged.

58. A proper balance between the role of institutions and that of the family in providing health care for the elderly—based on recognition of the family and the immediate community as elements in a well-balanced system of care—is important.

59. Existing social services and health-care systems for the aging are becoming increasingly expensive. Means of halting or reversing this trend and of developing social systems together with primary health care services need to be considered, in the spirit of the Declaration of Alma Ata.

Recommendation 6.—The trend towards increased costs of social services and health-care systems should be offset through closer coordination between social welfare and health care services both at the national and community levels. For example, measures need to be taken to increase collaboration between personnel working in the two sectors and to provide them with interdisciplinary training. These systems should, however, be developed, taking into account the role of the family and community—which should remain the interrelated key elements in a well-balanced system of care. All this must be done without detriment to the standard of medical and social care of the elderly.

60. Those who give most direct care to the elderly are often the least trained, or have insufficient training for their purpose. To maintain the well-being and independence of the elderly through self-care, health promotion, prevention of disease and disability requires new orientation and skills, among the elderly themselves, as well as their families, and health and social welfare workers in the local communities.

Recommendation 7.—(a) The population at large should be informed in regard to dealing with the elderly who require care. The elderly themselves should be educated in self-care; (b) Those who work with the elderly at home, or in institutions, should receive basic training for their tasks, with particular emphasis on participation of the elderly and their families, and collaboration between workers in health and welfare fields at various levels; (c) Practitioners and students in the human care professions (e.g. medicine, nursing, social welfare etc.) should be trained in prinicples and skills in the relevant areas of gerontology, geriatrics, psycho-geriatrics and geriatric nursing.

61. All too often, old age is an age of no consent. Decisions affecting aging citizens are frequently made without the participation of the citizens themselves. This applies particularly to those who are very old, frail or disabled. Such people should be served by flexible systems of care that give them a choice as to the type of amenities and the kind of care they receive.

Recommendation 8.—The control of the lives of the aging should not be left solely to health, social service and other caring personnel, since aging people themselves usually know best what is needed and how it should be carried out.

Recommendation 9.—Participation of the aged in the development of health care and the functioning of health services should be encouraged.

62. A fundamental principle in the care of the elderly should be to enable them to lead independent lives in the community for as long as possible.

Recommendation 10.—Health and health-allied services should be developed to the fullest extent possible in the community. These services should include a broad range of ambulatory services such as: day-care centres, out-patient clinics, day hospitals, medical and nursing care and domestic services. Emergency services should be always available. Institutional care should always be appropriate to the needs of the elderly. Inappropriate use of beds in health care facilities should be avoided. In particular, those not mentally ill should not be placed in mental hospitals. Health screening and counselling should be offered through geriatric clinics, neighbourhood health centres or community sites where older persons congregate. The necessary health infrastructure and specialized staff to provide thorough and complete geriatric care should be made available. In the case of institutional care, alienation through isolation of the aged from society should be avoided *inter alia* by further encouraging the involvement of family members and volunteers.

63. Nutritional problems, such as deficient quantity and inappropriate constituents, are encountered among the poor and underprivileged elderly in both the developed and the developing countries. Accidents are also a major risk area for the elderly. The alleviation of these problems may require a multisectoral approach.

Recommendation 11.—The promotion of health, the prevention of disease and the maintaining of functional capacities among elderly persons should be actively pursued. For this purpose, an assessment of the physical, psychological and social needs of the group concerned is a prerequisite. Such an assessment would enhance the prevention of disability, early diagnosis and rehabilitation.

Recommendation 12.—Adequate, appropriate and sufficient nutrition, particularly the adequate intake of protein, minerals and vitamins, is essential to the well-being of the elderly. Poor nutrition is exacerbated by poverty, isolation, maldistribution of food, and poor eating habits, including those due to dental problems. Therefore special attention should be paid to:

(a) Imrovement of the availability of sufficient foodstuffs to the elderly through appropriate schemes and encouraging the aged in rural areas to play an active role in food production;

(b) A fair and equitable distribution of food, wealth, resources and technology;

(c) Education of the public, including the elderly, in correct nutrition and eating habits, both in urban and rural areas;

(d) Provision of health and dental services for early detection of malnutrition and improvement of mastication;

(e) Studies of the nutritional status of the elderly at the community level, including steps to correct any unsatisfactory local conditions;

(f) Extension of research into the role of nutritional factors in the aging process to communities in developing countries.

Recommendation 13.—Efforts should be intensified to develop home care to provide high quality health and social services in the quantity necessary so that older persons are enable to remain in their own communities and to live as independently as possible for as long as possible. Home care should not be viewed as an alternative to institutional care; rather, the two are complementary to each other and should so link into the delivery system that older persons can receive the best care appropriate to their needs at the least cost.

Special support must be given to home care services, by providing them with sufficient medical, paramedical, nursing and technical facilities of the required standard to limit the need for hospitalization.

Recommendation 14.—A very important question concerns the possibilities of preventing or at least postponing the negative functional consequences of aging. Many life-style factors may have their most pronounced effects during old age when the reserve capacity usually is lower.

The health of the aging is fundamentally conditioned by their previous health and, therefore, life-long health care starting with young age is of paramount importance; this includes preventive health, nutrition, exercise, the avoidance of health-harming habits and attention to environmental factors, and this care should be continued.

Recommendation 15.—The health hazards of cumulative noxious substances—including radioactive and trace elements and other pollutions—assume a greater importance as life-spans increase and should, therefore, be the subject of special attention and investigation throughout the entire life-span.

Governments should promote the safe handling of such materials in use, and move rapidly to ensure that waste materials from such use are permanently and safely removed from man's biosphere.

Recommendation 16.—As avoidable accidents represent a substantial cost both in human suffering and in resources, priority should be given to measures to prevent accidents in the home, on the road, and those precipitated by treatable medical conditions or by inappropriate use of medication.

Recommendation 17.—International exchange and research co-operation should be promoted in carrying out epidemiological studies of local patterns of health and disease and their consequences together with investigating the validity of different care delivery systems, including self-care, and more care by nurses, and in particular of ways of achieving optimum programme effectiveness; also investigating the demands for various types of care and developing means of coping with them paying particular attention to comparative studies regarding the achievement of objectives and relative cost-effectiveness; and gathering data on the physical, mental and social profiles of aging individuals in various social and cultural contexts, including attention to the special problems of access to services in rural and remote areas, in order to provide a sound basis for future actions.

(b) Protection of elderly consumers

Recommendation 18.—Governments should:

(a) Ensure that food and household products, installations and equipment conform to standards of safety that take into account the vulnerability of the aged;

(b) Encourage the safe use of medications, household chemicals and other products by requiring manufacturers to indicate necessary warnings and instructions for use;

(c) Facilitate the availability of medications, hearing aids, dentures, glasses and other prosthetics to the elderly so that they can prolong their activities and independence;

(d) Restrain the intensive promotion and other marketing techniques primarily aimed at exploiting the meagre resources of the elderly.

Government bodies should co-operate with non-governmental organizations on consumer education programmes.

The international organizations concerned are urged to promote collective efforts by their Member States to protect elderly consumers.

(c) Housing and environment

64. Adequate living accommodation and agreeable physical surroundings are necessary for the well-being of all people, and it is generally accepted that housing has a great influence on the qual-

ity of life of any age group in any country. Suitable housing is even more important to the elderly, whose abodes are the centre of virtually all of their activities. Adaptations to the home, the provision of practical domestic aids to daily living and appropriately designed household equipment can make it easier for those elderly people whose mobility is restricted or who are otherwise disabled to continue to live in their own homes.

65. The elderly meet manifold problems in traffic and transport. Especially elderly pedestrians have to cope with objective or subjectively felt dangers that restrict and limit their mobility and participatory aspirations. The traffic circumstances should be adapted to older people instead of the other way around. Measures and facilities should include traffic education, speed limits especially in human settlements, traffic-safe environments, accommodations and means of transport, etc.

Recommendation 19.—Housing for the elderly must be viewed as more than shelter. In addition to the physical, it has psychological and social significance, which should be taken into account. To release the aged from dependence on others, national housing policies should pursue the following goals:

(a) Helping the aged to continue to live in their own homes as long as possible, provision being made for restoration and development and, where feasible and appropriate, the remodelling and improvement of homes, and their adaptation to match the ability of the aged to get to and from them and use the facilities;

(b) Planning and introducing—under a housing policy that also provides for public financing and agreements with the private sector—housing for the aged of various types to suit the status and degree of self-sufficiency of the aged themselves, in accordance with local tradition and customs;

(c) Co-ordinating policies on housing with those concerned with community services (social, health, cultural, leisure, communications) so as to secure, whenever possible, an especially favourable position for housing and aged vis-a-vis dwelling for the population at large;

(d) Evolve and apply special policies and measures, and make arrangements so as to allow the aged to move about and to protect them from traffic hazards;

(e) Such a policy should, in turn, form part of the broader policy of support for the least well-off sectors of the population.

Recommendation 20.—Urban rebuilding and development planning and law should pay special attention to the problems of the aging, assisting in securing their social integration.

Recommendation 21.—National Governments should be encouraged to adopt housing policies that take into account the needs of the elderly and the socially disadvantaged. A living environment designed to support the functional capacities of this group and the socially disadvantaged should be an integral part of national guidelines for human settlements policies and action.

Recommendation 22.—Special attention should be paid to environmental problems and to designing a living environment that would take into account the functional capacity of the elderly and facilitate mobility and communication through the provision of adequate means of transport.

The living environment should be designed, with support from Governments, local authorities and non-governmental organizations, so as to enable elderly people to continue to live, if they wish, in locations that are familiar to them, where their involvement in the community may be of long standing and where they will have the opportunity to lead a rich, normal and secure life.

Recommendation 23.—The growing incidence of crime in some countries against the elderly victimizes not only those directly involved, but the many older persons who become afraid to leave their homes. Efforts should be directed to law enforcement agencies and the elderly to increase their awareness of the extent and impact of crime against older persons.

Recommendation 24.—Whenever possible, the aging should be involved in housing policies and programmes for the elderly population.

(d) Family

66. The family, regardless of its form or organization, is recognized as a fundamental unit of society. With increasing longevity, four- and five-generation families are becoming common throughout the world. The changes in the status of women, however, have reduced their traditional role as caretakers of older family members; it is necessary to enable the family as a whole, including its male members, to take over and share the burden of help in and by the family. Women are entering and remaining in the labour force for longer periods of time. Many who have completed their child-rearing roles become caught between the desire and need to work and earn income and the responsibility of caring for elderly parents or grandparents.

Recommendation 25.—As the family is recognized as a fundamental unit of society, efforts should be made to support, protect and strengthen it in agreement with each society's system of cultural values and in responding to the needs of its aging members. Governments should promote social policies encouraging the maintenance of family solidarity among generations, with all members of the family participating. The role and contribution of the non-government organizations in strengthening the family as a unit should also be stressed at all levels.

Recommendation 26.—Appropriate support from the wider community, available when and where it is needed, can make a crucial difference to the willingness and ability of families to continue to care for elderly relatives. Planning and provision of services should take full account of the needs of those carers.

67. There is ample evidence of the high esteem in which older people are held in developing countries. Trends towards increasing industrialization and urbanization and greater mobility of the labour force indicate, however, that the traditional concept of the role of the elderly in the family is undergoing major change. World-wide, the over-all responsibility of the family to provide the traditional care and support needs of the aging is diminishing.

Recommendation 27.—Ways to ensure continuity of the vital role of the family and the dignity, status and security of the aging, taking into account all the internal and international events which might influence this status of security, are issues that deserve careful consideration and action by Governments and non-governmental organizations. Recognizing the predominance of older women, and the relatively greater numbers of widows than widowers throughout the world, particular consideration should be given to the special needs and roles of this group.

Recommendation 28.—Governments are urged to adopt an age/family-integrated approach to planning and development which would recognize the special needs and characteristics of older persons and their families. Older persons should be included in the governmental and other decisions-making processes in the political, social, cultural and educational areas among others, and children should be encouraged to support their parents.

Recommendation 29.—Governments and non-governmental bodies should be encouraged to establish social services to support the whole family when there are elderly people at home and to implement measures especially for low-income families who wish to keep elderly people at home.

(e) Social welfare

68. Social welfare services can be instruments of national policy and should have as their goal the maximizing of the social functioning of the aging. They should be community-based and provide a broad range of preventive, remedial and developmental services for the aging, to enable them to lead as independent a life as possible in their own home and in their community, remaining active and useful citizens.

69. In relation to elderly migrants appropriate measures should be taken to provide social services in accordance with their ethnic, cultural, linguistic and other characteristics.

Recommendation 30.—Social welfare services should have as their goal the creation, promotion and maintenance of active and useful roles for the elderly for as long as possible in and for the community.

70. In many countries where resources are scarce, thre is a general lack of organized social welfare services, particularly in the rural areas. Although the role of governments in providing such services is paramount, the contribution of non-governmental organizations is also of great importance.

71. In traditional societies, old people have always enjoyed a privileged position based on respect, consideration, status and authority. But this is starting to be upset under the influence of modern trends and that privileged position is now being questioned. It is therefore time to become aware of these changes and on that basis to define national aging policies that would avoid some of the problems concerning the elderly faced by some developed countries.

Recommendation 31.—Existing formal and informal organizations should consider the particular needs of the aging and allow for them in their programmes and future planning. The important role that co-operatives can play in providing services in this area should be recognized and encouraged. Such co-operatives could also benefit from the participation of elderly people as full members or consultants. A partnership should be formed between governments and non-governmental organizations designed to ensure a comprehensive, integrated, co-ordinated and multipurpose approach to meeting the social welfare needs of the elderly.

Recommendation 32.—The involvement of young people—in providing services and care and in participating in activities for and with the elderly—should be encouraged, with a view to promoting intergenerational ties. Mutual self-help among the able and active elderly should be stimulated to the extent possible, as should the assistance this group can provide to its less fortunate peers, and the involvement of the elderly in informal part-time occupations.

Recommendation 33.—Governments should endeavour to reduce or eliminate fiscal or other constraints on informal and voluntary activities, and eliminate or relax regulations which hinder or discourage part-time work, mutual self-help and the use of volunteers alongside professional staff in providing social services or in institutions for the elderly.

Recommendation 34.—Whenever institutionalization is necessary or inevitable for elderly persons, the utmost effort must be made to ensure a quality of institutional life corresponding to normal conditions in their communities, with full respect for their dignity, beliefs, needs, interests and privacy; States should be encouraged to define minimum standards to ensure higher quality of institutional care.

Recommendation 35.—In order to facilitate mutual help among the elderly and let their voices be heard, governments and non-governmental bodies should encourage the establishment and free initiative of groups and movements of elderly persons and also give other age groups opportunities for training in, and information on, the support of the elderly.

(f) Income security and employment

72. Major differences exist between the developed and the developing countries—and particularly between urban, industrialized and rural, agrarian economies—with regard to the achievement of policy goals related to income security and employment. Many developed countries have achieved universal coverage through generalized social security schemes. For the developing countries, where many if not the majority of persons, live at subsistence levels, income security is an issue of concern for all age groups. In several of these countries, the social security programmes launched tend to offer limited coverage: in the rural areas, where in many cases most of the population lives, there is little or no coverage. Furthermore, particular attention should be paid, in social security and social programmes, to the circumstances of the elderly women whose income is generally lower than men's and whose employment has often been broken up by maternity and family responsibilities. In the long term, policies should be directed towards providing social insurance for women in their own right.

Recommendation 36.—Governments should take apppropriate action to ensure to all older persons an appropriate minimum income, and should develop their economies to benefit all the population. To this end, they should:

(a) Create or develop social security schemes based on the principle of universal coverage for older people. Where this is not feasible, other approaches should be tried, such as payment of benefits in kind, or direct assistance to families and local co-operative institutions;

(b) Ensure that the minimum benefits will be enough to meet the essential needs of the elderly and guarantee their independence. Whether or not social security payments are calculated taking into account previous income, efforts should be made to maintain their purchasing power. Ways should be explored to protect the savings of the elderly against the effects of inflation. In determining the age at which pensions are payable, due account should be taken of the age of retirement, changes in the national demographic structure and of the national economic capacity. At the same time, efforts should be made to achieve continuous economic growth;

(c) In social security systems, make it possible for women as well as men to acquire their own rights;

(d) Within the social security system and if necessary by other means, respond to the special needs of income security for older workers who are unemployed or those who are incapable of working;

(e) Other possibilities of making available supplementary retirement income and incentives to develop new means of personal savings for the elderly should be explored.

73. Broadly related to the issues of income security are the dual issues of the right to work and the right to retire. In most areas of the world, efforts by older persons to participate in work and economic activities which will satisfy their need to contribute to the life of the community and benefit society as a whole meet with difficulties. Age discrimination is prevalent: many older workers are unable to remain in the labour force or to re-enter it because of age prejudice. In some countries this situation tends to impact women more severely. The integration of the aged into the machinery of development affects both the urban and rural population groups.

Recommendation 37.—Governments should facilitate the participation of older persons in the economic life of the society. For that purpose:

(a) Appropriate measures should be taken, in collaboration with employers' and workers' organizations, to ensure to the maximum extent possible that older workers can continue to work under satisfactory conditions and enjoy security of employment;

(b) Governments should eliminate discrimination in the labour market and ensure equality of treatment in professional life. Negative stereotypes about older workers exist among some employers. Governments should take steps to educate employers and employment counsellors about the capabilities of older workers, which remain quite high in most occupations. Older workers should also enjoy equal access to orientation, training and placement facilities and services;

(c) Measures should be taken to assist older persons to find or return to independent employment by creating new employment possibilities and facilitating training or retraining. The right of older workers to employment should be based on ability to perform the work rather than chronological age.

(d) Despite the significant unemployment problems facing many nations, in particular with regard to young people, the retirement age for employees should not be lowered except on a voluntary basis.

Recommendation 38.—Older workers, like all other workers, should enjoy satisfactory working conditions and environment. Where necessary, measures should be taken to prevent industrial and agricultural accidents and occupational diseases. Working conditions and the working environment, as well as the scheduling and organization of work, should take into account the characteristics of older workers.

Recommendation 39.—Proper protection for workers, which permits better follow-up for people of advanced age, comes about through a better knowledge of occupational diseases. This necessarily entails training medical staff in occupational medicine.

Similarly, pre-retirement medical checks would allow the effects of occupational disease upon the individual to the detected and appropriate steps to be planned.

Recommendation 40.—Governments should take or encourage measures that will ensure a smooth and gradual transition from active working life to retirement, and in addition make the age of entitlement to a pension more flexible. Such measures would include pre-retirement courses and lightening the work-load during the last years of the working life, for example by modifying the conditions of work and the working environment of the work organization and by promoting a gradual reduction of work-time.

Recommendation 41.—Governments should apply internationally adopted standards concerning older workers, particularly those embodied in Recommendation 162 of the International Labour Organization. In addition, at the international level, approaches and guidelines concerning the special needs of these workers should continue to be developed.

Recommendation 42.—In the light of ILO Convention No. 157 concerning maintenance of social security rights, measures should be taken, particularly through bilateral or multilateral conventions, to guarantee to legitimate migrant workers full social coverage in the receiving country as well as maintenance of social security rights acquired, especially regarding pensions, if they return to their country of origin. Similarly, migrant workers returning to their countries should be afforded special conditions facilitating their reintegration, particularly with regard to housing.

Recommendation 43.—As far as possible, groups of refugees accepted by a country should include elderly persons as well as adults and children, and efforts should be made to keep family groups intact and to ensure that appropriate housing and services are provided.

(g) Education

74. The scientific and technological revolutions of the twentieth century have led to a knowledge and information "explosion". The continuing and expanding nature of these revolutions has given rise also to accelerated social change. In many of the world's soci-

eties, the elderly still serve as the transmitters of information, knowledge, tradition and spiritual values: this important tradition should not be lost.

Recommendation 44.—Educational programmes featuring the elderly as the teachers and transmitters of knowledge, culture and spiritual values should be developed.

75. In many instances, the knowledge explosion is resulting in information obsolescence, with, in turn, implications of social obsolescence. These changes suggest that the educational structures of society must be expanded to respond to the educational needs of an entire life-span. Such an approach to education would suggest the need for continuous adult education, including preparation for aging and the creative use of time. In addition, it is important that the aging, along with the other age groups, have access to basic literacy education, as well as to all education facilities available in the community.

Recommendation 45.—As a basic human right, education must be made available without discrimination against the elderly. Educational policies should reflect the principle of the right to education of the aging, through the appropriate allocation of resources and in suitable education programmes. Care should be taken to adapt educational methods to the capacities of the elderly, so that they may participate equitably in and profit from any education provided. The need for continuing adult education at all levels should be recognized and encouraged. Consideration should be given to the idea of university education for the elderly.

76. There is also a need to educate the general public with regard to the aging process. Such education must start at an early age in order tht aging should be fully understood as a natural process. The importance of the role of the mass media in this respect cannot be overstated.

Recommendation 46.—A co-ordinated effort by the mass media should be undertaken to highlight the positive aspects of the aging process and of the aging themselves. This effort should cover, among other things:

(a) The present situation of the aged, in particular in rural areas of developed and developing countries, with a view to identifying and responding to their real needs;

(b) The effects of migration (both internal and international) on the relative aging of populations of rural areas, and its effects on agricultural production and living conditions in these areas;

(c) Methods to develop job opportunities for and adapt conditions of work to older workers. This would include developing or furnishing simple equipment and tools which would help those with limited physical strength to accomplish their assigned tasks;

(d) Surveys of the role of education and aging in various cultures and societies.

Recommendation 47.—In accordance with the concept of life-long education promulgated by the United Nations Educational, Scientific and Cultural Organization (UNESCO), informal, community-based and recreational-oriented programmes for the aging should be promoted in order to help them develop a sense of self-reliance and community responsibility. Such programmes should enjoy the support a national Governments and international organizations.

Recommendation 48.—Governments and international organizations should support programmes aimed at providing the elderly with easier physical access to cultural institutions censuses, surveys or vital statistics systems—are essential for the formulation, application and evaluation of policies and programmes for the elderly and for ensuring their integration in the development process.

79. Governments and organizations that are in a position to do so should develop an information base which would be more specific than the "sixty-and-over" one now in use and which would be of help in planning the development of and solving problems concerning the elderly. The base could cover social, age, functional and economic classifications, among others.

80. Household sample and other surveys and other sources of demographic and related socio-economic statistics provide important data for use in formulating and implementing policies and programmes for the elderly.

81. All countries that so request should be provided with the technical assistance needed to develop or improve data bases relating to their elderly and the services and institutions that concern them. The assistance should cover training and research in methodologies for collecting, processing and analysing data.

Recommendation 52.—Data concerning the aging could be developed along the line of a codification system which will give national Governments information tabulated by sex, age, income levels, living arrangements, health status and degree of self care, among others. Such data could be collected through the census, micro or pilot census or representative surveys. Governments are urged to allocate resources for that purpose.

Recommendation 53.—Governments and institutions concerned should establish or improve existing information exchange facilities, such as data banks in the field of aging.

2. Training and education

82. The dramatic increase in the number and proportion of older adults calls for a significant increase in training. A dual approach is needed: an international programme for training concomitant with national and regional training programmes that are particularly relevant in the countries and regions concerned. The needs of the elderly, as well as the implications of the aging of the population for development, need to be taken into account in developing education and training policies and programmes for all ages, especially the younger generation.

Recommendation 54.—Education and training programmes should be interdisciplinary in nature, as aging and the aging of the population is a multidisciplinary issue. Education and training in the various aspects of aging and the aging of the population should not be restricted to high levels of specialization, but should be made available at all levels. Efforts should be made to regulate the training skills and educational requirements for different functions in the field of aging.

83. The exchange of skills, knowledge and experience among countries with similar or comparable structures and composition, or having historical, cultural, linguistic or other links, with respect to their aging population would be a particularly fertile form of international co-operation. Besides the transfer of specific skills and technologies, the exchange of experience regarding the wide array of practices relating to aging could also constitute an area for technical co-operation among developing countries. In regions which include both developed and developing countries side by side, the rich opportunities for mutual learning and co-operation in training and research should be vigorously explored.

Recommendation 55.—Intergovernmental and non-governmental organizations should take the necessary measures to develop trained personnel in the field of aging, and should strengthen their efforts to disseminate information on aging, and particularly to the aging themselves.

Recommendation 56.—Retirees' and elderly people's organizations should be involved in planning and carrying out such exchanges of information.

Recommendation 57.—The implementation of several recommendations will require trained personnel in the field of aging. Practical training centers should be promoted and encouraged, where appropriate facilities already exist, to train such personnel, especially from developing countries, who would in their turn train others. These centers would also provide updating and refresher courses and act as a practical bridge between and among developed and developing regions; they would be linked with appropriate United Nations agencies and facilities.

Recommendation 58.—At national, regional and international levels, extra attention should be given to research and study undertaken in support of integrating the problems of aging in planning and policy formulation and management.

Recommendation 59.—Training in all aspects of gerontology and geriatrics should be encouraged and given due prominence at all levels in all educational programmes. Governments and competent authorities are called upon to encourage new or existing institutions to pay special attention to approriate training in gerontology and geriatrics.

3. Research

84. The Plan of Action gives high priority to research related to developmental and humanitarian aspects of aging. Research activities are instrumental in formulating, evaluating and implementing policies and programmes: (a) as to the implications of the aging of the population for development and (b) as to the needs of the aging. Research into the social, economic and health aspects of aging should be encouraged to achieve efficient uses of resources, improvement in social and health measures, including the prevention of functional decline, age-related disabilities, illness and poverty, and co-ordination of the services involved in the care of the aging.

85. The knowledge obtained by research provides scientific backing for a sounder basis for effective societal planning as well as for improving the well-being of the elderly. Further research is required, e.g. (a) to narrow the wide gaps in knowledge about aging

and about the particular needs of the aging, and (b) to enable resources provided for the aging to be used more effectively. There should be emphasis on the continuum of research from the discovery of new knowledge with due consideration of cultural and social diversity.

Recommendation 60.—Research should be conducted into the developmental and humanitarian aspects of aging at local, national, regional and global levels. Research should be encouraged particularly in the biological, mental and social fields. Issues of basic and applied research of universal interest to all societies include:

(a) The role of genetic and environmental factors;

(b) The impact of biological, medical, cultural, societal and behavioural factors on aging;

(c) The influence of economic and demographic factors (including migration) on societal planning;

(d) The use of skills, expertise, knowledge and cultural potential of the aging;

(e) The postponement of negative functional consequences of aging;

(f) Health and social services for the aging as well as studies of coordindate programmes;

(g) Training and education.

Such research should be generally planned and carried out by researchers closely acquainted with national and regional conditions, being granted the independence necessary for innovation and diffusion. States, intergovernmental organizations and non-governmental organizations should carry our more research and studies on the developmental and humanitarian aspects of aging, cooperate in this field and exchange their findings in order to provide a logical basis for policies related to aging in general.

Recommendation 61.—States, intergovernmental organizations and non-governmental organizations should encourage the establishment of institutions specializing in the teaching of gerontology, geriatrics and geriatric psychology in countries where such institutions do not exist.

Recommendation 62.—International exchange and research cooperation as well as data collection should be promoted in all fields having a bearing on aging, in order to provide a rational basis for future social policies and action. Special emphasis should be placed on comparative and crosscultural studies on aging. Interdisciplinary approaches should be stressed.

IV. RECOMMENDATIONS FOR IMPLEMENTATION

A. ROLE OF GOVERNMENTS

86. The success of this Plan of Action will depend largely on action undertaken by Governments to create conditions and broad possibilities for full participation of the citizens, particularly the elderly. To this end, Governments are urged to devote more attention to the question of aging and to utilize fully the support provided by intergovernmental and non-governmental organizations, including retirees' and elderly people's organizations.

87. Since wide divergencies exist with respect to the situation of the aging in various societies, cultures and regions—as reflected in different needs and problems—each country should decide upon its own national strategy and identify its own targets and priorities within the Plan. A clear commitment should be made at all levels of Government to take appropriate action to achieve those targets and give effect to those priorities.

88. Governments can play an important role with regard to the Plan of Action by evaluating and assessing the aging process from the individual and demographic points of view, in order to determine the implications for development of these processes in the light of the prevailing political, social, cultural, religious and economic situation.

89. The architects of national policies and strategies for the implementation of the Plan of Action should recognize that the aging are not a homogeneous group and be sensitive to the wide differences and needs of the aging at various stages of their lives. Governments should pay special attention to improving the lot of elderly women, who are often at a severe disadvantage.

90. The establishment of interdisciplinary and multisectoral machinery within Governments can be an effective means of ensuring that the question of the aging of the population is taken into account in national development planning, that the needs of the elderly are given the attention they merit, and that the elderly are fully integrated into society.

91. These actions will gain in effectiveness if their preparation, implementation and follow-up are well coordinated at various geopolitical levels. The coordination must flow from cooperation between those in positions of responsibility in all sectors and the representatives of pensioners and the aged, in order to ensure the participation of the latter when decisions of direct concern to them are being taken. Hence, it would be appropriate to consider the setting up of corresponding planning, programming and coordinating bodies at the national level.

92. In certain countries, some of the objectives of the Plan of Action have already been achieved; in others they may only be accomplished progressively. Moreover, by their very nature, some measures will take longer to implement than others. Governments are urged, therefore, to establish short-, medium- and long-term objectives with a view to facilitating implementation of the Plan, in the light of their resources and priorities.

93. Governments should, if necessary, retain in a suitable form (or encourage the formation of) the mechanisms established at the national level to prepare for the World Assembly on Aging, in order to be ready to facilitate the planning, implementation and evaluation of the activities recommended by the World Assembly.

B. ROLE OF INTERNATIONAL AND REGIONAL CO-OPERATION

1. Global action

94. International co-operation in the implementation of the programme of action on the establishment *inter alia* of a new international economic order and of the International Development Strategy for the Third United Nations Development Decade, based on the

peaceful co-existence of States having different social systems, is essential to achieving the goals of the Plan of Action and can take the form of bilateral and multilateral co-operation between Governments and by utilizing the United Nations system. Such co-operation could take the form of direct assistance (technical or financial), in response to national or regional requests, co-operative research, or the exchange of information and experience.

95. The General Assembly, the Economic and Social Council and all its appropriate subsidiary bodies, in particular the Commission for Social Development, the Governing Council of the United Nations Development Programme, and the legislative and policy-making bodies of the concerned specialized agencies and intergovernmental organizations are urged to give careful consideration to the Plan of Action and to ensure an appropriate response to it.

96. In view of the role that the Centre for Social Development and Humanitarian Affairs of the Department of International Economic and Social Affairs has been playing within the United Nations system in matters related to the aging, it should be strengthened in order to continue to serve as the focal point for activities in that respect; to this end the Secretary-General of the United Nations is requested, within the existing global resources of the United Nations, to give due consideration to the provision of appropriate increased resources for the implementation of the Plan of Action, which will be primarily at the national level.

97. The Administrative Committee on Co-ordination should consider the implications of the Plan of Action for the United Nations system with a view to continued liaison and co-ordination in implementing the provisions of the Plan.

98. The need to develop new guidelines in areas of concern to the elderly should be kept constantly under review in relation to the implementation of the Plan.

99. Governments, national and local non-governmental voluntary organizations and international non-governmental organizations are urged to join in the co-operative effort to accomplish the objectives of the Plan. They should strengthen their activities by encouraging the formation of and utilizing regular channels of communication at the national level for consulting with the elderly on policies and programmes that affect their lives. Governments are also urged to encourage and, where possible, support national and private organizations dealing with matters concerning the elderly and the aging of the population.

100. All States are invited to consider designating a national "Day for the Aging" in conformity with General Assembly resolution 36/20 of 9 November 1981.

101. The International Plan of Action on Aging should be brought to the attention of the appropriate United Nations bodies responsible for preparations for the International Conference on Population (1984), so that its conclusions and recommendations could be taken into account in preparing the proposals for the further implementation of the World Population Plan of Action.

(a) Technical co-operation

102. The United Nations, and in particular the United Nations Development Programme and the Department of Technical Co-op-

eration for Development, together with the specialized agencies, should carry out technical co-operation activities in support of the objectives of the Plan of Action. The Centre for Social Development and Humanitarian Affairs should continue to promote, and provide substantive support to, all such activities.

103. The voluntary Trust Fund for the World Assembly on Aging, established by General Assembly resolution 35/129, should be used, as requested by the General Assembly, to meet the rapidly increasing needs of the aging in the developing countries, in particular in the least developed ones. The payment of voluntary public and private contribution should be encouraged. The Trust Fund should be administered by the Centre for Social Development and Humanitarian Affairs.

104. Furthermore, as requested by the General Assembly in its resolution 36/20, the Fund should be used to encourage greater interest in the developing countries in matters related to aging and to assist the Governments of these countries, at their request, in formulating and implementing policies and programmes for the elderly. It should also be used for technical co-operation and research related to the aging of populations and for promoting co-operation among developing countries in the exchange of the relevant information and technology.

105. Aging is a population issue which affects development and which requires increasing international assistance and co-operation and, therefore, the United Nations Fund for Population Activities is urged, in co-operation with all organizations responsible for international population assistance, to continue and to strengthen its assistance in that field, particularly in developing countries.

(b) Exchange of information and experience

106. The exchange of information and experience at the international level is an effective means of stimulating progress and encouraging the adoption of measures to respond to the economic and social implications of the aging of the population, and to meet the needs of older persons. Countries with different political, economic and social systems and cultures and at different stages of development have benefited from the common knowledge of problems, difficulties and achievements and from solutions worked out jointly.

107. Meetings and seminars have proved to be most valuable in providing a regional and international exchange of information and experience and should be continued. These could focus, *inter alia,* on promoting technical co-operation among developing countries and on monitoring the implementation of the Plan of Action.

108. The Centre for Social Development and Humanitarian Affairs should co-ordinate the activities of regional and subregional research and development centres in the United Nations system, promote the preparation of information materials, as well as the constant exchange of information on problems and policies related to aging and the training of personnel, and facilitate activities related to technical co-operation among developing countries in collaboration with concerned Governments and regions.

109. With respect to the exchange of information about matters concerning aging, it is essential that standardized definitions,

terms and research methodologies be developed, the United Nations should treat these matters with all due importance.

110. The United Nations bodies concerned should encourage Governments and the international community to pay special attention to developing programmes, projects and activities that will give older persons the skills, training, and opportunties necessary to improve their situation and enable them to participate fully and effectively in the total development effort. Special attention should be given to training courses in technologies that will enable older persons to continue to work in agriculture.

111. The International Plan of Action on Aging should be transmitted to the unit in the United Nations Secretariat responsible for International Youth Year (1985) in order that that unit may bring the recommendations and conclusions of the World Assembly on Aging—particularly as they relate to intergenerational matters—to the attention of national planning committees concerned with developing ideas for the Youth Year.

(c) Formulation and implementation of international guidelines

112. The appropriate organizations should undertake studies on and review periodically the effectiveness of existing international guidelines and instruments related to the subject of aging, in order to determine their adequacy in the light of changing conditions in the modern work and the experience gained since their adoption.

2. Regional action

113. Effective implementation of the Plan will also require action at the regional level. All institutions having regional mandates are therefore called upon to review the objectives of the Plan and contribute to their implementation. In this respect, a central role should be played by the United Nations regional commissions.

114. In order to carry out the above-mentioned functions, Governments members of regional commissions should take steps to ensure that their regular programme of activities take into account the problems of aging.

115. Furthermore, in co-ordination with the conduct of the international review discussed above, the regional commission should organize the periodic review of regional plans.

C. ASSESSMENT REVIEW AND APPRAISAL

116. It is essential that assessment, evaluation and review should take place at the national level, at intervals to be determined by each country.

117. Regional appraisal and review should focus on the special role regional action can play and the particular advantages it can offer in such fields as training, research and technical co-operation among developing countries.

118. It is recommended that the Commission for Social Development should be designated the intergovernmental body to review the implementation of the Plan of Action every four years to make proposals for updating the Plan as considered necessary. The findings of this exercise should be transmitted through the Economic

and Social Council to the General Assembly for consideration. To assist the Commission in its work it should be provided with periodic reports on progress made within the United Nations system in achieving the goals and objectives of the Plan. The Centre for Social Development and Humanitarian Affairs should serve as the co-ordinator of this process.

Appendix D
Federal Educational Programs Serving Older Adults

Adapted from *Education and Training for Older Persons: A Program Guide*. Washington, D.C.: U.S. Department of Education, Office of Vocational and Adult Education, March 1981.

Department of Education

Program	Description	Legislative Authority
Office of Bilingual Education: Bilingual Education	Bilingual adult education programs; personnel development; planning and technical assistance; research and development.	Bilingual Education Act
Office of Career Education: Career Education	To make education as preparation for work a major goal of all who teach and all who learn by increasing the emphasis on career awareness, exploration, decision making and planning, and to do so in a manner to create equal opportunity.	Career Education Incentive Act
Office of Consumer Education: Consumer Education	Consumer education programs, curriculum development, demonstration projects, dissemination, preservice and inservice training, auxiliary services.	Consumer Education Act of 1978
Office of Environmental Education: Environmental Education	Environmental education programs; curriculum development; dissemination; preservice/inservice training; planning of outdoor ecological study centers; community education programs on environmental quality; preparation and distribution of materials.	Environmental Education Act of 1978
Office of Vocational and Adult Education: Vocational Education Basic Grants to States	Vocational education programs, work study programs, cooperative vocational education programs, energy education, placement services, industrial arts, support services for women, research, exemplary and innovative programs, curriculum development, vocational guidance and counseling, vocational education personnel training grants to overcome bias.	Vocational Education Act as amended, Subparts 2 and 3

Vocational Education Consumer and Homemaking	Consumer education, food and nutrition, family living and parenthood education, child development and guidance, housing and home management, clothing and textiles, and supportive auxiliary services.	Vocational Education Act as amended, Part A, Subpart 5
Bilingual Vocational Education	Bilingual vocational training programs and training allowances for program participants.	Vocational Education Act as amended, Part B, Subpart 3
Adult Education Grants to States	Education and training programs to assist adults in acquiring functional basic skills, completing secondary school and in becoming more employable, productive, and responsible citizens.	Adult Education Act as amended, Education Amendments of 1978, Title XIII, Part A, Adult Education
Discretionary Grants	Research, development, evaluation, and dissemination; special projects for elderly; programs for adult Indians; Indochina adult refugees, and adult immigrants.	Adult Education Act as amended, Education Amendments of 1978, Title XIII, Part A, Adult Education
Office Unspecified: Law-Related Education	Law-related education programs for non-lawyers; curriculum development; pilot and demonstration projects; dissemination; preservice and inservice training; involvement of law-related organizations/agencies/personnel.	Law-Related Education Act of 1978
Older Reader Services	Conduct of special library programs for elderly; purchase of special materials; provision of in-home visits by librarians; outreach services; provision of transportation; employment of elderly; training of librarians to work with elderly.	Library Services and Construction Act, as amended, Title IV

Department of Education (continued)

Program	Description	Legislative Authority
Office Unspecified (continued):		
Student Financial Aid and Student Loans	'Pell grants' and supplemental educational opportunity grants (10% of institutional allocations may be used for less-than-half-time students who are otherwise eligible).	Higher Education Act of 1965, as amended, Title IV, Student Assistance
	Special services to disadvantaged including basic education skills, counseling, tutorial services; exposure to career options; provision of education and financial aid information through educational opportunity centers, staff development.	
	Guaranteed and insured student loans.	
Women's Educational Equity	Demonstration, development, and dissemination activities that increase full participation of women in American society; guidance and counseling; activities to increase opportunities for unemployed and underemployed women; expansion of improvement of educational programs for women in vocational and career education.	Women's Educational Equity Act of 1978
Community Schools	Educational, cultural, recreational, health care, use of school facilities for community activities; preventive health, dental care and nutrition; special programs for older persons; services for handicapped or other health impaired clients; rehabilitation purposes; improved relations between schools and communities; leisure education.	Community Schools and Comprehensive Community Education Act of 1978

Continuing Education	Continuing education programs; removal of barriers caused by rural isolation; provision of legal, vocational, and health educational services; educational and occupational information and counseling services; dissemination of information on educational opportunities; community education activities; provision of postsecondary education to older individuals as well as other educational needs which have been inadequately served; services to women at the place of employment.	Higher Education Act as amended, Title I, Part B, Education Outreach Programs
Correction Education	Demonstration projects providing academic and vocational education to correction inmates.	Correction Education Demonstration Project Act of 1978
Federal Discretionary	Develop and evaluate innovative delivery systems to increase access of under-served adults; expand range of education and community resources used; stimulate and evaluate creative approaches to removal of access barriers; provide preservice and inservice training.	Higher Education Act as amended, Title I, Part B, Education Outreach Programs
Health Education	Health education programs to promote physical health and well-being and to prevent illness and disease.	Health Education Act of 1978

Department of Health and Human Services

Program	Description	Legislative Authority
Administration on Aging		
Nutrition Services	Establishment and operation of projects providing for congregate and/or home delivery of meals, including nutrition education and other supportive services.	Older Americans Act of 1965, as amended, Title III, Part C
Social Services	Provides funds for social services which may include continuing education; information and referral; personnel counseling; health education; consumer education; household management training; recreational arts and crafts; community education programs and services; legal services; home repair programs; pre-retirement and second career counseling; operation of multipurpose senior centers.	Older Americans Act of 1965, as amended, Title III, Part B
Training	Payment in whole or in part for short-term and in-service training courses, workshops, institutes, and other personnel development activities; conduct of seminars, conferences, symposiums, and workshops in field of aging; fellowships and stipends for post-secondary education and training courses preparing personnel for field of aging; preparation of curriculum materials; projects and activities designed to attract qualified persons to field of aging.	Older Americans Act of 1965, as amended, Title IV-A
Discretionary Projects and Programs	Projects that provide continuing education to older individuals to broaden their educational, cultural, and social awareness; pre-retirement education; social services for physically and mentally impaired older individuals; for the unmet needs of special populations of older persons; for operations of senior ambulatory care day centers offering health, therapeutic, education, nutrition, recreational, rehabilitation, and social services.	Older Americans Act of 1965, as amended, Title IV-C

Office of Human Development Services:		
Public Social Services	Provides funding for social and employment services for eligible older persons. Services must be included in State Title XX Plan in order to be funded.	Social Services Amendments of 1974
Rehabilitative Services Administration:		
Rehabilitation Services and Facilities Basic Support	Provides funding for provision of vocational training and supportive services to eligible older individuals.	Rehabilitation Act of 1972
Vocational Rehabilitation Service for Social Security Disability Beneficiaries		

Department of Labor

Program	Description	Legislative Authority
Bureau of International Labor Affairs:		
Trade Adjustment Assistance for Workers	Provides reimbursement for training costs and other employment services provided workers who are totally or partially unemployed because of increased imports	Trade Adjustment Assistance Act of 1974
Employment and Training Administration:		
Senior Community Service Employment Program	Provides funds for subsidized part-time community service for disadvantaged older persons as well as for transportation services and administrative costs.	Older Americans Act of 1965, as amended, Title V
Services for Older Workers	Programs to assist older workers in overcoming employment barriers; upgrading their skills; removing age stereotyping; and developing appropriate job opportunities.	Comprehensive Employment and Training Act, as amended, Title II, Part B, Sec. 215
Special Projects for Middle-aged and Older Workers	Payment of tuition and costs for second career programs to assess skill and work experience for purposes of formulating realistic second career objectives; provide second career and occupational upgrading counseling; assist in formulating second career objectives; and train for second career objectives.	Comprehensive Employment and Training Act, as amended, Title III, Section 308

Miscellaneous

Program	Description	Legislative Authority
Action:		
Foster Grandparents, Senior Companions and Retired Senior Volunteer Programs	*Foster Grandparents* provides stipend for low-income older persons who provide volunteer supportive services to children with special needs.	Domestic Volunteer Services Act of 1973
	Senior Companion program provides stipend for senior volunteers who serve as senior companions for elderly in residential and non-residential group care facilities.	
	Retired Senior Volunteers encourages the use of retired senior volunteers in a variety of community service activities.	
Community Services Administration:		
Senior Opportunities and Services Program	Funding for information and referral, residential repair and renovation, outreach activities, and operation of senior centers.	Community Services Act of 1974, Title II, Part B
Department of Commerce, Economic Development Administration:		
Public Works	Funds for construction of and/or renovation and improvements of senior centers.	Local Public Works Development and Investment Act, Title I
Department of Commerce, Small Business Administration:		
Service Corps of Retired Executives	Provides access to a pool of senior volunteers with business experience.	Unspecified

Appendix E
Education Amendments of 1976: The Lifelong Learning Act

Source: U.S. Code Congressional and Administrative News, Laws of 94th Congress, 2nd session, 1976, 90 Stat. 2086–2089.

P.L. 94–482

"PART B—LIFELONG LEARNING

"FINDINGS

20 USC 1015. "Sec. 131. The Congress finds that—

"(1) accelerating social and technological change have had impact on the duration and quality of life;

"(2) the American people need lifelong learning to enable them to adjust to social, technological, political and economic changes;

"(3) lifelong learning has a role in developing the potential of all persons including improvement of their personal well-being, upgrading their workplace skills, and preparing them to participate in the civic, cultural, and political life of the Nation;

"(4) lifelong learning is important in meeting the needs of the growing number of older and retired persons;

"(5) learning takes place through formal and informal instruction, through educational programs conducted by public and private educational and other institutions and organizations, through independent study, and through the efforts of business, industry, and labor;

"(6) planning is necessary at the national, State, and local levels to assure effective use of existing resources in the light of changing characteristics and learning needs of the population;

"(7) more effective use should be made of the resources of the Nation's educational institutions in order to assist the people of the United States in the solution of community problems in areas such as housing, poverty, government, recreation, employment, youth opportunities, transportation, health, and land use; and

"(8) American society should have as a goal the availability of appropriate opportunities for lifelong learning for all its citizens without regard to restrictions of previous education or training, sex, age, handicapping condition, social or ethnic background, or economic circumstances.

"SCOPE OF LIFELONG LEARNING

"Sec 132. Lifelong learning includes, but is not limited to, adult basic education, continuing education, independent study, agricultural education, business education and labor education, occupational education and job training programs, parent education, postsecondary education, preretirement and education for older and retired people, remedial education, special educational programs for groups or for individuals with special needs, and also educational activities designed to upgrade occupational and professional skills, to assist business, public agencies, and other organizations in the use or innovation and research results, and to serve family needs and personal development.

"LIFELONG LEARNING ACTIVITIES

"Sec. 133. (a) The Assistant Secretary shall carry out, from funds appropriated pursuant to section 101(b), a program of planning, assessing, and coordinating projects related to lifelong learning. In carrying out the provisions of this section, the Assistant Secretary shall—

"(1) foster improved coordination of Federal support for lifelong learning programs;

"(2) act as a clearinghouse for information regarding lifelong learning, including the identification, collection, and dissemination to educators and the public of existing and new information regarding lifelong learning programs which are or may be carried out and supported by any department or agency of the Federal Government:

"(3) review present and proposed methods of financing and administering lifelong learning, to determine—

"(A) the extent to which each promotes lifelong learning,

"(B) program and administrative features of each that contribute to serving lifelong learning,

"(C) the need for additional Federal support for lifelong learning, and

"(D) procedures by which Federal assistance to lifelong learning may be better applied and coordinated to achieve the purpose of this title;

"(4) review the lifelong learning opportunities provided through employers, unions, the media, libraries, and museums, secondary schools and postsecondary educational institutions, and other public and private organizations to determine means by which the enhancement of their effectiveness and coordination may be facilitated;

"(5) review existing major foreign lifelong learning programs and related programs in order to determine the applicability of such programs in this country;

"(6) identify existing barriers to lifelong learning and evaluate programs designed to eliminate such barriers; and

"(7) to the extent practicable, seek the advice and assistance of the agencies of the Education Division (including the Office of Education, the National Institute of Education, the Fund for the Improvement of Postsecondary Education, and the National Center for Education Statistics), other agencies of the Federal Government, public advisory groups (including the National Advisory Councils on Extension and Continuing Education, Adult Education, Career Education, Community Education, and Vocational Education), Commissions (including the National Commission on Libraries and Information Sciences and the National Commission on Manpower Policy), State agencies, and such other persons or organizations as may be appropriate, in carrying out the Commissioner's responsibilities, and make maximum use of information and studies already available.

The review required by clause (3) of this subsection shall include—

"(i) a comparative assessment of domestic and foreign tax and other incentives to encourage increased commitment to business and labor;

"(ii) a study of alternatives such as lifelong learning entitlement programs or educational vouchers designed to assist adults to undertake education or training in conjunction with, or in periods alternative to employment;

"(iii) review of possible modifications to existing Federal and State student assistance programs necessary to increase their relevance to the lifelong learning needs of all adults;

"(iv) the organization and design of funding for pre- and post-retirement training and education for the elderly; and

"(v) modifications to Federal and State manpower training, public employment, unemployment compensation, and similar funding programs so as to better facilitate lifelong education and training and retraining, for employment.

"(b) After consultation with appropriate State agencies, the Assistant Secretary is authorized—

"(1) to assist in the planning and assessment, to determine whether in each State there is an equitable distribution of lifelong learning services to all segments of the adult population;

"(2) to assist in assessing the appropriate roles for the Federal, State, and local governments, educational institutions and community organizations; and

"(3) to assist in considering alternative methods of financing and delivering lifelong learning opportunities, including—

"(A) identification of State agencies, institutions, and groups that plan and provide programs of lifelong learning,

"(B) determination of the extent to which programs are available geographically,

"(C) a description of demographic characteristics of the population served,

"(D) analysis of reasons for attendance in programs of lifelong learning, and

"(E) analysis of sources of funds for the conduct of lifelong learning programs, and the financial support of persons attending programs of lifelong learning.

"(c) The Assistant Secretary is authorized, with respect to lifelong learning, to assess, evaluate the need for, demonstrate, and develop alternative methods to improve—

"(1) research and development activities;

"(2) training and retraining people to become educators of adults;

"(3) development of curricula and delivery systems appropriate to the needs of any such programs;

"(4) development of techniques and systems for guidance and counseling of adults and for training and retraining of counselors;

"(5) development and dissemination of instructional materials appropriate to adults;

"(6) assessment of the educational needs and goals of older and retired persons and their unique contributions to lifelong learning programs;

"(7) use of employer and union tuition assistance and other educational programs, education and cultural trust funds and other similar educational benefits resulting from collective bargaining agreements, and other private funds for the support of lifelong learning;

"(8) integration of public and private educational funds which encourage participation in lifelong learning, including support of guidance and counseling of workers in order that they can make best use of funds available to them for lifelong learning opportunities; and

"(9) coordination within communities among educators, employers, labor organizations, and other appropriate individuals and entities to assure that lifelong learning opportunities are designed to meet projected career and occupational needs of the community, after consideration of the availability of guidance and counseling, the availability of information regarding occupational and career opportunities, and the availability of appropriate educational and other resources to meet the career and occupational needs of the community.

"(d) In carrying out the provisions of this section the Assistant Secretary is authorized to enter into agreements with, and to make grants to, appropriate State agencies, institutions of higher education, and public and private nonprofit organizations.

"(e) In carrying out the provisions of this section, the Assistant Secretary shall issue reports summarizing research and analysis conducted pursuant to this section, and shall develop the resources and capability to analyze and make recommendations regarding specific legislative or administrative proposals which may be considered by the President or by the Congress.

"REPORTS

"Sec 134. The Assistant Secretary shall transmit to the President and to the Congress a report on such results from the activities conducted pursuant to this part as may be completed by January 1, 1978, together with such legislative recommendations as he may deem appropriate. The Assistant Secretary shall similarly report annually thereafter."

References

Academy for Educational Development. *Never Too Old to Learn.* New York: 1974.

Adult Education, Vol. 2, No. 2 (December 1951).

Aging In All Nations: A Special Report on the UN World Assembly on Aging, Vienna, Senate Special Committee on Aging in conjunction with the American Association of Retired Persons, the Federal Council on the Aging, and the Administration on Aging. Washington, D.C.: 1985.

Ading In All Nations: A Special Report on the UN World Assembly on Aging, Vienna, Austria. Washington, D.C.: The National Council on the Aging, 1982.

Aging International. "What Motivates Students Attending Universities of the Third Age?" Washington, D.C.: International Federation on Aging, Vol. 8, No. 4 (1981).

Aging International. Washington, D.C.: International Federation on Aging, Vol. 12, Nos. 1–4, 1985–86.

Aging International. Washington, D.C.: International Federation on Aging, Vol. 13, No. 1, (Spring 1986).

Akins, Thomas. "Empowerment: Fostering Independence of the Older Adult." *Aging Network News.* Omni Reports, Ltd., Vol. II, No. 5 (October 1985), 1.

America in Transition: An Aging Society, 1984–85 edition. Special Committee on Aging, United States Senate, Washington, D.C.: Serial No. 99B, June 1985.

Annual Report, School of Social Work, Solothurn, Switzerland, 1985. Trans. Louis Lowy.

Apps, Jerold. *The Adult Learner on Campus: A Guide for Instructors and Administrators.* Chicago: Follett, 1981.

Arenberg, David L., and Elizabeth A. Robertson. "The Older Adult as a Learner." In *Learning for Aging,* Stanley M. Grabowski and W. Dean Mason, eds. Washington D.C.: Adult Education Association, 1974, 2–39.

Aristotle. *The Philosophy of Aristotle,* trans. Creed Wardman. New York: Mentor Books, 1963.

Atchley, Robert C. *The Social Forces in Later Life,* 4th edition. Belmont, CA: Wadsworth, 1985.

Axelrod, S., and C. Eisdorfer. "Attitudes Toward Old People." *Journal of Gerontology,* 16 (1961), 75–80.

Axinn, June, and H. Levin. *Social Welfare: A History of American Response to Need,* 2nd edition. New York: Longman, 1980.

Banfield, Robert E., and J.E. Morgan. *Early Retirement: The Decision and the Experience.* Ann Arbor: University of Michigan Institute of Social Research 1969.

Barclay, Peter M. *Social Workers: Their Role and Tasks.* London: National Institute for Social Work, Bedford Sq. Press, 1982.

Bass, R.K. "Personalization of Instruction Based Upon Cognitive Style Mapping: Implications for Educational Gerontology." *Educational Gerontology,* 3(1978), 109–24.

Bauer, B.M. *A Model of Continuing Education for Older Adults.* Unpublished Doctoral dissertation, University of Minnesota, 1975.

Beebe, Cora P., and John W. Evans. "Clarifying the Federal Role in Education." In *The Federal Role in Education: New Directions for the Eighties,* Robert A. Miller, ed. Washington, D.C.: The Institute for Educational Leadership, 1981, 39–48.

Bennis, Warren, K. Benne and R. Chin. *The Planning of Change,* 2nd edition. New York: Holt, Rinehart and Winston, 1969.

Benoit, Hanah. "The Right to L.I.F.E.: A Better Deal for Nursing Home Residents." *Boston Globe Magazine,* July 1982, 12–24.

Berg, Stig. "Intelligence and Terminal Decline." Paper presented at the XIII International Congress of Gerontology, New York, July 13, 1985.

Berkeley, William D. "The Horse's Mouth." *Between Classes* (Elderhostel Newsletter), Vol. 2, No. 3, April 1985, 2.

Bertalanffy, Ludwig Von. "General Systems Theory." In *System Change and Conflict,* N.J. Demerath, III and R.A. Peterson, eds. New York: The Free Press, 1967, 115–129.

Binstock, Robert H. "Interest-Group Liberalism and the Politics of Aging." *The Gerontologist,* 12(1972), 265–280.

———. "The Aging as a Political Force: Images and Reality." In *Aging: A Challenge to Science and Social Policy,* Vol. 2, *Medicine and Social Science,* A.J.J. Gilmore et al., eds. London: Oxford University Press, 1981, 390–396.

Binstock, Robert H., Martin A. Levin and Richard Weatherley. "Political Dilemmas of Social Intervention." In *Handbook of Aging and the Social Sciences,* 2nd edition, Robert H. Binstock and Ethel Shanas, eds. New York: Van Nostrand Reinhold, 1985, 589–618.

Bolton, Christopher. "Review Essay: Adult Education." *The Gerontologist,* Vol. 25, No. 4 (August 1985), 436.

Botwinick, Jack. *Aging and Behavior.* New York: Springer, 1973.

Brasseul, Pierre. "The Impact of Education for Older Adults on Traditional Education in France." Paper presented at the XIII International Congress of Gerontology, New York, July 17, 1985.

Brody, Elaine M. "Long Term Care of the Aged." *Health and Social Work,* 2(1979a), 29–39.

———. "Women's Changing Roles, the Aged Family and Long Term Care of Older People." *National Journal* (October 27, 1979b), 11828–33.

———. "Women in the Middle and Family Help to Older People." *The Gerontologist,* Vol. 21, No. 5 (1981), 471–80.

Brown, Les. *Annual State of the World Report.* Reported in *Time,* February 24, 1986.

Bruner, Jerome. *The Process of Education.* Cambridge, MA: Harvard University Press, 1961.

Bubolz, Elizabeth, and H. Petzold. *Bildungsarbeit mit Alten Menschen.* Stuttgart, W. Germany: Klett Publishers, 1976.

Bubolz-Lutz, Elizabeth. *Bildung im Alter (Education in Later Years),* 2nd edition, trans. Louis Lowy. Freiburg i/Br., Lambertus, 1984.

Burgess, Ernst W. *Aging in Western Culture: A Survey of Social Gerontology.* Chicago: University of Chicago Press, 1960.

Burkey, F.T. *Educational Interest of Older Adult Members of the Brethren Church in Ohio.* Unpublished Doctoral dissertation, Ohio State University, 1975.

Butler, Robert N. *Why Survive? Being Old in America.* New York: Harper & Row, 1975.

———. "The Life Review: An Interpretation of Reminiscence in the Aged." In *Philosophical Foundations of Gerontology,* P.L. McKee, ed. New York: Human Sciences Press, 1982.

Cahill, Pati. "The Arts, the Humanities and Older Americans: A Catalogue of Program Profiles." Washington, D.C.: The National Countil on the Aging, 1981.

Calhoun, R.O., and B.R. Gounard. "Meaningfulness, Presentation Rate, List Length, and Age in Elderly Adults' Paired Associate Learning." *Educational Gerontology,* 4(1979), 49–56.

Canestrari, R.E. "Paced and Self-Paced Learning in Young and Elderly Adults." *Journal of Gerontology,* 18(1963), 165–8.

Carkhuff, Robert R. *The Art of Helping: An Introduction to Life Skills.* Amherst, MA: Human Resource Development Press, 1973.

Carter, President James. "Message to the Congress." *Congressional Record,* February 28, 1978. Quoted in John T. Wilson, *Academic Science Higher Education and the Federal Government 1950–1983.* Chicago: University of Chicago Press, 1983.

Cattell, Robert B. "Theory of Fluid and Crystallized Intelligence: A Clinical Experiment." *Journal of Educational Psychology,* 54(1963), 1–22.

Champling, Jo, ed. "Editor's Introduction." In *Post Education Society: Recognizing Adults as Learners* by Norman Evans. Dover, NH: Croom Helm, 1985.

Clark, Margaret, and B. Anderson. *Culture and Aging.* Springfield, IL: Charles C. Thomas, 1967.

Cohen, Nathan E. *Social Work in the American Tradition.* New York: Dryden Press, 1958.

Cohen, Wilbur. "Political Implications of Education for Aging." In *Learning for Aging,* Stanley M. Grabowski and W. Dean Mason, eds. Washington, D.C.: Adult Education Association, 1974, 61–78.

Colvin, Ruth J., and Jane H. Root. *TUTOR: Techniques Used in the Teaching Of Reading,* rev. edition. New York: Literacy Volunteers of America, 1984.

Commager, Henry Steele. Quoted in L. Demkovich, "Social Security at 50." *Modern Maturity,* Washington, D.C.: August-September, 1985, 31.

Conant, James B. *The American High School Today.* New York: New American Library, 1959.

Cross, K. Patricia. *Planning Non-traditional Programs: An Analysis of the Issues for Postsecondary Education.* San Francisco: Jossey-Bass, 1974.

———. "Adult Learners: Characteristics, Needs and Interests." In *Lifelong Learning in America,* Richard E. Peterson and Associates, eds. San Francisco: Jossey-Bass, 1979.

Current Population Reports. Washington, D.C.: U.S. Bureau of the Census, 1980.

Cutler, Stephen J. "Membership in Different Types of Voluntary Associations and Psychological Well-Being." *The Gerontologist,* Vol. 16, No. 4 (1976), 335–39.

Davenport, Joseph, and Judith Davenport. "A Chronology and Analysis of the Andragogy Debate." *Adult Education Quarterly,* Vol. 35, No. 3(Spring 1985), 152–159.

DeHoyos, Genevive, and C. Jensen. "The Systems Approach in American Social Work." *Social Casework,* 66 (October 1985), 490–97.

Denny, Nancy Wadsworth. "A Review of Life Span Research with the Twenty Questions Task: A Study of Problem-Solving Ability." *Aging and Human Development,* Vol. 21, No. 3 (1985), 161–173.

Diekhoff, John S. *Schooling for Maturity: Notes and Essays on Education for Adults.* Chicago: Center for Study of Liberal Education for Adults, 1955.

Docksai, Ronald F. "The Department of Education." In *The Federal Role in Education: New Directions for the Eighties,* Robert A. Miller, ed. Washington, D.C.: The Institute for Educational Leadership, 1981, 133–50.

Donahue, Wilma T. *Education for Later Maturity: A Handbook.* New York: Whiteside and William and Morrow, 1955.

Dressel, P.L. "The Meaning and Significance of Integration." In *Handbook of Research on Teaching,* N.L. Gage, ed. Chicago: Rand McNally, 1963.

Drewes, Donald W. "Education and Training for Older Persons: A Planning Paper." Washington, D.C.: Department of Education, May 1981.

Duncan, D.R., and A.M. Barrett. "A Longitudinal Comparison of Intelligence Involving the Wechsler Bellevue I and the WAIS." *Journal of Clinical Psychology,* 17(1961), 318–19.

Dye, Thomas. *Understanding Public Policy,* 5th edition. Englewood Cliffs, NJ: Prentice-Hall, 1984.

Eisdorfer, Carl. "The WAIS Performance of the Aged: A Retest Evaluation." *Journal of Gerontology,* 18(1963), 169–72.

Eisdorfer, Carl, J. Nowlin and F. Wilkie. "Improvement of Learning in the Aged by Modification of Autonomic Nervous System Activity." *Science,* 170(1970), 15–22.

Elias, John L., and Sharan Merriam. *Philosophical Foundations of Adult Education.* Huntington, NY: Robert E. Krieger, 1980.

Encyclopedia of Social Work. National Association of Social Workers, New York, 1960, 1977.

Estes, Carroll L. *The Aging Enterprise.* San Francisco: Jossey-Bass, 1983.

Evans, Norman. *Post Education Society: Recognizing Adults as Learners.* Dover, NH: Croom Helm, 1985.

Fallows, James. "Entitlements." *The Atlantic Monthly,* November 1982, 51–59.

Feifel, H., ed. *The Meaning of Death.* New York: McGraw-Hill, 1959.

Firman, James P., and C.A. Ventura. "Feasible and Adaptable." *Synergist,* Vol. 10, No. 2 (1981), 35–36.

Fisher, Dorothy C. *Learn or Perish.* New York: Liveright, 1931.

Fozard, James L. "Predicting Age in the Adult Years from Psychological Assessments of Abilities and Personality." *Aging and Human Development,* Vol. 3, No. 2 (1972), 175–82.

Frankel, Charles. "Social Values and Professional Values." *Journal of Education for Social Work,* Vol. 5, No. 1 (Spring 1969), 29–35.

Frankl, Viktor E. *Man's Search for Meaning,* trans. Ilse Lasch. New York: Simon and Schuster, 1939.

Freire, Paulo. *Pedagogy of the Oppressed,* trans. Myra Bergman Ramos. New York: Continuum, 1984.

Friedlander, Walter, and Robert Z. Apte. *Introduction to Social Welfare.* 4th edition. Englewood Cliffs, NJ: Prentice-Hall, 1974.

Friend, Celia M. and John P. Zubek. "The Effects of Age on Critical Thinking Ability" (1958). Reprinted in *Experimental Studies in Adult Learning and Memory,* D. Barry Lumsden and Ronald Sherron, eds. New York: Hemisphere, 1975, 37–50.

Galbraith, John Kenneth. *The Affluent Society.* Boston: Houghton Mifflin, 1958.

Gallant, Robert V., Cathy Cohen and Thomas Wolff. "Change of Older Persons' Image: Impact on Public Policy Result From Highland Valley Empowerment Plan." *Perspective on Aging* (September/October 1985), 9–13.

Getzel, Jessica. "Resident Councils and Social Actions." *Journal of Gerontological Social Work,* 5(1983), 179–85.

Gier, Nicholas F. "Humanism as an American Heritage." *Free Inquiry,* Vol. 2, No. 2 (Spring 1982), 27–29.

Gilder, George. *The Nature of Wealth and Poverty.* New York: Bantam Books, 1981.

Glickman, Lillian L., Benjamin S. Hersey, and Ira I. Goldenberg. *Community Colleges Respond to Elders.* Washington, D.C.: Department of Health, Education, and Welfare, 1975.

Goodrow, B.A. *The Learning Needs and Interests of the Elderly in Knox County, Tennessee.* Doctoral dissertation, University of Tennessee, 1974.

Gounard, B.R., and I.M. Hulicka. "Maximizing Learning Efficiency in Later Adulthood: A Cognitive Problem-Solving Approach." *Educational Gerontology* 2(1977), 417–27.

Graebner, William, *A History of Retirement: The Meaning and Function of An American Institution, 1885–1978.* New Haven, CT: Yale University Press, 1980.

Green, R.E., and M.A. Enderline. "A New Bottle for Good Wine." *Lifelong Learning* (October 1980), 12–15, 31.

Greider, William. "The Education of David Stockman." *The Atlantic,* December 1981, 27–54.

Groombridge, Brian. "The Impact of Older Learners on Educational Systems: A British Perspective." Presentation at the XIII International Congress of Gerontology, New York, July 17, 1985.

Groombridge, Brian, and Jennifer Rogers. *Right To Learn: The Case for Adult Equality.* London: Arrow Books, 1976.

Gross, Ronald. *The Lifelong Learner.* New York: Simon and Schuster, 1977.

Haggstrom, Warren C. "The Power of the Poor." In *Poverty in America,* Ferman, Kornbluh and Haber, eds. Ann Arbor: University of Michigan Press, 1969, 457–475.

Harris, Louis, and Associates. *The Myth and Reality of Aging in America.* Washington, D.C.: National Council on the Aging, 1975.

————. *1979 Study of American Attitudes Toward Pensions and Retirement.* New York: Johnson and Higgins, 1979.

————. *Aging in the Eighties: America in Transition.* Washington, D.C.: National Council on the Aging, 1981.

Hartley, J.T., J.O. Harker and D.A. Walsh. "Contemporary Issues and New Directions in Adult Development of Learning and Memory." In *Aging in the 1980's: Selected Contemporary Issues in the Psychology of Aging.* Washington, D.C.: American Psychological Association, 1980.

Havighurst, Robert J. "Changing Status and Roles During the Adult Life Cycle: Significance for Adult Education." In *Sociological Backgrounds of Adult Education,* Hobert Burns, ed. Chicago: Center for the Study of Liberal Education for Adults, 1964.

————. "Adulthood and Old Age." In *Encyclopedia of Educational Research,* 4th edition, R.L. Ebel, ed. New York: Macmillan, 1969.

————. "An Exploratory Study of Reminiscence." *Journal of Gerontology,* 27 (1972), 235–53.

————. "Education Through the Adult Lifespan." *Educational Gerontology,* Vol. 1, No. 1(1976), 41–51.

Hayslip, Bert, Jr., and Kevin J. Kennelly. "Cognitive and Noncognitive Factors Affecting Learning among Older Adults." In *The Older Adult As Learner: Aspects of Educational Gerontology,* D. Barry Lumsden, ed. New York: Hemisphere, 1985.

Hiemstra, Roger P. "Continuing Education for the Aged: A Survey of Needs and Interests of Older People." *Adult Education,* 22 (1972), 100–109.

————. "Educational Planning for Older Adults: A Survey of 'Expressive' vs. 'Instrumental' Preferences." *International Journal of Aging and Human Development,* 4 (1973), 147–56.

————. *The Older Adult and Learning.* Lincoln: University of Nebraska, 1975. (ERIC Document Reproduction Service No. CE 006 003).

————. "Older Adult Learning: Instrumental and Expressive Categories." *Educational Gerontology* 1(July-September 1976), 227–231.

Horn, John L., and Robert B. Cattell. "Integration of Structural and Developmental Concepts of the Theory of Fluid and Crystallized Intelligence." In *Handbook of Multivariate Experimental Psychology,* Horn and Cattell, eds. Chicago: Rand McNally, 1966.

Horowitz, Amy. "Sons and Daughters as Caregivers to Older Parents: Differences in Role Performance and Consequences." In *The Gerontologist,* 25 (December 1985), 612–617.

Hudson, Robert B. "Tomorrow's Able Elders: Implications for the State." Paper presented as part of the Ollie Randall Symposium at the Scientific Meeting of the Gerontological Society of America, New Orleans, November 1985.

Hudson, Robert B., and J. Strate. "Aging and Political Systems." In *Handbook of Aging and the Social Sciences,* Robert H. Binstock and Ethel Shanas, eds. New York: Van Nostrand Reinhold, 1985, 554–85.

Hulicka, Irene M. "Age Differences in Retention as a Function of Interference." *Journal of Gerontology,* 22(1967), 180–84.

Hulicka, Irene M., and J.L. Grossman. "Age-group Comparisons for the Use of Mediators in Paired-associate Learning." *Journal of Gerontology,* 22(1967), 45–51.

Hultsch, D.F. "Adult Age Differences in the Organization of Free Recall." *Developmental Psychology,* 1(1969), 673–78.

———. "Changing Perspectives on Basic Research in Adult Learning and Memory." *Educational Gerontology,* 2(1977), 367–82.

Hultsch, D.F., and T. Hickey. "External Validity in the Study of Human Development: Theoretical and Methodological Issues." *Human Development,* 21(1978), 76–91.

Illich, Ivan. *De-Schooling of Society.* New York: Harper and Row, 1970.

"Improving the Federal Government's Responsibilities in Education." In *The Federal Role in Education: New Directions for the Eighties,* Robert A. Miller, ed. Washington, D.C.: The Institute for Educational Leadership, 1981, 77–83.

Itzin, Neva L. "Right to Life, Subsistence, and the Social Services." *Social Work,* Vol. 3, No. 4(October 1958), 3–11.

Jennings, John F. "The Federal Role in Paying for Education in the 80's." In *The Federal Role in Education: New Directions for the Eighties,* Robert A. Miller, ed. Washington, D.C.: The Institute for Educational Leadership, 1981, 5–13.

John, Martha Tyler. *Teaching and Loving the Elderly.* Springfield, IL: Charles C. Thomas, 1983.

Johnstone, John W.C., and Ramon J. Rivera. *Volunteers for Learning.* Chicago: Aldine, 1965.

Jones, Harry. "The Rule of Law and the Welfare State." *Columbia Law Review,* 58 (February 2, 1958).

Jones, H.E., and H.S. Conrad. "The Growth and Decline of Intelligence: A Study of a Homogeneous Group Between the Ages of Ten and Sixty." *Genetic Psychology Monographs,* 13(1933), 223–98.

Kahn, Alfred J. *Social Policy and Social Services,* 2nd edition. New York: Random House, 1979.

Kalish, Richard A. "The New Age-ism and the Failure Models: A Polemic." *The Gerontologist,* Vol. 19, No. 4 (1979), 398–402.

———. *Death, Grief and Caring Relationships,* 2nd edition. Monterey, CA: Brooks Cole, 1984.

Kane, Barbara, and G. Lebow. "The Aging Network Services (ANS)." Washington, D.C. Reported in the *Washington Post,* April 10, 1984.

Kane, Robert L., and R.A. Kane. *Assessing the Elderly,* 3rd edition. Lexington, MA: Lexington Books, 1983.

Kaplan, Max. "The Uses of Leisure." In *Handbook of Social Gerontology,* Clark Tibbits, ed. Chicago: University of Chicago Press, 1960.

Karp, David A. "Academics Beyond Midlife: Some Observations on Changing Consciousness in the Fifty- to Sixty-Year Decade." *Aging and Human Development,* Vol. 22, No. 2 (1985–86), 81–103).

Kastenbaum, Robert R.J. *Death, Society and Human Experiences,* 2nd edition. St. Louis, MO: C.V. Mosby, 1981.

Kasworm, C. "The Illiterate Elderly." Paper presented at National Adult Education Association Meeting, Anaheim, CA, 1981 (cited in Ventura and Worthy, 1982).

Kauffman, Earl, and Patrick Luby. "Non-Traditional Education: Some New

Approaches to a Dynamic Culture." In *Learning For Aging,* Stanley M. Grabowski and W. Dean Mason, eds. Washington, D.C.: Adult Education Association, 1974, 130–159.

Kidd, James R. *How Adults Learn.* New York: Associated Press, 1959.

Kingston, Albert J. "The Senior Citizen as College Student." *Educational Gerontology,* 8(1982), 43–52.

Knowles, Malcolm S. *Informal Adult Education.* New York: Association Press, 1950.

———. *Higher Education in the U.S.* Washington, D.C.: American Council on Education, 1969.

———. *The History of the Adult Education Movement in the United States,* rev. edit., New York: Krieger, 1977.

———. "Andragogy Revisited Part II." *Adult Education,* Vol. 30, No. 1 (Fall 1979), 52–3.

———. *The Modern Practice of Adult Education: Andragogy Versus Pedagogy.* New York: Association Press, 1970; 2nd edition 1980.

———. *Andragogy in Action.* San Francisco: Jossey-Bass, 1984.

Knox, A.B. *Development and Learning.* San Francisco: Jossey-Bass, 1977.

Knudson, Russell S. "Humanagogy Anyone?" *Adult Education,* Vol. 29, No. 4(Summer 1979), 261–2.

Konopka, Gisela. *Eduard C. Lindeman and Social Work Philosophy.* Minneapolis: University of Minnesota Press, 1958.

Korim, Andrew S. *Older Americans and Community Colleges: A Guide for Program Implementation.* Washington, D.C.: American Association of Community and Junior Colleges, 1974.

Kübler-Ross, Elizabeth. *On Death and Dying.* New York: Macmillan, 1969.

Laurence, M.H. "Memory Loss with Age: A Test of Two Strategies for Its Retardation." *Psychonomic Science,* 9 (1967), 209–210.

Lawson, K.H. *Philosophical Concepts and Values in Adult Education.* Nottingham, England: Department of Adult Education, University of Nottingham, 1975.

Lebel, J. "Beyond Andragogy to Geragogy." *Lifelong Learning: The Adult Years,* Vol. 1, No. 9(1978), 16–18.

Lewin, Kurt. "Frontiers in Group Dynamics." *Human Relations,* 1(1947), 5–41.

———. "Field Theory in Social Science." In *Frontiers in Group Dynamics,* D. Cartwright, ed. New York: Harper and Row, 1951, 221–303.

Lewontis, R.C. "The Inferiority Complex." *New York Review of Books,* No. 28 (1981), 13.

Lindeman, Eduard. *The Meaning of Adult Education.* New York: New Republic, 1926.

Londoner, Carroll A. "Survival Needs of the Aged: Implications for Program Planning." *International Journal of Aging and Human Development,* 2(1971), 113–17.

———. "Instrumental and Expressive Education: A Basis for Needs Assessment and Planning." In *Introduction to Educational Gerontology,* 2nd edition, Ronald H. Sherron and D. Barry Lumsden, eds. Washington, D.C.: Hemisphere, 1978, reprint 1985, 93–110.

Longman, Phillip. "Justice Between Generations." *The Atlantic Monthly,* June 1985, 73–81.

Lorge, Irving. "Capacities of Older Adults." In *Education for Later Maturity,* Wilma Donahue, ed. New York: Whiteside and William Morrow, 1955.

Lowenthal, Marjorie F., M. Thurber and D. Chiriboga. *Four Stages of Life*. San Francisco: Jossey-Bass, 1975.

Lowy, Louis. *Adult Education and Group Work*. New York: Whiteside and William and Morrow, 1955.

———. "The Group in Social Work with the Aging." *Social Work*, Vol. 7, No. 4 (1962), 43–50.

———. "The Senior Center: A Major Community Facility Today and Tomorrow." *Perspectives on Aging*, Vol. 3, No. 2(1974a). Reprinted in the *Congressional Record*, May 8, 1974.

———. *The Function of Social Work in a Changing Scoiety*. Boston, Charles River Books, 1976.

———. *Social Policies and Programs on Aging*, 6th printing. Lexington, MA: D.C. Heath and Co., 1980.

———. "Social Group Work with Vulnerable Older Persons: A Theoretical Perspective." *Social Work with Groups*, Vol. 5, No. 2 (Summer 1982). New York: Haworth Press, 21–32.

———. "Social Security Intergenerational Problem." *The World*, Boston University News, November 1982, 3–4.

———. *Sozialarbeit/Sozialpädagogik als Wissenschaft Im Anglo Amerikanischen Und Deutschsprachigen Raum*: Freiburg, W. Germany: Lambertus Verlag, 1983a.

———. "Continuing Education in the Later Years: Learning in the Third Age." *Gerontology and Geriatrics Education*, Vol. 4, No. 2 (Winter 1983b), 89–104.

———. "Multipurpose Service Centers," chapter 12 in *Handbook of Gerontological Services*, A. Monk, ed. New York: Van Nostrand Reinhold, 1985a.

———. *Social Work with the Aging*, 2nd edition. New York: Longman, 1985b.

Lumsden, D. Barry, ed. *The Older Adult as Learner: Aspects of Educational Gerontology*. New York: Hemisphere, 1985.

McClusky, Howard Y., and the Technical Committee on Education. *Education: Background and Issues*. Report for the 1971 White House Conference on Aging. Washington, D.C.: U.S. Government Printing Office, 1971.

McClusky, Howard Y. "Education for Aging: The Scope of the Field and Perspectives for the Future." In *Learning for Aging*, Stanley M. Grabowski and W. Dean Mason, eds. Washington, D.C.: Adult Education Association, 1974.

———. "Cognitive Performance and Mental Ability: Implications for Learning in the Later Years." *Alternative Higher Education*, Vol. 5, No. 1 (Fall 1980), 18–29.

Mace, N.L., and P.U. Rabins. *The Thirty-Six Hour Day: A Family Guide to Caring for Persons with Alzheimer's Disease, Related Dementing Illness and Memory Loss in Later Life*. Baltimore: Johns Hopkins Press, 1982.

Mackay, James L., and Leroy Hixon. "Toward a Better Understanding of How to Teach Older Adults." *Adult Leadership*, 25(1977), 148–160.

Manton, Kenneth C., and Korbin Liu. "The Future Growth of the Long Term Care Population: Projections Based on the 1977 Nursing Home Survey and the 1982 Long Term Care Survey." In *America in Transition: An Aging Society*, 1984–85 edition, An Information Paper, Special Committee on Aging, U.S. Senate, Serial No. 99-B, June 1985.

Marcus, Edward E. *Effects of Age, Sex, and Socioeconomic Status on Adult Education Participants' Perception of the Utility of their Participation*. Doctoral dissertation, University of Chicago, 1976.

Maslow, Abraham. *Toward a Psychology of Being.* Princeton, NJ: Van Nostrand, 1968.

Melden, A.I. "Are There Welfare Rights?" In *Income Support: Conceptual and Policy Issues,* Peter G. Brown, Conrad Johnson and Paul Vernier, eds. Totowa, NJ: Rowman and Littlefield, 1982, 259–278.

Merriam, Sharan, and D. Barry Lumsden. "Educational Needs and Interests of Older Learners." In *The Older Adult As Learner: Aspects of Educational Gerontology,* D. Barry Lumsden, ed. New York: Hemisphere, 1985.

Merton, Robert K., G.G. Reader and P.L. Kendall, eds. *The Student Physician: Introduction to Studies in the Sociology of Medical Education.* Cambridge, MA: Harvard University Press, 1957.

Miles, C.C., and W.R. Miles. "The Correlation of Intelligence Score and Chronological Age from Early to Late Maturity." *American Journal of Psychology,* 44(1932), 44–78.

Miller, Robert A., ed. *The Federal Role in Education: New Directions for the Eighties.* Washington, D.C.: The Institute for Educational Leadership, 1981.

Moody, Harry R. "Philosophical Presuppositions of Education for Old Age." *Educational Gerontology,* 1(1976), 1–16.

———. "Education and the Life Cycle: A Philosophy of Aging. In *Introduction to Educational Gerontology,* Ronald H. Sherron and D. Barry Lumsden, eds. Washington, D.C.: Hemisphere, 1978, pp. 31–47.

———. "Philosophy of Education for Older Adults." In *The Older Adult As Learner: Aspects of Educational Gerontology,* D. Barry Lumsden, ed. New York: Hemisphere, 1985, 25–49.

———. "Education in An Aging Society." *Deadalus* (Winter 1986).

Moore, Francis D. "Who Should Profit from the Care of Your Illness?" *Harvard Magazine,* Vol. 88, No. 2 (Nov.-Dec. 1985), 43–55.

Morris, Robert. *Rethinking Social Welfare: Why Care for the Stranger?* New York: Longman, 1986a.

———. Book Review of *Losing Ground: American Social Policy 1950–1980. Social Work,* Vol. 31, No. 1 (1986b), 74.

Morris, Robert, and Scott A. Bass. "The Elderly as Surplus People: Is There a Role for Higher Education?" *The Gerontologist,* Vol. 26, No. 1 (February 1986), 12–18.

Motenko, Aluma. "The Gratifications and Frustrations of Older People Caring for a Spouse with Alzheimer's Disease." Dissertation in progress, Boston University, School of Social Work and Department of Sociology.

Murray, Charles. *Losing Ground: American Social Policy, 1950–1980.* New York: Basic Books, 1984.

National Center for Education Statistics. *Participation in Adult Education,* 1981. Unpublished data. Cited in *Education for Older Adults: A Synthesis of Significant Data,* C.A. Ventura and E.H. Worthy, Jr., eds. Washington, D.C.: National Policy Center on Education, Leisure and Continuing Opportunities for Older Americans and the National Council on the Aging, 1982.

National Center for Education Statistics. "The Condition of Education," 1983 edition. Washington, D.C.: U.S. Department of Education, 1983.

National Center for Health Statistics, 1981 and 1982. Reported in U.S. Senate Special Committee on Aging, 1984.

Neugarten, Bernice L. "Personality Changes during the Adult Years." In *Psychological Backgrounds of Adult Education,* R.G. Kuhlen, ed. Chicago: Center for Study of Liberal Education for Adults, 1963, 43–76.

————. "Personality and Aging." In *Handbook of the Psychology of Aging,* J. Birren and K. Warner Schaie, eds. New York: Van Nostrand Reinhold, 1977, 626–49.

————. "Time, Age and the Life Cycle." *American Journal of Psychiatry,* 136 (1977), 887–894.

Neugarten, Bernice L., ed. *Age or Need? Public Policies for Older People.* Beverly Hills, CA: Sage, 1982.

Nielsen, Kai. *Reason and Practice: A Modern Introduction to Philosophy.* New York: Harper & Row, 1971.

Nozick, Robert. *Philosophical Explanations.* Cambridge, MA: Belknap Press, Harvard University, 1981.

The Older We Get . . . An Action Guide to Social Change. Boston: Unitarian Universalist Service Center, July 1985, 86–88.

Owens, W.A. "Age and Mental Abilities: A Second Adult Follow-up." *Journal of Educational Psychology,* 57(1966), 311–25.

Parsons, Talcott. *The Social System.* New York: Free Press, 1964.

Parsons, Talcott, and E. Shils, eds. *Toward a General Theory of Action.* New York: Harper and Row, 1962.

Paterson, R.W.K. *Values, Education and the Adult.* London: Routledge & Kegan Paul, 1979.

Peck, Robert. "Psychological Developments in the Second Half of Life." In *Psychological Aspects of Aging,* J.E. Anderson, ed. Washington, D.C.: American Psychological Association, 1956.

Periodical on Aging 84, Vol. 1, No. 1, Department of International Economic and Social Affairs. New York: United Nations, 1985.

Peterson, David A. *Facilitating Education for Older Learners.* San Francisco: Jossey-Bass, 1983.

————. "A History of Education for Older Learners." In *The Older Adult as Learner: Aspects of Educational Gerontology,* D. Barry Lumsden, ed. New York: Hemisphere, 1985a.

————. Book Review "Adult Education." *The Gerontologist,* 25 (December 1985b), 657.

Philibert, Michel. "A Philosophy of Aging from a World Perspective." In *Perspectives on Aging: Exploding the Myths,* Pricilla W. Johnston, Coord. ed. Cambridge, MA: Ballinger, 1981.

————. "Contemplating the Development of Universities of the Third Age." In *Mutual Aid Universities,* Eric Midwinter, ed. Dover, NH: Croom Helm, 1984.

Pieper, Martha Heineman. "The Future of Social Work Research." *Social Work Research Abstracts,* NASW, 12 (1985), 3–11.

Pisco, Valena, and White, eds. "The Condition of Education," 1983 edition. Washington, D.C.: U.S. Department of Education, National Center for Education Statistics, 1983.

Powell, A.H., Jr., C. Eisdorfer and D. Bogdonoff. "Physiologic Response Patterns Observed in a Learning Task." *Archives of General Psychiatry,* 10(1964), 192–95.

Preston, Samuel H. "Children and the Elderly in the U.S." *Scientific American,* Vol. 251, No. 6 (December 1984), 44–9.

Rabbit, P. "Age and the Use of Structure in Transmitted Information." In *Human Aging and Behavior,* G.A. Talland, ed. New York: Academic Press, 1968, 75–92.

Rachal, J. "The Andragogy-Pedagogy Debate: Another Voice in the Fray." *Lifelong Learning: An Omnibus of Practice and Research,* Vol. 6, No. 9 (May 1983), 14–15.

Radcliffe, David. "Educational Gerontology and Lifelong Education." Presentation at the XIII International Congress of Gerontology, New York, July 17, 1985.

Rappaport, Julian. "In Praise of Paradox: A Social Policy of Empowerment over Prevention." *American Journal of Community Psychology,* Vol. 9, No. 1 (1981), 1–25.

————. "Studies in Empowerment: Steps Toward Understanding and Action." *Prevention in Human Services,* Vol. 3, No. 213 (1984), 3.

Rawls, John. *A Theory of Justice.* Cambridge, MA: Harvard University Press, 1971.

Reich, Charles. "The New Property." *Yale Law Journal,* 73 (April 1964), 773–787.

Richardson, Penelope L. "The Political Decision-Making Process in a Technological Society." In *Strategies for Lifelong Learning: A Symposium of Views from Europe and the USA,* Per Himmelstrup, John Robinson and Derrick Fielden, eds. Joint publication of the University Centre of South Jutland, Denmark, and the Association for Recurrent Education, UK, 1981.

Riegel, Klaus F., and R.M. Riegel. "Development, Drop, and Death." *Developmental Psychology,* 6(1972), 306–19.

Riley, M., and A. Foner. *Aging and Society: An Inventory of Research Findings.* New York: Russell Sage, 1968.

Roazen, Donna. Excerpts from interview with Curt G. Curtin, in "College-Age Students: Fifty-Plus," Curt G. Curtin. Unpublished manuscript, Westfield State College, Westfield, MA, February 1985.

Romaniuk, Jean Gasen. *The Older Adult in Higher Education: An Analysis of State Public Policy.* Washington, D.C.: National Policy Center on Education, Leisure and Continuing Opportunities for Older Persons and the National Council on the Aging, 1982.

Rosenmayr, Leopold. *Die Späte Freiheit (The Late Freedom).* Berlin, W. Germany: Severin und Siedler Verlag, 1983.

Rotberg, Iris C. "Federal Policy Issues in Elementary and Secondary Education." In *The Federal Role in Education: New Directions for the Eighties,* Robert A. Miller, ed. Washington, D.C.: The Institute for Educational Leadership, 1981, 23–36.

Rothman, Jack. "Three Models of Community Organization Practice: Their Mixing and Phasing." In *Strategies of Community Organization,* 3rd edition, Lox, Erlich, Rothman and Tropman, eds. Itasca, IL: Peacock, 1979, 25–45.

Schein, Edgar H. "The Mechanisms of Change." In *Planning of Change,* 2nd edition, Warren Bennis, K. Benne and R. Chin, eds. New York: Holt, Rinehart and Winston, 1969, 31–33.

Schonfield, David, and Betty-Anne Robertson. "Memory Storage and Aging" (1966). Reprinted in *Experimental Studies in Adult Learning and Memory,* D. Barry Lumsden and Ronald Sherron, eds. New York: Hemisphere, 1975.

Schulz, James H. *The Economics of Aging,* 3rd edition. Belmont, CA: Wadsworth, 1985.

Seltzer, Mildred, Sara Corbet and Robert Atchley. *Social Problems of the Aging.* Belmont, CA: Wadsworth, 1978.

Shanas, Ethel. "The Family and Social Class." In *Old People in Three Industrial Societies,* Ethel Shanas et al., eds. New York: Atherton, 1968.

Sheats, Paul H., Clarence D. Jayne and Ralph B. Spence. *Adult Education: The Community Approach.* New York: Dryden, 1953.

Sherron, Ronald H., and D. Barry Lumsden, eds. *Introduction to Educational Gerontology,* 2nd edition. Washington, D.C.: Hemisphere, 1985.

Shulman, Lawrence. *The Skills of Helping Individuals and Groups.* Itasca, IL: Peacock, 1984.

Silverman, P.R. *Mutual Self-Help Groups: Organization and Development.* Beverly Hills, CA: Sage, 1980.

Simmons, K., J. Ivry and M.M. Seltzer. "Agency-Family Collaboration." *The Gerontologist,* Vol. 25, No. 4 (August 1985), 343–346.

Siporin, Max. *Introduction to Social Work Practice.* New York: Macmillan, 1975.

Staffelnhof Seminar Proceedings, 1977–85. Reussbühl (Lucerne), Sozialstation in Littau, Kanton-Secretary A. Vonwyl, Director Sister Canesia; A. Hunziker, editor.

Stanford, E. Percil, and Antonia Dolar. "Federal Policy in Education for Older Adults." In *Introduction to Educational Gerontology,* 2nd edition, Ronald H. Sherron and D. Barry Lumsden, eds. New York: Hemisphere, 1985, 151–173.

Staples, Lee. *The Roots to Power.* New York: Praeger Special Studies, 1984.

The State of Families 1984–85. New York: The Family Service of America, 1985.

Taylor, Paul. "The Coming Conflict As We Soak the Young To Enrich the Old." The *Washington Post,* January 5, 1986, D1, D4.

Terman, L.M., and M.H. Oden. *The Gifted Group at Mid-life.* Stanford, CA: Stanford University Press, 1955.

Thorndike, E.L., et al. *Adult Learning.* New York: Macmillan Co., 1928.

Tibbitts, Clark. "Education." In *Academic Gerontology: Dilemmas of the 1980s,* Harold R. Johnson, ed. Ann Arbor: Institute of Gerontology, University of Michigan, 1980.

Timmerman, Sandra. "Education for Older Persons in the USA." Paper presented at the XII International Congress of Gerontology, Hamburg, Germany, July 11–17, 1981.

Toch, Hans. "The Care and Feeding of Typologies and Labels." *Federal Probation,* 34 (September 1970), 15–19.

Tough, A. "Major Learning Efforts: Recent Research and Future Directions." *Adult Education,* 28(1978), 250–263.

Towle, Charlotte. *Common Human Needs.* Chicago: University of Chicago Press, 1965.

Treas, Judith, and Sherry Berkman. "Life Span, Human Development and Old Age." In *Handbook of Gerontological Services,* A. Monk, ed. New York: Van Nostrand Reinhold, 1985, 24–43.

Truax, Charles B., and Robert B. Carkhuff. *Toward Effective Counseling and Psychotherapy: Training and Practice.* Chicago: Aldine, 1967.

United Nations, Department of International, Economic and Social Affairs. *Periodical on Aging,* Vol. 1, No. 1 (1985).

U.S. Department of Education, Office of Vocational and Adult Education. *Education and Training for Older Persons: A Program Guide.* Washington, D.C.: March 1981.

The 1971 U.S. White House Conference on Aging. "A Report to the Delegates from the Conference Sections and Special Concerns Sessions, November 28–December 2." Washington, D.C.: U.S. Government Printing Office, 1971.

The 1981 U.S. White House Conference on Aging. "Report of Technical Committee on Creating an Age-Integrated Society: Implications for the Educational Systems." Washington, D.C.: U.S. Government Printing Office, 1981.

———. "Chartbook on Aging." Washington, D.C.: U.S. Government Printing Office, 1981.

———. *Final Report,* Vol. 2. Washington, D.C.: U.S. Government Printing Office, 1981.

Ventura, Catherine. "Education for Older Adults: A Catalogue of Program Profiles." Washington, D.C.: The National Council on the Aging, and the National Policy Center on Education, Leisure and Continuing Opportunities for Older Americans, 1982.

Ventura, Catherine, and Edmund H. Worthy, Jr. "Education for Older Adults: A Synthesis of Significant Data." Washington, D.C.: The National Council on the Aging and the National Policy Center on Education, Leisure and Continuing Opportunities for Older Americans, 1982.

Vernier, Paul. "Rights to Welfare as an Issue in Income Support Policy." In *Income Support: Conceptual and Policy Issues,* Peter G. Brown, Conrad Johnson and Paul Vernier, eds. Totowa, NJ: Rowman and Littlefield, 1982, 219–232.

Warren, Roland. "Types of Purposive Change." Papers in Social Welfare. Waltham, MA: Brandeis University, 1965.

Wass, H., and C.A. West. "A Humanistic Approach to Education of Older Persons." *Educational Gerontology,* 2(1977), 407–16.

Watzlawick, Paul, Janet H. Beavin and Don D. Jackson. *Pragmatics of Human Communication: A Study of Interactional Patterns, Pathologies and Paradoxes.* New York: Norton, 1967.

Weinstock, Ruth. *The Graying of the Campus.* New York: Educational Facilities Laboratories, 1978.

Weiss, Ann Burak. "Long Term Care Institutions," chapter 19 in *Handbook of Gerontological Services,* A. Monk, ed. New York: Van Nostrand Reinhold, 1985, 635–456.

Whatley, L.F. *Expressive and Instrumental Educational Interests of Older Adults as Perceived by Adult Educators, Gerontologists, and Older Adults.* Unpublished Master's thesis, University of Georgia, 1974.

Wilensky, Harold L., and Charles N. Lebeaux. *Industrial Society and Social Welfare.* New York: The Free Press, 1965.

Wilson, John T. *Academic Science, Higher Education, and the Federal Government, 1950–1983.* Chicago: University of Chicago Press, 1983.

Winter, Julie. "Vorbereitung auf das Alter als Aufgabe des Schweizerischen Bildungswesens." In *Betrifft: Sozialpädagogik in der Schweiz.* P. Cassée, H. Cristen, M. Furrer, H. Kilchsperger and H. Tanner. Bern and Stuttgart: Verlag Haupt, 1984.

Wlodowski, Raymond I. *Enhancing Adult Motivation to Learn.* San Francisco: Jossey-Bass, 1985.

Wolk, Ronald A. *Alternative Methods of Federal Funding for Higher Education.* Berkeley, CA: Carnegie Commission on Higher Education, 1968.

Woodruff, Diana S., and David A. Walsh. "Research in Adult Learning: The Individual." *The Gerontologist,* 15(October 1975), 424–430.

Wooten, Roberta H. "Family Services: Family Life Education." *Encyclopedia of Social Work,* 7th issue. National Association of Social Workers, 1977, 423–428.

Yeo, G. "Eldergogy: A Specialized Approach to Education for Elders." *Lifelong Learning: The Adult Years,* Vol. 5, No. 5(Spring 1982), 4–7.

Index

About the Authors

Louis Lowy, Ph.D. (Harvard University) and M.S.W. (Boston University), is now Professor Emeritus at Boston University. He has been Professor and Associate Dean at Boston University School of Social Work for many years. He also was a faculty member of the university's Faculty of Arts and Science and its School of Public Health. He continues to be a faculty and research affiliate at the Boston University Gerontology Center, of which he was a co-founder, serving as its co-executive director from its founding in 1974 until 1977.

Dr. Lowy has been chair of the Professional Advisory Committee of the Massachusetts Executive Office of Elder Affairs since its inception in 1973 and has been instrumental in designing its home care programs for the state and housing and educational programs in the South End of Boston. He has been involved in gerontological social policy-making and gerontological social work practice as well as education in a variety of social welfare agencies and several policy-planning bodies in many parts of the country. He has been active as a consultant to numerous community agencies here and abroad and has conducted many educational and training programs in gerontology, social welfare policy, and social work throughout the United States, Canada, West Germany, Switzerland, Austria, Norway, France, The Netherlands, Belgium, and Israel as a visiting professor.

Dr. Lowy has been an officer of the Gerontological Society of America, the Northeastern Gerontological Society, and the National Association of Social Workers, and has been a member of many other professional associations. He has been the recipient of many awards, including the Metcalf Award of Boston University for Excellence in Teaching and Scholarship and the Werthman Medal for social welfare achievements in West Germany, and has been listed in *Who's Who in America* in every publication from 1980 to 1986.

Dr. Lowy is the author of many books, chapters, and articles on gerontology, social work, and education, among them, *Social Work with the Aging,* second edition, and *Social Policies and Programs on Aging* (sixth printing by Lexington Books), a text which also received the Journal of Nursing award in 1981. Presently Boston University is setting up a Louis Lowy Chair in Social Welfare Policy and Gerontology.

Darlene O'Connor formerly directed the home care program for Elder Services of Berkshire County, Inc., in Massachusetts, and prior to that served as Assistant for Professional Affairs at the University of Massachusetts Medical Center. She has also taught English at Southern Illinois University at Carbondale. A scholarship recipient at the XIII International Congress of Gerontology in 1985, she is a member of the Gerontological Society of America and the National Council on the Aging, and is active in many organizations in Massachusetts, including the Chicopee Council on Aging, the Gray Panthers of the Pioneer Valley, Tri-Valley Elder Services, and the Literacy Education for the Elderly Project. Ms. O'Connor holds B.A. and M.A. degrees in English and is a doctoral candidate at the Florence Heller School for Advanced Studies in Social Welfare at Brandeis University.